MIMESIS
INTERNATIONAL

DESIGN MEANINGS

N. 1

Book series edited by Renato Troncon
(Design Research Lab, Dipartimento di Lettere e Filosofia, Università di Trento)

"Whenever anyone asks why I am so passionate about activism,
I ask them to consider the alternative: passivity."

Anita Roddick 2001, XIX

DESIGNING ACTIVISM
AN INTRODUCTION

Tom Bieling

Self-evidently, the design of products, technologies, services, systems, virtual worlds and tangible objects always implicitly transmits role models and values. Design and the images it disseminates, often unreflectively, are hence unavoidably political. There is no doubt that the scope of action for designers also involves increasing awareness of the sociopolitical dimension of their design activities, in particular when it is a question of recognizing the power of their designs to exclude (or include), and of critically interrogating this power (Bieling 2019a).

It is *"design's ability to operate through 'things' and 'systems' that makes it particularly suitable for dealing with contemporary societal, economic and environmental issues."* (Fuad-Luke 2009, 2). Thus design is an effective force in shaping not only material culture, but also societal values and human behavior (Ericson/Mazé 2011, 12). Design as a 'critical practice' appears for instance in the context of social engagement, political activism, or civil disobedience (Magrini 2014, 144). This book is concerned with design activism both as "social action and political agency" (Julier 2008, 814). The central questions are what role activism can play in design, and vice versa, what is the benefit of using design in activism?

In recent years, under the banner of design activism, an emerging and increasingly popular approach to the intersection between civic engagement and various facets of sustainability[1] is being pushed into the foreground. Assembled under this concept are various activities that share the outlook that design can and should create socially, politically, economically and ecologically sustainable processes.

Ann Thorpe defines activism as *"taking intentional action to instigate change on behalf of a neglected group"* (Thorpe 2008, 1524). Social change should be supported here in that challenges to society can be addressed within a community and can thus receive more public attention. As such, existing norms of the (consumer) society are put into question and renegotiated to develop new solutions through design activism (Markussen 2011, 1). This perspective on the social sustainability[2] of design makes use of methods that do not touch upon the societal consensus but are

---

1   Here I refer to the cultural, political, social, ecological and economic dimensions of sustainability.

2   Design activism is occasionally used as a synonym for socially sustainable design (Markussen 2013), with the objection to create *"long-lasting prosperity and well-being for human and ecological systems"* (Thorpe 2008).

rather often disruptive and provocative, to make some of the social wrongs clear by other means. According to Ann Thorpe, design directly borrows techniques from activist practices and develops them further (Thorpe 2008). Design activism wishes to develop a "counter narrative," to demonstrate alternative proposals for the future and to furthermore provide impetus for their implementation (Bieling et al. 2014a).

In doing so, as Sara Hendren states, design activism uses the *"language of design to address, provoke and create political debate. Instead of solving problems in the manner of industrial design, or organizing forms as in graphic design, activist design might create a series of questions or proposals using artifacts or media for unresolved ends: to provoke, or question, or experiment in search of new political conditions. It might use and enrich different tools located in the field of visual communications, material cultures or practices of social, political and campaigning movements and organisations. The point of these artifacts is contestation, discourse and action, not a tidy fix."* (Hendren 2015).

Besides raising awareness, changing perceptions and behavior (Fuad-Luke 2009, 86), the objectives of a socially and politically engaged design obviously depends on the context and its particular perspective. Design is not activism and activism is not design. But the common ground, the shared space is large and growingly important (Malzacher 2012). It might be considered to be a space that offers a chance for design to be *"engaged, connected and relevant. [...] a space that offers activism a change not to get stuck in ideology, routine and functionarism, a chance to stay unpredictable and sharp."* (Ibid.) Because activism is a dynamic process: *"It starts when groups within society call for change, and society responds – either resisting, or incorporating the values encapsulated by activism"* (Thorpe 2008, 1524). With this book we want to capture design's role at the leading edge of this process (ibid.) and take a close look at what happens when the differences between design and activism lose importance (Malzacher 2012).

Social and political Dimension of Design

In recent years, the social and political dimensions of design have seemed to increasingly gain importance (again)[3], with design no longer being understood only as the design of single objects or signs, but rather as the design of systems, processes, experiences, interventions and interactions (c.f. Herlo et al. 2018, 219) as well as formats for critical discourse and/or decision-making in social, urban, cultural, or ecological contexts (ibid.; Mareis 2010; Erlhoff/Marshall 2008). With a broad variety of labels such *Social Design* (Banz 2016; Sachs 2018), *Design for Social Innovation* (Manzini 2007) or what Bazon Brock and Lucius Burckhart discussed as *Socio-Design* in the 1970 (Brock 1985, 446). Or more recently *Transformation Design* (Jonas et al. 2015; Sommer/Welzer 2016; Yee et al. 2017), and *Transition Design* (Irwin 2015; Irwin et al. 2015), which are all examples that stand for a certain kind of paradigm shift in design, that runs as follows: get rid of a „user-centred" (or even

---

3   The concept "social" is understood here in its general sense as concerning what is common and related to aspects of cohabitation.

worse: consumer-centred) Design, and focus on a rather community- or society-centred Design instead. A tendency, which has been identified by some protagonists from within and beyond design research as a "social turn".[4] What all these concepts have in common is an approach of such topics *"with a mixture of practical, factual, theoretical, and normative stances vis-à-vis the context of overarching change processes, influenced by digitalization, quite often in an attempt to position design as a 'game changer'."* (Herlo et al. 2018, 219f)

Change, as Alastair Fuad-Luke puts it, implies *"moving from 'state A' of a system to 'state B'. This may involve a transformation of the system and its target audiences or social groups, but often also involves the transformation of the individual activists too"* (Fuad-Luke 2009, 6). Fuad-Luke embeds both these notions of transformation in a working definition of activism: *"Activism is about [...] taking actions to catalyse, encourage or bring about change, in order to elicit social, cultural and/or political transformations. It can also involve transformation of the individual activists."* (ibid.)

A "socially active design," as Alastair Fuad-Luke has called it, focuses on society and its transformations toward a more sustainable way of living, working and producing (Fuad-Luke 2009, 78). Ezio Manzini describes the necessity for cultural change that can be propelled by a new awareness in society and by establishing new models of behavior (Manzini 1997, 43-51). Design can play an important role here in that its artifacts – in the form of products, services or interventions – can create awareness and can motivate alternative patterns of behavior. As such, design is required to reflect on the scope of its actions and on the responsibility of the designed artifact's possible effects. It is a question of the social responsibility of design and the potential to design social responsibility (Bieling et al. 2014a, 35). Against this backdrop Unteidig et al. diagnose *"a break in today's discourse about the political agency of design: While historically designers have attempted to induce social change by designing objects, today (social) design understands itself as a change agent in a much more direct relation to the social."* (Unteidig et al. 2017).

These points of intersection are being reflected upon in design in a number of ways, such as in Participatory Design (Sanders & Stappers 2008; Schuler/Namioka 1993; Simonsen/Robertson 2013), Design Infrastructuring (Björgvinsson et al. 2010) and Design Activism (Fuad-Luke 2009; Thorpe 2008). The principal orientation of Participatory Design is to integrate different groups of participants in the design process and to thereby create equal roles for the designers and "non-designers." These "non-designers" can be potential end users, employers, public representatives or members from other interest groups. They can be subsumed under the concept "stakeholder," which is to say, every participant possessing a certain, (in)direct interest in the design process, its conception, realization, implementation or resulting consequences. They can be closely integrated in the design (research) process in a variety of ways (Sanders 2013). Two main directions of participatory design have

---

4   The term *Social Turn* was coined by the art historian Claire Bishop in her essay *The Social Turn: Collaboration and Its Discontents* (Bishop 2006), to describe the recent return to socially engaged art that is collaborative, often participatory and involves people as the medium or material of the work.

become popular: Aside from the primary political motivations that can be found in movements, such as DIY ("do-it-yourself") and open source, participatory design has gained importance in the product development stage in order to, for example, develop idea generation.[5] Liz Sanders has concentrated more on orientation methods for the processes of product development where stakeholders become involved in the process to increase the marketability of the product or service (Sanders 2006). In contrast, a more political oriented variant of participatory design can be found in Pelle Ehn (Ehn 2001; Björgvinson et al. 2010) and Ezio Manzini (Manzini 2007). Here the focus is on the inclusion of citizens in societal processes as well as the authorization for independent improvements of living conditions. This variant is deeply rooted in the Scandinavian and American labor movements (Ehn/ Kyng 1987) and is based on the principle of including different groups in social and technological development processes. Ehn proposes "Design Infrastructuring" as a further development of participatory design. The concept's goal is to form longer-term, sustainable infrastructures to facilitate social innovation (Ehn, 2009). According to Wolfgang Zapf, social innovations are *"new ways to achieve goals, especially new forms of organization, new regulations and new lifestyles, which change the direction of social transformation, [and] are better at solving problems than earlier practices, and which are therefore worth imitating and institutionalizing"* (Zapf 1989). In particular the *"values of social progress, like social equality, equity and integration"* are implied (Rammert 2010).

In fact, these infrastructures can be places where the participants meet to discuss problems and develop approaches for solutions in an open, communal design process. Other structures or tools may arise for communities who have the goal to empower the participants for their own behavior. Consequently, this extends far beyond the idea of a 'traditional' design project, which has a predicted short- or middle-termed result that is closed (Bieling et al. 2014b).

Non-affirmative Design

In many regards today, humankind enjoys better health, longer life spans, and greater access to informational, social, cultural, and material goods than ever before (c.f. Antonelli/Hunt 2015, 7) *"As such, design has been rightfully trumpeted as a force for good [...] Yet, this narrative, albeit comforting and easy to digest, troubles in its simplicity. Throughout history, design has both perpetuated and mediated violence, giving rise to tools that harm, control, manipulate, and annihilate [...]."* (ibid.) Max Borka characterises design as a „double-headed monster" (Borka 2016, 30). He considers design to be „janus-faced" – one side precious, the other one dirty (ibid., 42). As an example, he names nuclear power, which on the hand can be regarded progressive, on the other hand dangerous. And if we think of inhumane working conditions or pollution

---

5   Crowd sourcing, which is mostly web-based, and where tasks or problems are implicitly or explicitly transferred to an unidentified group of users that then works together, is an example.

in the context of production, distribution and waste removal of designed goods, it becomes obvious that ordinary sneakers (for instance) can occasionally be more dangerous than a gun. Critically reflecting on design requires to be aware of this duality (or what Borka calls the 'shady side').

To question, for example, issues of gender and class, power and welfare, or authorship and ownership, has been practiced in emerging genres of 'social' and 'activist' design (Ericson/Mazé 2011, 12), as well as in more interrogative design approaches such as *critical* and *speculative design*. As conceptions of design have changed over time, situating it into more social systemic contexts (demanding more responsibility for future developments), Ludwig Zeller draws a distinction: *"while most of this is addressed with approaches such as ethnographic or participatory methods, which directly relate to the actual world, these new questions also bring up a host of speculative, narrative, and imaginative approaches [...]. These emerging fields use a notion of 'non-affirmative' design that refuses to function with the status quo of our world, instead using narrative and persuasive methods to foster imagination and change, respectively."* (Zeller 2018, 38). Here we can see an important link to design activism, which – as Fuad-Luke puts it – is *"imagination and practice applied [...] to create [...] counter-narrative[s] aimed at generating and balancing positive social, institutional, environmental and/or economic change."* (Fuad-Luke 2009, 27). The implication is that design activism *"voices other possibilities than those that already exist with a view to eliciting societal change and transformation."* (ibid.)

However, this also means to make things visible, graspable and intelligible, to provide a basis for activism. As James Bridle states, *"those who cannot perceive the network cannot act effectively within it, and are powerless.[6] The job, then, is to make such things visible."* (Bridle 2012) Undoubtedly this is what design can do.[7] It can *"reconnect the disconnected and make new connections. [It] can challenge the underlying, implicit ethics of the explicit forms we create. [...It..] can disturb current narratives. [It] can rupture the present with counter-narratives[8] [and] contribute to reformist approaches. It has the ability to catalyse societal transformations. Design is critical imagining."* (Fuad-Luke 2009, XXI).

Design as Activism – Activism as Design

Over the last decades, the number, diversity and vigour of popular movements has increased (Harding 2001, 5) and the world has witnessed a global rise of a comparably new activism, in which political protest often takes the form of impulsive, non-

7   As Arianna Huffington comments on his (art) project *Drone Shadows*, a series of one-to-one renderings of military drone aircraft outlined in chalk: *"He makes us see – or, more important, unable not to see."* (Huffington 2015, 128).

8   These counter-narratives might be a starting point to give rise to counterpublics (c.f. Michaelsen 2014, 394) and finally what Tim Gee describes as counterpower (Gee 2011). It can also foster the beginnings of a "counter-hegemony", too, that is *"the critical questioning of dominant norms as well as the formation of alternative political ideas and communal solidarity within civil society."* (c.f. Michaelsen 2014, 395)

institutional, mass action (Weibel 2014). Frequently empowered by networked communication these social protest movements (and individuals) manage to succeed in interrupting established systems of power (ibid).[9] The increasing use of designerly tools, creative methods and artisitic expressions by these movements sometimes culminates in a kind of *artivism*[10] (Ullrich/Bieling 2016) or what Peter Weibel calls *performative democracy*[11] which he considers to be perhaps the twenty-first century's first new art form (Weibel 2014).

The designerly (sometimes artistic) use of methods, tools, products and materials might help people in expressing themselves, communicating with a wider public, and building up as well as supporting networks inside and outside social movements (c. f. Zik 2014, 536). Further, design can have a direct impact on perception, experience, emotions and thus actions or its recipients. This circumstance enables design to go beyond its usage for practical purposes (ibid.) And apart from contributing as a channel for political expression or carrying symbolic values, design is capable to hold structural importance not least in the social dynamics of activist contexts.

Dietrich Heissenbüttel describes the difficult position minorities, the socially weak, peripheral regions, and people or topics that 'have no lobby' are often confronted with. *"Democracy aside, they remain underrepresented in a dual sense, because their concerns are not sufficiently visible and they lack representation of their interests. [...] The first step for mobilizing the public consist of drawing attention to a topic. For this, and for every other step, images are needed, since [...] pictorial representations are able to draw people's gaze and to 'set a scene' where there are complex circumstances, so they can be grasped at a glance."* (Heissenbüttel 2014, 474). Some popular examples we find in the distinctive images of resistance – posters, graphics, stickers, t-shirts, memes, street art, paintings, murals on walls, that hold a prominent place in the world's visual heritage.[12] And often thin is the line here between underground- and pop-culture.

Yet, the visual culture seems a bit like an obvious, almost classic design field of operation. Of courses design engages not only with graphic or physical forms, but also architectural, speculative, explorative or strategic, among other forms. It encompasses not only visual or tangible objects, but also user interfaces, information architectures, communications protocol (Antonelli/Hunt 2015, 7), public spaces, or

---

9   At least for a short moment in history, as Peter Weibel states.

10   A combination of the words art and activism. Currently most well known representatives are artist-/activist-groups such as *Zentrum für politische Schönheit* ("policital beauty"), *Tools for Action*, *Peng Collective*, *Enmedio*, *Etoy*, *Jody*, *Dashndem*, the *Yes Men* or some of the works by John Jordan, James Bridle, Arthúr van Balen, Liam Young, und Ai Weiwei.

11   *"A new form of public art is emerging, namely public politics. We are witnessing the evolution of a 'performative democracy'."* (Weibel 2014, 25).

12   Peter Weiss's *Die Ästhetik des Widerstands* [The Aesthetics of Resistance] (Weiss 1975) can be read as an attempt to reconstruct the history of a critical, society-oriented art (Heissenbüttel 2014, 474), that has been used as a reference for various theories, projects and exhibitions ever since. In a recent publication, for instance, Basil Rogger et al. pick up the notion of the *Aesthetics of Resistance*, reflecting on present and past forms of protest, and marginalized communities' practices of resistance, showing *"how protest draws on irony, subversion and provocation from a position of powerlessness, for pricking small but palpable pinholes into the controlling system of rule"* (Rogger et al. 2018).

service structures. Amongst these fields design has the potential to provoke strong, controversial, or subtle social reactions, covering a broad range of expression. Judy Seidman states that *"People have responded to repression and exploitation by developing their own voice across every form of creative media – in theatre, poetry, music, dance, and visual imagery. For each of these forms, people sought for and found images, metaphors, symbols, techniques and styles of expression."* (Seidman 2008, 11). We have seen many of these more recently, in the protest movements from *Occupy* to *Gezi*, from *Tahrir* to *G20*, from Artúr van Balen/Tools for Action's *Inflatables* to the Hong Kong *Umbrella Movement*.

A prominent feature of many of these actions and movements is the extensive use of design strategies and artistic practices – on a rhetorical level often combined with humor, satire and irony, and on a technical level operating with state-of-the-art (social) media, documentation and distribution channels. This obviously embraces more functions than a mere communication strategy. As Ragip Zik observed in the context of the Gezi Park Movement, *"Protesters embraced creative methods and art quickly became an indispensable part of the movement. Apart from the political content it had, art was instrumentalized as a public and individual medium, creating new opportunities within the movement; it thus took on a fundamental role in structuring the forms of protest."* (Zik 2014, 535).

A characteristic feature of these movements is the collaborative approach. Often 'professionals' and 'non-professionals' (e.g. in terms of political or design-professional experience) act together and learn from each other. Sometimes not least driven by designers providing appropriate tools and formats. With the design-activist (as well as with the 'artivist'), the field of actors has broadened. This can be regarded as both a social and technological phenomenon. Peter Weibel states that 'innovation' and 'creativity' are democratized, as 'user innovation' and 'user-generated-content' no longer influence only the world of mass media, but also the art world and design fields (Weibel 2014, 57). Both art and design will become a 'democratized user-centered innovation system' (Hippel 2005). *"Information and communication technologies open the gates to a century of the emancipated user who wants to be duly recognized in the worlds of art and politics."* (Weibel 2014, 57). He further states that the participation of the audience in art and design *"has morphed into the participation of the citizens in the sphere of politics."* (Weibel 2014, 25). This goes along with a general tendency, the rise of the 'citizen artists', the 'citizen scientists', and probably the 'citizen designers' too. *"Scientists as well as ordinary citizens can become artists, just as citizens and artists can participate in scientific projects, and artists and scientists can participate as citizens in politics."* (Weibel 2014, 26f.)

As the field of design has been discussed about, reflected upon and interpreted as a political actor in many ways, from various perspectives and with different nuances for more than a century (Unteidig et al. 2017), 'political' (in this sense) is not a narrow view of political parties and their respective philosophies and beliefs (Fuad-Luke 2009, 6), but *"is a wider view of the citizen contributing to a broad political dialogue within society, where the question being asked is 'in what sort of society do we want to live?' Design is implicitly embedded in this question and so all design can be considered political."* (ibid.)

Design and its conceptual, functional, aesthetic, speculative and interventional concepts can assert an oppositional public sphere (c.f. Hoffmann 2014, 184), it can actively interfere in common definitions, understandings and opinion making, and it can create effective outrage through critical, alternative and interrogative concepts, thoughts, and prototypes. This offers opportunities for ideological engagement (in a good or in a bad sense) and societal transformation through the mechanisms, logics and activities of design (c.f. Ericson/Mazé 2011, 12). However, as Ericson and Mazé indicate: *"The critique posed by such critical practices is not of design, as such, but of design blindly serving historical convention or hegemonic ideologies. [...] It may not be up to design to resolve the large-scale problematics of the prevailing social, political or economic order – but, by finding and articulating underlying ideas and implications, critical practices render these more accessible to understanding debate – and change."* (ibid.).

The Role of Technology

To what extent design activist projects should be rather classified and valued as design projects or political action, is not always easy to say. In fact, this can be regarded as part of their strategy, too, because eventually they are both (Ullrich/Bieling 2017). This becomes even more obvious in the context of mass digitalization, artificial intelligence, and the increasing importance of information- and communication-technologies. As technology has infiltrated the world in which we live, *"societal development and its political mobilization takes place with and through technology. It defines a space for political intervention."* (Bunz 2014, 187).

But how can we conceive of political intervention with technology today? Raising awareness might be an important step, but is probably not enough. As Ann Thorpe states, *"to move beyond simply 'raising awareness' activism has to build power to make change. In simple terms, power struggles are usually enacted through several means (often combined), particularly organized money, organized people, and from a design perspective, organized representations, materials and spaces. This is another reason why it is important for design activists to think of their work in social movements terms."* (Thorpe, chapter IV). This is surely related to social and design questions, and progressively a technological question, too: *"How can the individual play a leading role in the use of technology and eventually in the future of our digital society?"* (Magrini 2014, 148) According to the activist media artworks of Christoph Wachter and Mathias Jud,[13] Boris Magrini argues that *"giving back to the consumers the keys to the tools of the digital era, and an understanding of the context that regulates these tools"* would be an important move to also *"give them the responsibility to question and reshape the paradigms, the moral values, and the social behavior of our contemporary society"* (ibid.)

The tools Wachter and Jud develop in their critical artistic and design work, often focusing on applications in real-life contexts, are mostly open-source projects that

---

13   In particular to their projects *Picidae*, *New Nations*, and *qual.net* that have been collected under the title of a series "Tools for the next revolution".

have a practical function and can be effectively used by people. Often their projects uncover forms of restricted participation, internet censorship, social in-/exclusion and an attempt to resolve the dependency on (digital, analog) infrastructure. Their tools are used by communities worldwide, including Syria, China, North Korea, Egypt, Tunisia or Iran. Basically these *Tools for the next Revolution* focus on underprivileged individuals and communities, providing them with practical and useful instruments, and as Magrini emphasizes *"their work is not devoid of criticism, nonetheless: Apart from offering actual alternatives to commercial solutions, the[se] works aim at raising awareness of the condition of the digital society and our dependency on private corporations who are not only producing and selling electronic devices, but strongly influencing behavior associated with their use, creating software and brands dependencies, as well as influencing the laws regulating their consumption".* (Magrini 2014, 146). Approaches like these offer a rich ground to explore the politics of digital (as well as visual or interface) culture for instance, but also the alternative processes and spaces – often radically participatory – that frequently accompanies it. Furthermore it can provide both inspiration and a counterpoint to professionalised design discourse. So, after all, such positions could be used both implicitly and explicitly, to support movements for progressive social change.

However to regard a design project or activist object as political just because it addresses precise political topics and local political difficulties would be simplistic (c.f. Magrini 2014, 150). Approaches like the work of Wachter and Jud mentioned above, are political as they *"originate from the desire to politicize the aspects of our contemporary life, more particularly the ones that we constantly forget to consider under a political angle."(ibid).* Digital technologies and electronic devices such as smartphones, tablets, computers, self-driving cars or smart watches, need to be viewed and reclassified in a broader political context *"to ensure that the circumstances of their consumption and their meaning for our society are correctly understood"(ibid.).* Instead of pitting the consumer against powerful corporations and the authorities, [projects like the *Tools for the next Revolution*] invite the consumers to actively participate in the political, economic, and cultural system in which they live. [Thus] unmistakably, the [artists/authors/ creators/designers] affirm the responsibility of the individual in shaping our society and the moral values upon which it is based."(ibid.)

Therefore testing possibilities as well as using design as a means of analyzing social processes and power structures, making them public, and helping to rethink them (Holten 2013, 106) is merely one aspect of design activism. Here we begin to understand, what Carl DiSalvo means, when he describes political design as something, that occurs when the object or processes of design activism is used to reveal and contest existing configurations and conditions of society (DiSalvo 2010). Actually, this one goes even a little step further, as it clarifies that design activism is something, that enables people themselves to take action.[14]

---

14   Ezio Manzini for instance propagates an approach to address social challenges, and to improve individual lives as well as those of communities by means of a collaborative, democratic design practice. He argues for *"the real possibility of changing the rules of the game: of acting politically on everyday life, not by*

According to Mercedes Bunz one could summarize by saying, that in these cases *"political intervention and opposition are located in a social gap that is opened with and through technology. In addition, these examples indicate another interesting shift: technology that allows for participatory action is replacing negative critique that distances itself. Political intervention with technology goes beyond simple opposition by using and appropriating technological developments. Precisely because technology shapes society, one shouldn't leave it to 'the others' – whoever they may be. So one thing remains important: getting involved."* (Bunz 2013, 196)

Design Activism in Theory and Practice

This is a book about how the worlds of design and activism (could) inspire each other. The main goal is to encourage a continuous debate and investigation of research related to design (in theory and practice) and its position within social, activist movements. What is the benefit of using design in activism? What is design's role in the course of social movements? What role can and does activism play in design? What are the contemporary expressions of design activism (c.f. Fuad-Luke 2009, 77)? Who can be a design-activist?[15] And is there an emergent typology of design activism?[16] In this book we shall elaborate these questions through analyzing the use of design e.g. for the communication, information, problematization, visualization, interaction, gamification or management in activist contexts and purposes. We will have a closer look at the approaches, methods, tactics and strategies used in this field. This will help us to better understand the rituals, structures and meanings of design (&) activism in history and the present. And it shall help us to derive arguments and examples for the transformative potential of future design activism.

Structure of the Book

The selection of essays is organized into five overarching chapters that place them within the context of different aspects, perspectives and approaches of Design (&) Activism.

Chapter **I Context** provides the theoretical foundation for the relationships of design and activism, as well as for the similarities and differences between them. By introducing design and activism as cultural acts, it sets a theoretical framework and overview. How is theory informing action, and action informing theory? The authors discuss different varieties of participation, activism and democracy

---

demanding something, but by putting into practice new ways of doing things." (Manzini 2019)

15   In her essay, Ann Thorpe points out that in a global connected world change, and consequently activism, do not come either solely from the top or solely from the bottom of society. According to this, Guy Julier proclaims that you do not necessarily have to be a designer to be a design-activist (Julier 2016).

16   Ann Thorpe provides an overview of *"how sociologists understand activism and show its relevance to design"* and offers a typology of action for design activism (Thorpe 2008, 1524).

in the context from a designerly perspective, ranging from civic disobedience and resistance, to aspects of civic participation, e.g. in terms of political opinion formation and decision making. At this, it shall also become clearer, what areas of design are included in the fields of activism, and which are not.

Chapter **II** *Spaces and Things* outlines how design (&) activism appears and functions in the public and private sphere. This includes online-, offline and hybrid spaces, because increasingly we can witness the *"occupation of public spaces by private persons, as well as the publication of nonpublic information by private persons. [And] the lines dividing the private from the public sphere are blurring."* (*Weibel 2014, 25f)* Be it in local urban spaces or through the global mass media, people seek a public presence in order to articulate global interests and concerns (ibid.). And Design is strongly involved in making these spaces in/accessible.[17] Against this backdrop, this chapter aims to discover the (critical) role of artifacts in design activism. In terms of 'civil disobedience' – as Ann Thorpe describes in her essay – the design twist is that the 'disobedient' element is not the designers and their physical presence, for example at a sit-in, but the materials and symbols they use and produce. The specificity of design interventions as political-aesthetic acts, as Anke Hoffmann puts it, is *"grounded in the real as opposed to the symbolical"* (Hoffmann 2014, 179). Such interventions *"transcend the symbolic in order to act in the real world of everyday life, or in real places and spaces. They relate to concrete political or social situations, and through their heterogenous strategies effect intrusions and disruptions in functional or seemingly closed systems. In doing so, they create oppositional public spheres, out of which new, alternative modes of experience and action can result. Interventions are open-ended inventories that cannot be completely controlled or guided, but which are especially open to confrontations. Such dispute transmits the critical stance into social discourse. An intervention's effectiveness can often be measured by the resistance it elicits on the part of the system or state"* (ibid.) or certain user- and non-user-groups. Thus, artifacts and spaces can assume activist roles, too, which shall be further enquired here.[18]

Chapter **III** *Tools and Strategies* offers ideas and concepts of how activism is constituted in specific contexts. By tracing design strategies in politics and political strategies in design, this chapter is focused on questions like how to do activism? How to design activism? How to 'activate' design? There is a broad range of (often subversive) methods and strategies that have been practiced and discussed within and beyond the design field over a long period. For instance *Culture Hacking* (Düllo/Lieb 2005), *Culture Jamming* (Lasn 1999; see also Adbusters, subvertising / antipreneurs), *Appropriation / Recontextualization* (c.f. Evans 2009), *Subversive Affirmation / Over-identification* (c.f. Arns/Sasse 2006), *Détournement / recuperation*[19] (Debord/Wolman

---

17   *"Artefacts also embed ideas of inclusion or exclusion of individuals or particular social groups. So it is possible to talk about an 'including artefact' and an 'excluding artefact."* (Fuad-Luke 2009, 85)

18   The mission is to help designers and social movement actors to gain a better understanding of the spatial and material possibilities of design's role in activism. *"It makes design activism more accessible within the field of design, and also to wider constituencies."* (Thorpe 2011).

19   *Détournement* takes place, when terms from a clearly defined environment are used in a new context. Guy E. Debord and Gil J. Wolman described and practiced it as one of the leading strategies of situationism (c.f. Landwehr 2014, 228)

1956), *Counter Publicity / Tactical Media* (see Critical Art Ensemble), *Disinformation*[20] (Mindfuck / Fnord; c.f. Shea/Wilson 1976) or *Semiological guerilla / Communications Guerilla*[21] (Eco 1967).[22]

Talking about strategies in the design context, especially with a social and political notion, we should also talk about tactics of course. Michel De Certeau distinguishes between strategies and tactics, calling strategy „*the calculation (or manipulation) of power relationships that become possible as soon as a subject with will and power (a business, an army, a city, a scientific institution) can be isolated."* (De Certeau 1984, 35 f.). Strategies belong to the ones in power. Tactic, on the other hand *"is the art of the weak"*, that fights that power: it *"operates in isolated actions, blow by blow. It takes advantage of ,opportunities' and depends on them, being without any base where it could stockpile its winnings, build up its own position, and plan raids."(ibid.)*. But both terms – tactics and strategies – are correct here, for at least three reasons. First, there is the notion of design strategy or strategic design, not least important when it comes to collaborating with or with 'the institution', which may be well explained as "strategy as a tactic". Then there is the aspect of transferring knowledge from the field of design activism research back into design education, which could be described as a design educational strategy.[23] And then finally there is what Florian Malzacher calls an interest in *"the consequent use of certain tactics, the combination of certain tactics, the invention of tactics follow strategies or form strategies."* (Malzacher 2012).

How does Design Activism happen and what does it take – in terms of design acts, actions and activities? What is the relationship between design practice, studies and explorations in design activism?[24] Potential fields to be discussed here, are related to aspects such as Designing Social Interactions, the Art of Resistance, Relocating Design Agency, Transforming Modes of Production, Materializing Societal Structures or Occupying the Margins of Design (c. f. Ericson/Mazé 2011,

---

20 Targeted dissemination of false information - nowadays also related to the term *Fake News*. Method stemming from psychological warfare (c.f. Landwehr 2014, 227).

21 Operating with invented encyplopedia entries or collectively used invented identities. Refers back to Roland Barthes: *"Is not the best subversion to distort the codes rather than destroy them"*(Barthes 1980; c.f. Landwehr 2014, 230).

22 There are numerous subversive methods and strategies that have been practiced and discussed since the mid-20th century. The ones listed here illustrate that there is often no distinct categorization into the fields of art, design, politcs, business, or media (Daniels 2014, 166 f).

23 The transfer of knowledge to the scholars of Design Research is important to build an *"intellectual tradition within the discipline, and to contribute to the accumulated body of knowledge"* (Fallman 2008, 9). This might also involve the design researcher in taking part in and contributing to the fields of practice as well as ongoing discourses of design activism, be it on a theoretical or methodological level, or from a design historical or design philosophical point of view.

24 According to Daniel Fallman the process of a design research project can be seen as a triangular model defined by the activity areas of "design practice", "design studies" and "design exploration", aiming at what is "real", "true" and "possible" respectively. The corners of this model lead to the three external interfaces: industry, academia and society at large. During an ongoing design research project, the researcher can move and drift through the different areas of activity in loops and trajectories - thereby changing the point of view on the researched matter - that differ in terms of perspective of research outcome and its tradition of research motivation and methods (Fallman 2008).

8). Especially the 'marginal' can be reclaimed and activated as an ideological – and powerful – force in design (ibid., 151). For instance, if we think of the perceptual change of disability (Bieling 2018), gender (Brandes 2017; Bieling 2019b) or ageing. But (how) can the principles of (design) activism also be transferred to other fields, that are not necessarily related to political activism or civic disobedience? Chapter **IV *Principles and Practices*** gives some examples. As the types of tactics and concepts found in conventional activism apply to design activism as well (c.f. Thorpe's essay), we will get to know instances of transferring (design) activist approaches into different contexts. *"Activism describes the work of framing or revealing a problematic or challenging issue through disrupting routines, social practices, or systems of authority; this disruption characterizes activism as being unconventional or unorthodox – outside traditional channels of political change. Social movement activists often turn to disruption as a form of influence because their other resources are limited."* (ibid.). Design activists use disruptive methods to try to bring about change in other arenas.[25]

So what is to be done? After having discussed the potential, the chances and opportunities of the links between the cultural and political practices of design and activism, Chapter **V *Reflections and Projections*** shall now focus on the difficulties, challenges, pitfalls and complexity. To what extent can design help solve *"problems that politics and societies themselves have ignored for so long?"* (Malzacher 2012). And why should designers know what to do when nobody else does? (ibid.). What about the instrumentalization, the misuse and appropriation of design activism, e.g. by companies or the political opponent? The recent revival auf rightist movements and ideologies in some parts of our world has partly disclosed strategies of appropriating leftist tactics, topics, terminologies and (visual) appearances. A similar phenomenon we witness in the context of global brands quickly appropriating aesthetics or ideas, signs, symbols or objects of design activism in a parasitical way (c.f. Julier 2016). Obviously capitalism is extremely good in what it does: *"It is distinguished by the fact that it can incorporate the most radical form of an opposition movement, make a business out of it (and become the exact opposite through mainstreaming)"* (Welzer 2014). As Guy Julier states *"It is fair to say that design activists do some of the work of capitalism, whether they like it or not."* (Julier 2016).

This also raises the question, what roles the *"personal value systems of designers play in the design process and its methods? Should they be suppressed in favor of enabling the widest possible range of diverse perspectives"* (Jonas 2015), which – as Herlo et al. observe – might be in itself an ideological program (Herlo et al. 2018, 228). Or is a *"conscious reflection and application of moral and political positions a prerequisite for design to understand itself as being political?"* (ibid.) But what exactly political design is, what it wants and can accomplish, is always an object of a wider social negotiation (Hoffmann 2014, 178f).[26] After all, the possibilities of design activism, both as

---

25 Usually but not necessarily in those, where the issues are *"typically cash poor and value rich."* (ibid.)

26 In reference to art, Hoffmann states that *"politically committed art can only be described as articulating and taking a critical stance towards the dominant systems of power. In this respect, it sees itself nowadays also as a counter movement against the advance of neoliberalism and the established art system. Political art seeks*

practical action but also as political agency (Julier 2008, 813) are discussed. We shall conclude with reflections, that may be extended as an inspiration or reference within an ongoing discussion on the changing definition of design and the role of designers today (Ericson/Mazé 2011, 9). Ideally this might help people and institutions from within and beyond the design field to develop a different understanding of the tasks, limits and potentials of design.

The Essays

Design activism has been the object of increasing attention over the last decade, which is not least witnessed by a growing number of publications, networks and conferences focusing on the topic. In particular research has been dedicated to defining what design activism is and how it should be conceived of in its resistance to different systems of power and authority. Along this line, a theoretical distinction is often introduced between forms of design activism that works *inside* existing systems of power and those forms that work *outside* being staged as confrontational or subversive to that system. The inside/outside pair is also reflected in other accounts as a difference between design activism encouraging either consensus or dissensus. In his essay, however, **Thomas Markussen** avoids such spatialisations and dichotomies, and comes up with a more nuanced explanation of how design activism always and by necessity is tangled up in forces of power and politics. More specifically, he proposes the notions of 'impure politics' and argues that design activism must be understood as caught up in imbalances of autonomy and instrumentalisation, dissensus and consensus. Besides that, he makes a point clear: Just because designers critically engage with the political or the social does not per se make their practice activist. Focusing on the urban environment, he further provides analyses of some design activist projects to substantiate his claims.

Michael Erlhoff criticises a mere heroic attitude regarding the role of design as social and as a tool of activism. The "stupid mistake" in most of the discourse on the political and social dimensions of design derives from a deep misunderstanding of what design actually is and does. As basically everything is designed, everything we regard as 'normal' is, indeed, a result of design. And that is the crucial point in the political discourse on design which is so urgently needed. As 'norm' is given and moves and shapes us beneath our conscious awareness. Of course, when protesting against norms, and the normal, we have to understand what Kurt Schwitters explained nearly 100 years ago: not the protest against normality is chaotic, normality is.

Can designerly and artistic practices still play a critical role in a society where the difference between art and advertising have become blurred and where artists

---

to be art beyond representation and description by conveying a different form of effectiveness and visibility, and therefore particularly chooses strategies of active participation in shaping the world and in criticizing society." (Hoffmann 2014, 178f).

and cultural workers have become a necessary part of capitalist production? In her essay on artistic activism and agonistic spaces **Chantal Mouffe** discusses several perspectives on the relation(s) between art and politics in terms of two separately constituted fields: the aesthetic dimensions in the political, and the political dimensions in art. Mouffe pleads for designers (and artists) to take up strategies of engagement to challenge the dominant neo-liberal consensus. Under post-fordist conditions, designers working inside the system are totally instrumentalized and, transformed into businessmen; they are bound to contribute to the reproduction of the system. Resistances are still possible, but they can only be located outside the institutions. Next to this strategy of 'withdrawal from institutions', there is another strategy which is the one she advocates, a strategy of 'engagement with institutions'.

Rejecting the economically narrowed neoliberal definition of democracy, **Gui Bonsiepe** claims for the potential of design to promote democracy. He uses a simple interpretation of the term *democracy* in the sense of participation so that dominated citizens transform themselves into subjects opening a space for self-determination, and that means a space for a project of one's own accord. Formulated differently: democracy reaches farther than the formal right to vote, similarly the notion of freedom reaches farther than the possibility to chose between a hundred varieties of smart phones. *Design and Democracy* introduces a concept of design activities which aim to interpret the needs of social groups and to develop viable emancipative proposals in the form of material and semiotic artifacts.

In attempting to address methods and perspectives combining artistic labour, design and political participation, **Gavin Grindon**'s focus is not on the area of performance or dialogue but on objects, probably the most neglected and apparently problematic category for such work. In his essay he critically examines the art and design of social movements[27] and how we might understand and engage with them as designers and citizens. The role of artefacts and material culture in social movement is a mostly untold story, as design and non intentional design[28] objects have gone mostly uncollected, unpreserved, thus excluded from their place in the making of history. Though he avoids the term, we might think of these as 'activist objects' in the sense that they are active, bound up with the agency of social change, and therefore inevitably relevant for the public.

Public space is the part of a city structure open to everyone. Public space is, because we are civic society. Its meaning turned into a political battlefield, its use and the shaping of it are the future subjects of negotiations. In cities, public space is the network of streets, squares and parks that constitutes and represents urban communities. Demographic change, values and principles of the human condition

---

27   More precisely: the art and design objects produced within activist social movements.

28   Non Intentional Design (NID) is a phrase formulated by Uta Brandes and Michael Erlhoff, describing the everyday, unprofessional redesign of professionally designed objects, e.g. through conversion or misappropriation (vgl. Brandes/Erlhoff 2006). NID results for instance when an object is used in a manner different from the prescribed (and therefore restricted) functional intention (Brandes 2008). Uta Brandes has also described this as the „production of things through use", as NID examines the generation of function and the meaning of objects in and through use (Brandes et al. 2009, 10).

are directly expressed by plural forms of its inhabitation and adaptation. Despite scepticism virtual space has not taken over or replaces physical space, only amended. **Barbara Hoidn** asks, which measures are required to defend the right to public space in the long run, to anchor it as a democratic value and right in contemporary urban development policy? She points out that the discussion surrounding the composition of public space and its significance for contemporary urban society has just begun. Publicness has to be tolerated. It is obvious that quality and function of public spaces must be taken seriously as distinct and independent dimensions in urban planning.

Using the example of Tear Gas, **Anna Feigenbaum** takes us from military labs and chemical weapons expos to union assemblies and protest camps, to show how policing with poison came to be. Teargas, is a chemical weapon that went from the battlefield to the streets, designed to force people out from behind barricades and trenches, and has become the most commonly used form of "less-lethal" police force. In 2011, the year that protests exploded from the Arab Spring to Occupy Wall Street, tear gas sales tripled. Most tear gas is produced in the United States, and many images of protestors in Tahrir Square showed tear gas canisters with "Made in USA" printed on them, while Britain continues to sell tear gas to countries on its own human rights blacklist. Feigenbaum sketches out the different perspectives and positions of stakeholders (e.g. executive authority, companies, protesters, bystanders) and concludes with a concrete grass-roots-research project (RiotID), a civic media project designed to help people identify, monitor, and record the use of riot-control agents against civilians, monitor human rights violations, and help people medically respond to the effects of exposure and injury.

Mikala Hyldig Dal focuses on the iconography of activism during the Egyptian revolution of 2011, discussing spatial, social and artistic practices in and around Cairo's *Tahrir Square* that has emerged as a global icon of civil resistance against military rule. During the first revolutionary phases "the core utopian city", as protestors coined the public space around Tahrir, constituted a space to which both political theorist Hannah Arendt's and cultural critic Jaques Ranciére's concepts of (aesthetic) political practice can be applied. Among the political desires most intimately connected with the early revolutionary movement was that of a re-thinking of the polis from a top-down hierarchical structure, in which the majority of the population possessed no representation nor any means of gaining one, to a "space of appearance". The "space of appearance" as conceived by Arendt signifies the active practice of citizenship in the formation of an ideal polis. It is a space where individuals gather to conduct their political agency in a mode of joint voicing. It is a tentative space that depends on the active participation of the temporary inhabitants that constitute it; when these seize to affirm the space through continued activity it seizes to exist. The budding civil society acting within the framework of the *space of appearance* negotiates new terms of visibility, its practitioners define a shared language within their common space by asserting experiential forms of the political and so, in the sense of Ranciére's, actively touch upon the *aesthetic core of politics*. Activists on the square during and in the wake of the revolution embraced collective image making, insitu galleries, large-scale performances, poetry citing and chants, music making and theater playing as tools of political agency. The practices that we know from art, design and cultural institutions were established as central in the renegotiation of public space and in the subversion of autocratic power structures for which the utopian space of Tahrir stood and still stands. If no longer in the form of a fixed geographical site, then at least as a possibility that informs the place in which it once existed.

Common "failures" of artistic activism are outlined and analysed by **Stephen Duncombe** and **Steve Lambert**. Based upon the authors' long experience as practitioners, researchers, and trainers, a number of perils of the practice are identified, including: good intentions, political expressionism, art and activism as lifestyle, raising awareness and other information delusions, media coverage as a marker of success, faith that conversations change the world, and an outdated belief in shock value. The overarching mistake is to see what are really means to greater ends as ends in themselves. The essay concludes with advice and a simple exercise to help artistic activists avoid some of these pitfalls and "fail better".

Further suggestions are given by **Harald Gruendl**, who asks what it needs to change the destructible design attitude of the market economy. Gruendl argues, that it needs a new mindset of designers, consumers and producers which do ask what is needed rather than what can be sold. Open design instead of copyrights, circular design and social design are the tools of a design revolution. And design activists are on the forefront of a design transition towards an economy of commons. Gruendls best practices, collected in this essay, are not meant to be understood as tips or advices, but rather as field reports from system interventions, in order to encourage other designers to take action.

How can graphic design be conceived a political and social practice? In her essay, **Cathy Gale** explores the emergence of creative collectives as an antidote to the contingencies of current market-led practices in graphic design practice and pedagogy. Historically, isolated modes of professional practice have been sought (and taught) as the route to hero status (amongst one's peers) and commercial success through differentiation. Yet this dominance is dependent on individualistic rather than co-operative approaches in a competitive over-crowded field leading to anxious states of capitalism realism. The design collective represents a way to overcome these limitations through cohesion and shared ideals, whether for pragmatic cost-saving ends, or for a more critical purpose. By embedding notions of design activism and political reflection into the design curriculum the power of written and visual forms of design activism are examined. The same persuasive pictorial strategies employed in visual communication to increase consumer engagement and gain commercial advantage are developed here as a visual rhetoric to provoke discourse in two pedagogic contexts. First, the design manifesto project, 'Word As Weapon', secondly, the 'Wall of Words' exhibition.

When the question of a connection of design and activism is asked, the question of a Rhetoric of Subversion emerges as well. **Pierre Smolarski** argues that rhetoric can be seen as an art of identification and that is – first of all – an art of affirmation.

Nonetheless there are both subversive means (for example in guerrilla marketing) and also subversive motives (ends) as in forms of culture jamming, and the success of both is bound to their ways to offer cues of identification. A rhetoric of subversion will show which strategies are successfully possible. In the heart of this rhetorical enquiry stands one of the master tropes of the present days (in entertainment, commercials, forms of protest and also in design) and its counterpart: irony and authority.

Alastair Fuad-Luke explores how *design-led* activism is deploying disruptive, fabulative and generative practices in its attempts to unbalance Integrated World Capitalism (IWC), a term coined by Felix Guattari, today understood as neoliberal transnationalism. IWC dominates what Petra Hroch calls 'images of thought' generating an undifferentiated, capitalized, designed, materialized, hegemonic world-view. This worldmaking is underlain by *pharmaka design*, that is, designed things as, paradoxically, medicine *and* poison; a means to meet real needs yet a means to meet false needs, or destroy others' (human and other-than-human) freedoms; a stimulant yet also a palliative, sedative, toxin and placebo. Lacking the ethics of true-cost economics, this ubiquitous designed world hides ugliness, is undemocratic, is de-futuring and accelerating social injustice, human and ecological disaster. These practices not only challenge the ideology of IWC but also inquire as to who designs, what the designing does, and how designing helps possibilities emerge. Design-led activism is activist in conceptualized, actualized and realized worlds while simultaneously being activist *on* these worlds of design itself. Design-led activism re-conceptualises and re-materialises design as interventions, interruptions, irritations through unexpected acts, paralogic moves and processes. Emergent practices are demonstrated through a selection of contemporary case studies.

Ann Thorpe explores political and social elements of design activism through the lens of transport and mobility. Using a variety of case studies, she examines the idea of 'disruptive events' that activists typically use in attempts to change patterns of power. What activist tactics are in use? What forms of power are in play? Looking at areas in transport such as disability and ageing, spatial equity, gender, health and environment, Thorpe explores how we frame design activism in the context of the transport system. Argumenting with some exemplary positions of contemporary art, **Marcel René Marburger** analyses artistic expressions whose substantial quality is generated through the performing act rather than their aesthetic appearance. Subsequently, the author argues for new variants of artistic resistance – in particular for a shift away from communicational matters towards the act itself. Marburger ascribes the capacities to realize this shift from communication to action especially to designers and pleads for a collaboration between artists and designers to organize future resistance more effectively.

Is there a unique kind of design activism in the Americas? This is the guiding question in **Fernando Luiz Lara**'s essay. The latest OECD report on inequality shows that the three most unequal countries of the so-called "developed" countries are in the Americas: United States, Chile and Mexico in that order. Add Brazil, Colombia, Venezuela, and Peru to those three and we have the following picture:

the Americas are much more unequal than the rest of the world, including most of Africa and the Middle East. This alone would induce the need for strong design activism in that continent. With a rooted history of exclusion (and erasure), the Americas also have developed in the last 50 years a tradition of participation and activism that, despite its successes, has been mostly invisible in the design scholarship. The essay analyzes several cases, including the contemporary *colectivos* that are taking matters in their own hands and pushing architecture away from its elitists quarters and straight to the streets. Lara states that we might be experiencing the very end of starchitects' era, and instead experiencing the dawn of a humbler, connected and socially aware practice of architecture. However, in library shelves, textbooks and syllabus reading lists there are still hundreds of titles celebrating the elitist genius of the past traditions and not enough exposure of the impact made by a new more of socially engaged architecture. Lara's essay can be regarded as a contribution to the latter.

As the role of design has been expanding over time, responsibility and areas of influence of designers in confronting with society have also been changing. **Maziar Rezai** gives an overview of the changing role and definition of designers as activist-designers, containing some significant cases of the last few years, such as the experience of the Arab Spring to challenge and examine the concept of 'activist-designer'. Therefor he subdivides design activism into two different contexts, which he denominates as "Design by Act" and "Design Intellectualism". His essay aims at gaining a better understanding of how the activist designer can effectively work and interact within social and political contexts. Therefor Rezai analyzes several significant cases from Egypt, Iran, Sweden, and Bahrain.

The global rise of design since the 1980s is a cause and symptom of the seepage of neoliberalisation into everyday life. Neoliberalism and design are almost inextricably co-dependent. Can they be decoupled? **Guy Julier** expounds that vast swathes of what is called design activism actually fall short of proposing, let alone enacting, new economic and environmental arrangements, however. Without these, become mere gestures that ultimately collude in mainstream ideological ambitions. Social movements that have prefigured or followed-on from the 2008 economic crisis have more explicitly explored new formats for economic and social life, but if we get closer to design's professional sphere, with all its neoliberal-friendly ethos of service-mode project-based working and its embeddedness with flexible accumulation, it seems that the possibilities for radical, re-directive practices wear a bit thinner. Julier's essay expands on what working in this shadow-world of being both inside and outside neoliberal arrangements produces in terms of design activism and asks what limits this practice has and how these limitations might be overcome. To truly 'fuck neoliberalism', then, design activists working in this space must reflexively design the conditions of their own protection and, thus, longevity. This is different from the notion of leveraging under-used assets as a resilience-producing tactic – a favourite of neoliberal-friendly forms of social innovation and social entrepreneurship. Instead, infrastructures might be developed alongside objects. This means designing also democratic systems of deliberation and representation, trustworthy feedback loops and ways of responding to unpredictable threats. Alternative territories and temporalities of responsibility may then co-emerge.

References

Antonelli, Paola / Hunt, Jamer (2015): *Design and Violence.* New York: MoMa.

Arns, Inke / Sasse, Sylvia (2006): Subversive Affirmation: On Mimesis as a Strategy of Resistance. In: East Art Map. London.

Banz, Claudia (Ed.) (2016): *Social Design – Gestalten für die Transformation der Gesellschaft.* Transcript, Bielefeld.

Bieling, Tom (2018): Design and Inclusion. In: Ralf Michel (Ed.): *Integrative Design: Essays and Projects.* Board of International Research in Design, Basel: Birkhäuser.

Bieling, Tom (2019a): *Inklusion als Entwurf. Teilhabe orientierte Forschung über, für und durch Design.* Board of International Research in Design. Basel: Birkhäuser.

Bieling, Tom (Hg.) (2019b): *Gender (&) Design. Theorien und Praktiken zur Geschlechterkonstruktion und -gestaltung.* Milano: Mimesis.

Bieling, Tom / Sametinger, Florian & Gesche Joost (2014a): Social Dimensions of Design Research; in: Baltic Horizons, No 21 (118), II. Social, ethical and political Aspects of Research in Design; October 2013, EuroAcademy Series Art & Design, Euroakadeemia, Tallinn, Estonia, 35–40.

Bieling, Tom; Joost, Gesche; Sametinger, Florian (2014b): Die soziale Dimension; in Fuhs, Brocchi, Maxein & Draser (Hg.): *Die Geschichte des nachhaltigen Designs*; VAS, Bad Homburg, 218 – 229.

Bishop, Claire (2006): The Social Turn: Collaboration and Its Discontents. International Art Forum, Feb. 2006, Vol. 44, No. 6. New York.

Björgvinsson, Erling / Ehn, Pelle / Hillgren, Per-Anders (2010): Participatory design and democratizing innovation. In *Proceedings of the 11th Biennial Participatory Design Conference*, 41-50. http://portal.acm.org/citation.cfm?id=1900448 ACM [28.06.2011].

Borka, Max (2016): *Brutal schön – Brutal Beauty. Gewalt und Gegenwartsdesign.* Berlin: Kerber.

Brandes, Uta (2008): Non Intentional Design. In: Erlhoff, Michael / Marshall, Tim (Hg.): *Perspectives on Design Terminology.* Birkhäuser, Basel, 270–272.

Brandes, Uta (2017): *Gender Design – Streifzüge zwischen Theorie und Empirie.* Birkhäuser, Basel.

Brandes, Uta / Erlhoff, Michael (2006): *Non Intentional Design.* DAAB, Köln.

Brandes, Uta / Stich, Sonja / Wender, Miriam (2009): *Design by Use: The Everyday Metamorphosis of Things.* Board of International Research in Design, Birkhäuser, Basel.

Bridle, James (2012): Under the Shadow of the Drone. BookTwo, Oct 11, 2012 https://booktwo.org/notebook/drone-shadows/ [accessed 17.09.2018].

Brock, Bazon (1985): *Ästhetik als Vermittlung – Arbeitsbiographie eines Generalisten.* Ostfildern: DuMont.

Bunz, Mercedes (2014): Technology as Political Intervention. In: Dominik Landwehr (Hg.): *Political Interventions*; Edition Digital Culture 1, Christoph Merian Verlag, Basel, 186–196.

Debord, Guy-Ernest / Wolman, Gil J. (1956): A User's Guide to Détournement. (Originally: "Mode d'emploi du détournement", *Les Lèvres Nues* #8 (May 1956)).

De Certeau, Michel (1984): *Practice of Everyday Life.* University of California (3rd Edition 2011).

Diaz-Kommonen, Lily (2002): *Art, Fact and Artifact Production – Design Research and Multidisciplinary Collaboration*; Helsinki: UIAH.

DiSalvo, C. (2010). Design, Democracy and Agonistic Pluralism. In Proceedings of the Design Research

Society Conference 2010. Montreal.

Düllo, Thomas / Lieb, Franz (Hrsg.) (2005): *Cultural Hacking. Kunst des strategischen Handelns.* Wien/New York: Springer.

Eco, Umberto (1967): Für eine semiologische Guerilla. In: Umberto Eco: *Über Gott und die Welt.* München 1996.

Ehn, Pelle (2001): On the Collective Designer; keynote lecture at Cultural Usability Seminar, UIAH Helsinki, April 2001; as quoted in Diaz-Kommonen 2002, 41.

Ehn, Pelle (2009): Design Things and Living Labs. Participatory Design and Design as Infrastructuring. In Multiple Ways to Design Research. Research cases that reshape the design discipline. Proceedings of the Swiss Design Network Symposium 2009; Lugano, 52–64.

Ehn, Pelle / Kyng, Morten (1987): The Collective Resource Approach to Systems Design. In Gro Bjerknes, Pelle Ehn & Morgegn Kyng (Eds.): *Computers and Democracy.* Aldershot, Brookfield, 17–57.

Ericson, Magnus / Mazé, Ramia (2011): *Design Act – Socially and politically engaged Design today – critical roles and emerging tactics.* Sternberg, Berlin.

Erlhoff, Michael / Marshall, Tim (Eds.): *Design Dictionary – Perspectives on Design Terminology.* Basel: Birkhäuser.

Evans, David (Ed.) (2009): *Appropriation. Documents of Contemporary Art.* Cambridge Mass.

Fallman, Daniel (2008): The Interaction Design Research Triangle of Design Practice, Design Studies, and Design Exploration. Design Issues: Volume 24, Number 3 Summer 2008, Massachusetts Institute of Technology. Cambridge/MA: MIT Press.

Fuad-Luke, Alastair (2009): *Design activism: beautiful strangeness for a sustainable world.* London: Earthscan.

Gee, Tim (2011): *Counterpower: Making Change Happen.* London: World Changing; Edition Unstated edition.

Harding, Thomas (2001): *The Video Activist Handbook.* London: Pluto.

Havel, Václav (1978): *The Power of the Powerless.* Reprint (2018), Vintage Classics. London: Random House.

Heissenbüttel, Dietrich (2014): Protests everywhere? In: Peter Weibel (Ed.): *Global Activism – Art and Conflict in the 21st Century.* ZKM Karlsruhe / MIT Press, Cambridge, MA / London, England, 462–482.

Hendren, Sara (2015): Notes on Design Activism. Accessible Icon.

Herlo, Bianca / Unteidig, Andreas / Joost, Gesche (2018): Community Now? Conflicts, Interventions, New Publics. In: *Unfrozen – a Design Research Reader by the Swiss Design Network.* Zürich: Triest, 215–230.

von Hippel, Eric (2005): *Democratizing Innovation.* Cambridge (MA): MIT Press, as quoted in Weibel 2014, 57.

Hoffmann, Anke (2014): Tactics of Appropriating Reality. In: Dominik Landwehr (Hg.): *Political Interventions;* Edition Digital Culture 1, Christoph Merian Verlag, Basel, 176–185.

Holten, Johan (Ed.) (2013): *Macht der Machtlosen – Power of the powerless.* Staatliche Kunsthalle Baden-Baden. Köln: Walther König.

Irwin, Terry (2015): Transition Design: A Proposal for a New Area of Design Practice, Study and Research. Design and Culture Journal, 9/2015. Abingdon: Taylor & Francis.

Irwin, Terry / Kossoff, Gideon / Tonkinwise, Cameron (2015): Transition Design: An Educational Framework for Advancing the Study and Design of Sustainable Transitions. 6th International Sustainability Transitions Conference (8/2015), University of Sussex, UK.

Jonas, Wolfgang (2015): Social Transformation Design as a form of Research Through Design (RTD): Some historical, theoretical, and methodological remarks. in: Wolfgang Jonas, Sarah Zerwas, and Kristof von Anshelm (Eds.): *Transformation Design: Perspectives on a New Design Attitude.* Board of International Research in Design. Basel: Birkhäuser, 114–133.

Jonas, Wolfgang / Zerwas, Sarah / von Anshelm, Kristof (2015): *Transformation Design – Perspectives on a New Design Attitude.* Board of International Research in Design. Basel: Birkhäuser.

Julier, Guy (2008): Design activism as a tool for creating new urban narratives. In: Proceedings of *Changing the Change* Conference, Turin July 2008, 813–822.

Julier, Guy (2016): Radical Design. Vitra Design Museum. October 2016.

Landwehr, Dominik (Ed.): *Political Interventions.* Edition Digital Culture 1. Basel: Christoph Merian / Migros Kulturprozent.

Lasn, Kalle (1999): *Culture Jam. The Uncooling of America.* New York: Eagle Brook.

Magrini, Boris (2014): Beyond mere Tools. In: Dominik Landwehr (Hg.): *Political Interventions*; Edition Digital Culture 1, Christoph Merian Verlag, Basel, 140–151.

Malzacher, Florian (2012): Truth is concrete. Theorie zur Praxis – Reader in Progress. Opening Introduction for the 24/7 Marathon camp on artistic strategies in politics and political strategies in art. 21. – 28.09.2012 at Steirischer Herbst, Graz.

Manzini, Ezio (1997): Leapfrog – designing sustainability. Domus, 01, 43-51.

Manzini, Ezio (2007): Design Research for Sustainable Social Innovation, in: Ralf Michel (Ed.): *Design Research Now*, Basel: Birkhäuser.

Manzini, Ezio (2019): *Politics of the Everyday (Designing in Dark Times).* New York: Bloomsbury.

Mareis, Claudia (2010): Entwerfen, Wissen, Produzieren. Designforschung im Anwendungskontext. Bielefeld: Transcript, 9–32.

Markussen, Thomas (2011): The Disruptive Aesthetics of Design Activism: Enacting Design between Art and Politics. NORDES – Nordic Design Research Conference 2011, Helsinki.

Markussen, Thomas (2013): The Disruptive Aesthetics of Design Activism: Enacting Design between Art and Politics. Design Issues Vol. 29, No 1 (2012).

Michaelsen, Marcus (2014): Beyond the 'Twitter Revolution': Digital Media and Political Change in Iran. In: Peter Weibel (Ed.): *Global Activism – Art and Conflict in the 21st Century.* ZKM Karlsruhe / MIT Press, Cambridge, MA / London, England, 384–395.

Murray, R., J. / Caulier-Grice / Mulgan, G. (2010): *The Open Book of Social Innovation.* NESTA/Young Foundation, London.

Rammert, W. (2010): *Die Innovationen der Gesellschaft. In Soziale Innovationen.* VS Verlag für Sozialwissenschaften.

Rancière, Jacques (2006): *The Politics of the Aesthetics.* London/New York: Continuum.

Rogger, Basil / Voegeli, Jonas /Widmer, Ruedi & Zurich University of the Arts, Museum für Gestaltung Zürich (Eds.) (2018): *Protest. The Aesthetic of Resistance.* Zürich: Lars Müller Publ.

Sachs, Angeli (Ed.) (2018): *Social Design – Partizipation und Empowerment.* Museum für Gestaltung, Zürich: Lars Müller Publ.

Sanders, Elisabeth B.N. (2006): Scaffolds for building everyday creativity. In: Frascara, J. (Hrsg.) *Design for Effective Communications: Creating Contexts for Clarity and Meaning.* Allworth Press, New York.

Sanders, Elisabeth / Stappers, Pieter-Jan (2008): Co-creation and the new landscapes of design. Co-Design, 4(1), 5-18.

Sanders, Elisabeth (2013): Perspectives on participation in design. In: C. Mareis, M. Held, G. Joost (Ed.) *Wer gestaltet die Gestaltung?* Bielefeld: transcript.

Schuler, Douglas / Namioka, Aki (Eds.) (1993): *Participatory Design – Principles and Practices.* London: Taylor & Francis.

Seidman, Judy (2008): *Red on Black: The Story of the South African Poster Movement.* Johannesburg: Real African Publishers.

Shea, Robert / Wilson, Robert Anton (1976): *Illuminatus!* London: Sphere Books.

Simonsen, Jesper / Robertson, Toni (Eds.) (2013): *Routledge International Handbook of Participatory Design.* London: Routledge.

Sommer, Bernd / Welzer, Harald (2016): *Transformationsdesign – Wege in eine zukunftsfähige Moderne.* München: Oekom.

Staatliche Kunsthalle Baden-Baden (2012): *Bilderbedarf – Braucht Gesellschaft Kunst? – The Civic and the Arts.* Walther König, Köln.

Steirischer Herbst & Florian Malzacher (Eds.) (2014): *Truth is concrete – A Handbook for Artistic Strategies in Real Politics.* Berlin: Sternberg.

Thorpe, Ann (2008): Design as activism: A conceptual tool. In: Proceedings of *Changing the Change* Conference, Turin July 2008, 1523–1535.

Thorpe, Ann (2008b): Is there a Fourth Sector?, quoted in Thorpe 2008.

Thorpe, Ann (2011): Defining Design as Activism. Submitted to the Journal of Architectural Education.

Thorpe, Ann (2012): *Architecture & Design versus Consumerism – How Design Activism confronts Growth.* London: Taylor & Francis.

Ullrich, Wolfgang / Bieling, Tom (2017): "Die Kunst als fünfte Gewalt im Staat? – Ein Gespräch über Artivismus". In: DESIGNABILITIES Design Research Journal, (9) 2017. PDF Download: https://designabilities.files.wordpress.com/2017/09/designabilities_wolfgangullrich_tombieling_artivismus_sept2016-17.pdf. [Full version of a shorter text initially published in Ullrich/Bieling 2016].

Ullrich, Wolfgang / Bieling, Tom (2016): "Die Kunst als fünfte Gewalt im Staat? – Ein Gespräch über Artivimus"; in: Die Referentin – Kunst und kulturelle Nahversorgung; Referentin #5, September 2016, Linz, Österreich, 10–13.

Unteidig, Andreas / Domínguez Cobreros, Blanca / Calderon-Lüning, Elizabeth & Gesche Joost (2017): Digital commons, urban struggles and the role of Design. Design for Next. EAD12, Rome.

Weibel, Peter (Ed.) (2014): *Global Activism – Art and Conflict in the 21st Century.* ZKM Karlsruhe / MIT Press, Cambridge, MA / London.

Weiss, Peter (1975): *Die Ästhetik des Widerstands,* Frankfurt a. M.: Suhrkamp.

Welzer, Harald (2014): Gesche Joost in dialog with Harald Welzer / 150 Years of the MAK. From Arts and Crafts to Design. Museum für Angewandte Kunst, Wien. Juni 2014.

Yee, Joyce / Jefferies, Emma / Michlewski, Kamil (2017): *Transformations – 7 Roles to drive Change by Design.* Amsterdam: BIS.

Zapf, Wofgang (1989): Über soziale Innovationen. *Soziale Welt,* 40, ½, 170-183.

Zeller, Ludwig (2018): The B1/B2 Manifesto: Refining Dichotomies in Post-utopian Design Research. In: *Unfrozen – a Design Research Reader by the Swiss Design Network.* Zürich: Triest, 37–61.

Zik, M. Ragip (2014): Raising Resistance: Reinterpreting Art within the Gezi Movement. In: Peter Weibel (Ed.): *Global Activism – Art and Conflict in the 21st Century.* ZKM Karlsruhe / MIT Press, Cambridge, MA / London, 535–543.

I. CONTEXT

THE IMPURE POLITICS OF DESIGN ACTIVISM

Thomas Markussen

Design activism is the topic of a growing number of publications, networks and design conferences. As a result, there exist today various notions of what design activism is and not least what can be expected of design activist practices, which are the two issues I will be primarily interested in here.

It is not unusual to find general assertions made of design activism's overlap with social design and participatory design, approaches that are likewise engaged with the needs of marginalized groups and designing for non-commercial ends (See e.g. Armstrong et al. 2014; Banz 2016; Björgvinsson/Ehn/Hillgren 2012, 127–44; Thorpe/Gamman 2011, 217–30). Moreover, design activism is often presented as the antidote to the unsustainable condition of living resulting from unruly forces of Neoliberalism, global capitalism and over consumption (Julier 2013, 215–36). In this sense, design activism easily gets conflated with design for sustainability and social innovation (See e.g. Fuad-Luke 2009; Manzini 2015; Thorpe 2012). However, just because designers critically engage with the political or the social does not *per se* make their practice activist. Hence, in spite of a common goal (a more sustainable environmental and social future), there is a key difference between design activism and these other design practices' engagement with the political and social (See also Markussen 2017, 160–74). Notably, this difference hinges upon what I will refer to as the 'politics of design activism', i.e. its ability through critical aesthetic practice to contest and unsettle existing systems of power and authority.

Several authors have delved into this topic, some of whom explicitly speak of 'design activism' (Fuad-Luke 2009; Fuad-Luke 2013; Julier 2013; Markussen 2013; Thorpe 2008; Thorpe 2012), while others use cognate terms such as 'design as politics' (Fry 2011), 'adverserial design' (DiSalvo 2012) and 'agonistic participatory design' (Björgvinsson/Ehn/Hillgren 2013). Yet, there are subtle variations in how design's potential for effecting change is conceptualised.

In order to account for these variations, Fuad-Luke has proposed a coarsely grained meta-theoretical framework, where current theories of design activism are divided into one out of two approaches (Fuad-Luke 2013). More specifically, Fuad-Luke makes a distinction between theories conceiving of design activism as working *within* a paradigm of power and control and design activism working *outside* the paradigm. When design activism works within the paradigm it *"adopts a consensus over dissensus approach, while outside the paradigm the approach is one of dissensus over consensus"* (Fuad-Luke 2013, 471).

In what follows, I will demonstrate that we need to be cautious in making such spatial dichotomies because they easily lead to two incompatible ideological representations of design activism, both of which, although dominant in current design research, are not at ease with the actual practice of design activism. While the consensus over dissensus approach enslaves design activism to the hegemony of existing systems of power, the dissensus over consensus approach often leads to overblown claims of design activism being able to obliterate that power through revolt and anarchy.

To substantiate my argument, I shall first provide some theoretical background for understanding the meaning of the concepts 'dissensus' and 'consensus'. This theoretical background will be modelled upon Jacques Rancière's political philosophy, notably his distinction between 'politics' and 'the police'. The basic tenet of Rancière's thought is that critical aesthetic practices – whether in design activism or critical art – can truly call existing paradigms of power into question, and for this reason they enact dissensus and politics, but these practices are inescapably bound up with these paradigms. Hence, for Rancière, it does not make sense to speak of an 'inside' and 'outside' of a paradigm. The politics of aesthetic practices is an 'impure politics', as I will show below. For now, suffice it to say, that the notion of impure politics allows me to position design activist practice in-between hegemony and anarchy and, in so doing, to make the theorization of design activism more attuned with design activist practice.

Theoretical background: Pure and impure politics

The offer of Rancière's philosophy to design research is a valuable explanation of how design in general and design activism in particular can be understood as an inherently aesthetic and political practice. Aesthetic for Rancière refers not to "a theory of sensibility, taste or pleasure" (Rancière 2004, 22). Instead, aesthetics refers to those forms that "determine what presents itself to sense perception" (ibid., 13). Rancière therefore asserts that aesthetic is about "the distribution of the sensible". Such a distribution entails that a sensible space and time are given as shared, and at the same time, divided and partitioned among the entities (people, artefacts, systems, institutions) identified as forming part of it (Vallury 2009, 229). Through this distribution a perceptual field is configured so that it enables certain social orders, ways of participating, doing, making, speaking, acting, and being. Politics, on the other hand, occurs when the sensible is redistributed, when culturally entrenched ways of being, saying and doing are disturbed so that it opens up for new modes of subjectivization and inscription" in a shared space (ibid). In this way politics enacts what Rancière refers to as *dissensus* (Rancière 2010, 38). Yet, to fully grasp what dissensus means, it is necessary to understand that politics and dissensus in Rancière's work are defined in diametrical opposition to the notions of 'police' and 'consensus'.

'Police' is used by Rancière to denote the organisation of powers and a broad set of procedures that allows a specific system to govern. Formally, the police can be manifested through the passing of acts and laws, the organization of political parties into parliaments, election procedures and so on. However, orders of the police are not reducible to the arena of political science. The police permeate the whole of a society and are often only implicitly felt in how a social formation distributes bodies and things into places and roles in certain ways. Policing takes place everywhere: through the organization of healthcare services, educational systems, urban planning, and policy-making, but also in how people daily interact and communicate with each other. What is characteristic of police orders is that they are structured hierarchically into a social order, which sets conditions for who has the right to speak and to listen, who is excluded and included, and what is deemed right and wrong. To establish such conditions the police perform ways of counting empirical parts of the social formation. People are divided into actual groups by their difference in birth, ethnicity, different functions, locations and interests that are counted as constituting the social body (ibid., 35). Although such ways of counting can only be conventional the police works through sophisticated processes of naturalization that seeks to legitimize and make self-evident this counting and distribution of parts (cf. Chambers 2013, 66). This is how the police are tightly coupled to the notion of consensus: that which is taken as univocal, but which could be otherwise (cf. Rancière 2010, 149).

Politics is the disrupting of the police order. A moment of dissensus that disturbs the self-evidence of the given order of domination so that a reconfiguring of positions, roles of identity and power can take place (ibid., 37). But there are divergent interpretations of what exactly this disruption consists in and how one should conceive of its potential for changing the police order. For the sake of clarity, let us say, that among Rancière scholars there exists a *pure politics* and an *impure politics* interpretation.

According to the pure politics interpretation, which can be found, for instance, in Tood May's work, politics is the actions of a wronged group or individuals who protest against the inequalities of the hierarchically structured policing order (May 2008). In this account the police are conceived of in pejorative terms and is often associated with repressive orders of domination or Neoliberal government. Politics is the force of the people, a way for them to radically call into question the injustices of the police (through revolt, riot and protest) and eventually to obliterate it by reclaiming total equality. Although May argues convincingly that politics is the way of safeguarding democratic politics there is a short distance from his notion of total equality to anarchy. Moreover, politics and police in his account come to represent what Sloterdijk elsewhere refers to as "a fire of pure burning oppositions": good versus evil, friend against enemy, the people versus the state, and so on (Sloterdijk 2005). Politics and police cannot co-exist, only one survives by overturning the other.

The impure politics interpretation is set up against and as a critique of this account. One of its proponents is Chambers who argues that for Rancière "politics *cannot be uncoupled from police; it only appears in this blended form"* (Chambers 2013, 49). Note however that for Chambers this blending should not be taken in the sense of 'merging' (ibid., 49). Politics is a moment of rupturing the police that makes a "wrong" or "miscount" perceivable in the policing order. It's potential for changing the police order lies precisely in letting this dis-sensus be acknowledged, but what comes after cannot be predicted. Politics occur as *"a possible event with repercussions that can never be anticipated"* (ibid., 8). This means that Chambers does not subscribe to the idea that politics is a conflict between the people and the authorities; nor that it can be instrumentalised to achieve certain political goals or state of affairs, e.g. the overturning of the police. Because, as he says, *"Politics can do nothing else than this: renegotiate and reconfigure the police order"* (ibid., 65).

In this account, the police are taken in a neutral and non-pejorative sense based on the assumption that "police orders are not only bad" (ibid., 10). Whether a reconfiguration of the police order happens relies on how dissensus – the making perceivable of a wrong – is accommodated by the police. The central critique of Neoliberalism as a policing order is that it seeks to eliminate every occurrence of dissensus by cordoning it off into a confined and controlled space in its prevailing order of counted parts (ibid., 29). This does not lead to change, but to sustaining hegemony as the status quo.

Why is this disagreement in philosophy relevant for design research? In what follows below, I demonstrate that it is important, because it allows for increasing understanding of how dominant ideas and theories of design activism diverge.

Design activism as pure politics and anarchy

In *Design as politics*, Fry provides a discouraging account of the miserable condition of our world at large, identifying the true causes of the crisis and why the model of what he appropriately terms 'defuturing' is only going to make things worse. The entire project of the book is described as *"the transformation of design and of politics combining, for all agents of change, to become the means by which the moment and process of Sustainment (the overcoming of the unsustainable) is attained"* (Fry 2011, viii). For this transformation to happen, designers need to shift attention from institutionalised politics to action in "the realm of the political". This is what 'design as politics' stands for: *"an engagement with the political nature of the world around us"* (Fry 2011, 102–3).

Notwithstanding Fry preferably speaks of 'design as politics' and not 'design activism', it goes without saying that his proclamation can be seen as being explicitly concerned with the question that I have set out to explore. What can we expect of design activism? According to Fry we should expect massive change. Faced with mal-functioning democracy, as the existing system of governance design must be used as means for exceeding and replacing democracy, because it is "unable to deliver Sustainment".[1] Drawing upon Carl Schmitt's political theory, Fry asserts

---

1   Fry uses 'democracy' in the singular to denote Neoliberal democracy.

that a "superior form of politics" must replace democracy. The shaping of such a politics is placed in the hands and minds of 'creative communities' who *should put themselves before the challenge of developing new realizable (rather than utopian) political imaginaries"* (Fry 2011, 103). Further, to support the implementation of this politics, we need to invent a new kind of institutional form: a planetary institution – like the United Nations, but entirely transformed.

Disregarding the question of whether this is a utopian or realisable project, I shall focus on how such an account can be seen as a vivid example of pure politics. Thus, basing the discussion on the theoretical backbone extracted from Ranciére's philosophical work, one can argue that democracy for Fry is conceived of as an ill-functioning policing order. It is a system of power exercised through unsustainable logics of marketization and capitalism weighting economic value over environmental and social value. By claiming that the aim is to contest and replace democracy, Fry represents design as politics as the elimination of democracy. Or to use the wordings of Fuad-Luke: Fry takes an overtly "dissensus over consensus approach" (Fuad-Luke 2013, 471). But what does such a notion of design entail?

It is hard to avoid seeing Fry's "superior form of politics" as yet another police order with the 'creative communities' acting as a new ruling class and a sovereign planetary institution. Creativity is in this way instrumental to securing this order. As a matter of fact creativity becomes the instrument for exercising power and inevitably there will be those allocated positions, roles and places for deeming what counts as Sustainment and what not. One could of course counter argue that such a hierarchy would be avoided if one declares that everyone of us is recognised as being equally creative or capable of designing. However the radical consequence of such a view would be a creative anarchy of DIY freaks and not Sustainment with a capital 'S', but endless political imaginaries of sustainment.

The point here is not that I do not share Fry's acute diagnosis and frustration with Neoliberal democracy. It is rather to question the ideological representation of the politics of design as consisting in the complete overturning of this political system. Neoliberalism and the growth model of economics can surely be held much responsible for the miseries of the status quo. But, as Julier remarks, it is rather doubtful whether design activism is actually capable of effecting massive change *"to a post-neoliberal environment where power relations, the role of capital, and care for the environment are radically different"* (Julier 2013, 227). The reason is, Julier says, that Neoliberalism is flexible and "adept at exploiting crises".

What Julier is hinting at here is a common observation in political theory, namely that political uprising and protest, due to crises, is used affectively by capitalist power to uphold and outmanoeuvre all kinds of opposition, so that it "continues to function, its institutions and power still intact" (ibid.).

Alternatively, as mentioned in the beginning, Fuad-Luke suggests that design activism can also work within the existing paradigm of power adopting a consensus over dissensus approach. As a proponent of this approach, Fuad-Luke points out Ann Thorpe's book *Architecture & Design versus Consumerism* with the telling subtitle *How Design Activism confronts Growth* (Thorpe 2012). This line of thought would seem to be consistent with Julier's emphasis on design activism being inextricably bound up with Neoliberal forces and deserves further scrutiny.

Hegemony and the taming of design activism

In her book Thorpe provides a thorough analysis and diagnosis of the current state of the world that is almost identical with Fry's, but her account of how design activism can effect the necessary change are both tempered and exemplified in abundance with numerous projects within architecture and design. Generally, Thorpe defines design activism as taking *"action on an issue that is neglected or excluded, but socially or environmentally important"* (Thorpe 2012, 190). Insofar as the bringing about of social and environmental values are used as her primary classification criteria, design activism ends up being a rather vast category for Thorpe, including i) design activism "that focuses on making the business case for social and environmental design", ii) design activism that takes place "in non-profit groups as well as public or government arenas" and iii) design activism taking the form of design for sustainability and social innovation organised in networks such as DESIS[2] (Thorpe 2012, 7). However, at stake here is a hotchpotch of approaches that, although sharing a concern for the social and environmental, clearly needs to be differentiated.

Elsewhere I have demonstrated that "making a business case for social design" lives up to what is commonly understood as social entrepreneurship and not design activism (Markussen 2017, 163–65). Thus, in their systematic review of 122 articles on social entrepreneurship and social innovation, Philips and her colleagues found that social entrepreneurship is essentially defined by the attempt not only to perform socially to help a needy group, but also financially (Philipps et al. 2014). In addition other authors see social entrepreneurship as a result of what is referred to as a 'market error' (Christensen/Morgen 2010, 7–23; Dees 1998; Hockerts 2006; Weerawardena/Sullivan 2006). The assumption here is that commercial market forces are unable to meet social needs, either because those needing services cannot pay for them (Austin/Stevenson/Wei-Skillern 2006, 2) or because the nature of social problems are too wicked to be addressed from a business and profit seeking approach (Weisbrod 1975). As examples of social entrepreneurship one can think of Muhammad Yunus' micro-credits or Internet platforms such as MyC4, which supports peer-to-peer investment to help underprivileged people in developing countries set up a business.

Social innovation, on the other hand, arises because of a 'system error' or organisational inertia that make a society respond to its challenges in a delayed, insufficient or erroneous manner (Lawrence/Lorsch 1967). Social innovations are the result of complex collaborative processes *"shaped by the collective sharing of knowledge between a wide range of organizations and institutions that influence*

---

2   DESIS is an International Design Network for Social Innovation and Sustainability founded by Ezio Manzini.

developments in certain areas to meet a social need or to promote social development"
(Philipps et al., 449). Another defining trait is that social innovations are usually
the result of a new combination or hybrids of existing elements or services rather
than new in themselves (Manzini 2015; Mulgan 2014). Although social innovation
and social entrepreneurship may thus be regarded according to different premises,
they are likened to each other in their ability to achieve large scale transformations
enabling others to copy the idea and distribute it through a number of significant
imitations and implementations (Christensen/Morgen 2010; Martin/Osberg 2007).

This is unlike social design, which is usually confined to fostering change on a
micro scale for a limited group of disadvantaged people. The notion of social value
in social design refers to the improving of interpersonal relations and well being at
the level of the individual, family, or community, and is most often not transferrable
to large-scale transformations (Markussen 2017, 165–69). For the same reason,
Thorpe and Gamman argue for lowering expectations to "good enough design"
rather than massive change (Thorpe/Gamman 2011).

In spite of their differences, social entrepreneurship, social innovation and social
design are all subjected to certain logics and powers of instrumentalisation. Taking
Europe as the geopolitical focus, social entrepreneurship is spurred by the logic of
commodifying social needs thereby exploiting a missed market opportunity; social
innovation by the logic of fixing recurrent system errors in shrinking welfare states
to maintain welfare services and infrastructure; and social design is harnessed by a
logic of founding new partnerships between the public sector and civic society to
retain basic delivery of welfare services.

Ann Thorpe (2012) conflates design activism with these three other approaches.
As a consequence, design activism ends up being represented as a design practice
tamed by the very same orders of domination and hegemony that are criticised in
the first place for having caused the urgent need for change. This becomes perhaps
most evident in her use of two examples from architecture. More specifically,
Thorpe highlights OMA's Seattle Public Library[3] (Thorpe 2012, 93) and Renzo
Piano's California Academy of Sciences (Thorpe 2012, 159) as two architectural
projects that have been capable of attaining respectively social inclusion and eco-
friendliness. The measures and hard facts certainly does not belie the social and
environmental achievements of the two buildings: In the first instance library usage
has increased more than 65 percent, drawing in people from Seattle's two largest
communities, African American and Hispanic; and it must be appreciated, in the
second instance, that a natural science museum produces 50 percent less waste
water or that it uses natural lighting in 90 percent of occupied spaces. What is
questionable though is whether these projects made by two starchitect companies
are exemplifying design activism confronting growth.

What is forfeited here is that the idea of design practices taking a consensus
over dissensus approach yields an image of design activism being enslaved to the
hegemony of the existing system of power and growth. Clearly, the two architectural

---

3   OMA is short for Office for Metropolitan Architecture, co-founded by Rem Koolhaas in 1975.

projects must be seen as parts in a wider economic system of clients and architects, cities using iconic buildings competitively for branding purposes and to boost their event economical bottom lines and livability index. Returning to the thought of Ranciére, one can see such a system as a very powerful policing order that delimits social inclusion and environmental values to confined corners in the economy and existing system of production. If we understand the politics of design activism as referring to the enacting of dissensus, then design activism introduces a logic that, although bound up with it, is entirely heterogeneous to that of the policing order (Rancière 1999, 31). In what remains, I shall elaborate on this third view.

Design activism in-between anarchy and hegemony

Drawing on previous work, I argue that design activism should be recognised as an aesthetic dissensual practice of its own. Because design activism also engages with the political and social does not make its practices identical with, for instance, social design or social innovation. Furthermore, by criticising a pure politics interpretation of design, I also argue that design activism is not about an institutional overturning or taking over of power. Rather the aesthetic dissensus lies in the subtle way design activism is able *"to cut across and expose hierarchies – hierarchies that control both practice and discourse – so that zones can emerge where processes of subjectivization might take place"* (Markussen 2013, 45). By introducing the notion of impure politics, I aim here to elaborate further on this interpretation of design activism.

First of all, design activism involves a messy clash between two logics. It is a practice where an individual or a collective assert their position in a way, to cite Davide Panagia, "that ruptures the logic" of the existing social order (Panagia 2001). Such a rupture holds a potential for emancipation, but not a promise that it will actually happen. Emancipation begins with a perceived wrong that let us understand that what is hierarchically structured as an apparently self-evident order can be undermined or contradicted by a logic of no structure, of equality (cf. Rancière 2009, 13). It is by introducing this second logic heterogeneous to that of the existing order that design activism - unlike social design and social innovation – is able to wrist itself out if the instrumentalising logic of governance and policy-making.

Secondly, it is important to notice that the disruption of the social order through aesthetic dissensus should be considered as a "short lived" moment or event (Chambers 2013, 8; Corcoran 2010, 5). Nevertheless, this does not make design activism less valuable than social innovation and social design, where outcomes are often said to have long-term effects. Design activism effects a momentary dis-identification or opening up of a gap between prescribed ways of doing and making and unanticipated ways of doing and making. In this opening up established roles, spaces and practices become malleable to renegotiation and new identities and silenced subjects can make themselves be heard.

Thirdly, the politics of design activism is an impure politics. It may reveal and contest the exclusion of the poor, the vulnerable, the homeless, the refugee, the discriminated, etc., but new processes of exclusion and inclusion and the exercising of power will inevitably follow. At best, the repercussions of design activism lead to police orders doing good and not bad things.

An example from the field of urban activism will allow me elucidate this view and bring these theoretical reflections down to street level. In 2011, the design activist collective Bureau Detours installed Dennis Design Center as a temporary urban installation on Prague's Boulevard in Copenhagen for about two weeks. Dennis Design Center, which was part of the Metropolis festival, consisted in two freight containers fully equipped with wood, tools, bicycle barbecues and around 20 carpenters, designers, artist, architects, teachers, among others, who invited local citizens in to take part in "designing useable designs inspired by local demand and site specific issues".[4] According to a newspaper article published at around the time of its opening, in a few days Dennis Design Center had led to a transformation of a toxic site to a place where the locals took part in reshaping the area, discussions on contemporary urban planning and collective street cooking events (Kjær 2011).

Playing deliberately with the similarity in English between the pronunciation of Dennis Design Center and the Danish Design Center, Bureau Detours' installation contested the national institutionalised promoting of design in business and industry. With a tongue-in-cheek hoax Dennis was presented as the founder of the Design Center, depicted with a portrait of a knight-looking design hipster and described as "a weird, but most clever, 2.20 meter tall design enthusiast from Rotterdam in the Netherlands", who had asked the collective to collaborate with him (Haack/Aude/Muchenberger 2012, 26–27). Dennis was of course unable to attend the opening, but a fictional speech authored by him was read aloud. In Dennis Design Center citizens met design at street level and they collaborated with the activist collective in the making of free DIY furniture or the welding together of tall bikes. In this way, Dennis Design Center became a momentary zone where new processes of subjectification and ways of making and doing took place. Local citizens were actively engaged in processes of making and manufacturing their own products under the label Dennis Design. Through such activities Dennis Design Center contested and revealed as hollow the glorified branding image of Danish Design being promoted by the Danish Design Center as socially inclusive, rooted in true craftsmanship and design for the people. The free DIY furniture coming out of Dennis Design Center made perceivable a wrong or disjunction between Danish Design Center's naming of Danish Design as democratic and the expensive furniture classics of Danish Design put on display as status symbols on pedestals in glamorous showrooms and magazines. In the gap that was opened up by this aesthetic dissensus, it became possible, if only for a moment, to let Danish Design take visible and audible form as furniture being designed not for an equalized notion of a unified people, but for and by a multitude of local residents.

This project also provides a paramount example of the impure politics of design

---

4   See the Bureau Detours website located at http://www.in-situ.info/en/artists/bureau-detours/works/en/
      dennis-design-center-39.

activism. On the 20th of August 2011, on the day of the closing of Dennis Design Center, Bureau Detours officially received an email from the Danish Design Center, demanding that the collective would stop using the name Dennis Design Center and erase it on their website (Gudme 2011). Allegedly, this was because 'Dennis' phonetically sounds like 'Danish' in English, and Danish Design Center claimed the copyright. Bureau Detours was then given an ultimatum until the 6th of September. If they did not live up to this demand, they were threatened that the Danish Design Center would withdraw their invitation to the collective to exhibit work during the Copenhagen Design Week later that year. After an open meeting, the parties agreed however that there was "room for yet another design center, a practical of the kind" (Haack/Aude/Muchenberger 2012, 21). So, when Dennis Design Center re-opened its freight containers for a wider public at the Milan Design Week in 2012 it was with the acceptance of the Danish Design Center.

I will leave it an open question whether or not aesthetic dissensus here is cancelled out through a forceful global design event economy. Suffice it to say, that what the example so brilliantly shows is that in design activism politics and policing are unmistakably intertwined in a messy and impure way. Dennis Design Center does not enact its contestation in the pure anarchistic form of an institutional overturning of the Danish Design Center, nor it is enslaved by it. It enacts aesthetic dissensus through a momentary interruption of the hierarchies and ways of doing and making allocated by this policing order.

Concluding remarks

By introducing central analytical concepts from Rancière's political philosophy I have attempted to clarify some of the discrepancies characteristic of the current theorization of design activism. Notably, I have demonstrated that caution should be taken in not overestimating the politics of design activism; nor is design activism's engagement with the political and social reducible to that of social design and social innovation. To avoid ending up in either a pure politics interpretation or a hegemonic taming of design activism, I have tried to position a third interpretation. A critique of this interpretation could be that because it is concisely modeled upon Rancière's conceptual apparatus, it risks becoming too narrow and unable to exhaustively account of the multifaceted ways in which design activism is practiced and conceptualized. True, this is only a point of departure that needs to be reworked, criticised and challenged by the outcomes of actual activist practices.

This work was supported by the Danish Council for Independent Research [grant number DFF-4180-00221].

References

Armstrong, Leah / Jocelyn Bailey / Guy Julier and Lucy Kimbell (2014): Social Design Futures: HEI Research and the AHRC.

Austin, James / Stevenson, Howard and Jane Wei-Skillern (2006): Social and Commercial Entrepreneurship: Same, Different, or Both?, Entrepreneurship Theory and Practice, 30 (2006), 1–22.

Banz, Claudia (2006): *Social Design: Gestalten für die Transformation der Gesellschaft.* Bielefeld: transcript Verlag.

Björgvinsson, Erling / Ehn, Pelle and Per-Anders Hillgren (2012): Agonistic Participatory Design: Working with Marginalised Social Movements, CoDesign, 8 (2012), 127–44.

Chambers, Samuel A. (2013): *The Lessons of Rancière.* Oxford University Press.

Christensen, Poul Rind / Morgen, Anja Sinding (2010): Socialt Entreprenørskab–lappeløsning Eller Innovation?, Ledelse & Erhvervsøkonomi, 75 (2010), 7–23.

Corcoran, S., (Ed.) (2010): Editor's Introduction, in Dissensus: On Politics and Aesthetics. London & New York: Continuum Intl Pub Group.

Dees, J. Gregory (1998): *The Meaning of Social Entrepreneurship.* Kansas City & Palo Alto: Kauffman Foundation & Stanford University.

DiSalvo, Carl (2012): *Adversarial Design.* MIT Press.

Fry, Tony (2011): *Design as Politics.* Oxford & New York: Berg.

Fuad-Luke, Alastair (2009): *Design Activism: Beautiful Strangeness for a Sustainable World.* CSIRO, Routledge.

Fuad-Luke, Alastair (2013): Design Activism: Challenging the Paradigm by Dissensus, Consensus and Traditional Practices', The Handbook of Design for Sustainability.

Gudme, P. N. (2011): Designcenter Vil Beskytte Sig Mod Dennis Design, Politiken, 3 September 2011.

Haack, S. / Aude, U. and A. Muchenberger (Eds.) (2012): Dennis Design Center - W.I.P. (Bureau Detours)

Hockerts, Kai (2006): Entrepreneurial Opportunity in Social Purpose Business Ventures, in Social Entrepreneurship. Springer, pp. 142–54.

Julier, Guy (2013): From Design Culture to Design Activism, Design and Culture, 5 (2013), pp. 215–36.

Kjær, B. (2011): Dennis Design Center Er Åbnet På Amager, Politiken, 11 August 2011

Lawrence, Paul R. / Lorsch, Jay W. (1967): 'Differentiation and Integration in Complex Organizations', Administrative Science Quarterly, pp. 1–47

Manzini, Ezio (2015): *Design, When Everybody Designs: An Introduction to Design for Social Innovation.* MIT Press.

Markussen, Thomas (2017): Disentangling "the Social" in Social Design's Engagement with the Public Realm, CoDesign, 13, pp. 160–74.

Markussen, Thomas (2013): The Disruptive Aesthetics of Design Activism: Enacting Design Between Art and Politics, Design Issues, 29.

Martin, Roger L. / Osberg, Sally (2007): Social Entrepreneurship: The Case for Definition, Stanford Social Innovation Review, 5, pp. 28–39.

May, Todd (2008): Political Thought of Jacques Ranciere: Creating Equality: Creating Equality. Edinburgh University Press.

Mulgan, Geoff (2014): Design in Public and Social Innovation: What Works and What Could Work Better, Article Publié Sur www.nesta.org. UK.

Panagia, Davide (2001): Ceci n'est Pas Un Argument: An Introduction to the Ten Theses, Theory & Event, 5.

Phillips, Wendy / Lee, Hazel / Ghobadian, Abby / O'Regan, Nicholas and Peter James (2014): Social Innovation and Social Entrepreneurship A Systematic Review', Group & Organization Management, pp. 428– 461.

Rancière, Jacques (1999): *Disagreement: Politics and Philosophy.* University of Minnesota Press.

Rancière, Jacques (2004): *The Politics of Aesthetics.* London & New York: Continuum.

Rancière, Jacques (2009): *The Emancipated Spectator.* London & New York: Verso Books.

Rancière, Jacques (2010): *Dissensus: On Politics and Aesthetics,* ed. by Steven Corcoran. Continuum Intl Pub Group.

Sloterdijk, Peter (2005): Against Gravity: Bettina Funcke Talks with Peter Sloterdijk, Bookforum February/March, URL (Consulted May 2011): http://www. Bookforum.com/Archive/Feb_05/ Funcke. html.

Thorpe, Adam / Gamman, Lorraine (2011): Design with Society: Why Socially Responsive Design Is Good Enough, CoDesign, 7 (2011), pp. 217–30.

Thorpe, Ann (2012): *Architecture & Design Versus Consumerism: How Design Activism Confronts Growth.* Routledge.

Thorpe, Ann (2008): Design as Activism: A Conceptual Tool' (presented at the Changing the Change, Turin, Italy.

Vallury, Raji (2009): Politicizing Art in Rancière and Deleuze: The Case of Postcolonial Literature, in *Jacques Rancière: History, Politics, Aesthetics,* ed. by Gabriel Rockhill and Philip Watts. Durham & London: Duke University Press.

Weerawardena, Jay / Sullivan Mort, Gillian (2006): Investigating Social Entrepreneurship: A Multidimensional Model, Journal of World Business, 41 (2006), pp. 21–35.

Weisbrod, Burton (1975): Towards a Theory of the Nonprofit Sector, in *Altruism, Morality and Economic Theory.* New York: Russell Sage, ed. by E. S. Phelps. New York: Russel Sage Foundation.

YELLOW SUBMARINES
DESIGN AGAINST NORMALITY AND INFORMATION

Michael Erlhoff

Some preliminary remarks

Design, or what we call design today, has always been a very important part of political articulation and protest. But, design has also always been an important part of all kinds of governmental or economic power because authorities always need signs to express and to explain their power and status in hierarchical societies: Costumes, buildings, flags, interiors, crowns, even gestures and behaviour etc. And, on the other hand, there have always been the signs related to protest: the uniforms of liberation armies, pamphlets by rebelling farmers, communication devices of 19th century democratic movements, and, closer to our present concept of design, all the activities of the 1917 Russian Revolution, the political statements of Dada and Surrealism, the activism of resistance or the Situationists and 1968 activism.

That is: the role of design in social and political movements has always been ambivalent and it has been impossible to simply associate design either with the inhumane or with the humanistic and ethical side.

By the way, some artists (in those days there were no designers) of the early Soviet Union at the beginning of the 1920s obviously knew about this ambiguity and tried out some new ways of explaining protest and rebellion. For example, one night they smeared red paint on all the plants in several public parks in Moscow in order to change the landscape architecture into symbols of the revolution. But, in contrast to authoritarian gestures of building monuments, the artists had used a type of paint that would be washed away by the rain. After a few days, the red paint in the parks was gone, but it stayed in people's minds. Or: being forced by the Leninist bureaucracy to create public sculptures of the heroes of the revolution, the artists used a material that was not waterproof: it is easy to imagine what these public sculptures, meant to be lasting monuments, would look like after some really rainy days. The government immediately set up wooden barricades to block the view onto those naturally destroyed, and now very bizarre-looking, sculptures. (Useless, because in the Russian winter, people needed wood to make fires, and so they regarded the wooden barricades as a perfect resource.)

As refreshing as this kind of subversive design might have been, we also have to be aware of the fact that there were times when design was indeed more helpful in supporting authoritarian, inhumane and racist governments, in particular the Italian Fascists and the German National Socialists. And this happened during a time when design was still young, when an awareness of design had yet to fully establish itself. The Bauhaus already existed before 1933 and had changed the political and social perception of design. Some of the Bauhaus people (in particular Mies van der Rohe, Herbert Bayer and Ernst Neuffert) actually worked for the Nazi government. Indeed, the German National Socialist politicians, or at least some of them, were highly aware of the intrinsic competences of design and used them in various ways: again, there were uniforms, banners and flags, there were weapons and city planning, but there was also language, there were gestures and the organisation and ornamentalisation of human crowds, or the system for marking the Jewish population. All of this was a result of design – of corporate design or branding, of communication design, product design and even service design.

Design can be very cruel or can be an accessory to depress, ruin and kill people – and well-designed guns may kill better and faster.

This had to be stated as a kind of introduction to this essay in order to avoid misunderstandings and to criticise a mere heroic attitude regarding the role of design as social and as a tool of activism.

Normal normality and informed information

No doubt, design is inevitably social. Firstly, because it is only realised when it is used (probably the most significant difference between radically useless fine arts and design). And secondly, because everything we tend to call 'normal' is designed: the pavement we walk on, the shoes made for walking, the traffic signs guiding us through the traffic, the GPS system moving us around the globe, smartphones and laptops, the trees alongside avenues, our spectacles sharpening our view, glasses for drinking wine, books, magazines and Twitter, the sounds surrounding us, the tactile structures, the smells of objects and in shopping malls. Simply everything is designed, even the layouts of parliaments and courts.

But there's even more: each governmental law and regulation is published via design, institutions or companies use design for their publications, each news item comes to us by design. And each piece of information is shaping us 'in form'. Indeed, to be informed means to be brought into a specific form (design) somebody or something wants us to be in. And we are never asked whether we like that form or whether we would prefer something else.

'Normal' does not simply happen: it is the result of norms, rules and regulations. But, as normal is normal, it cannot be avoided; even worse, when we take normal as normal we do not question it, do not think about it and do not criticise it. It is just normal.

Nevertheless, this normality is a result of design because institutions, governments and companies use design to change abstract instructions into visible, tangible and usable instructions so that human beings can follow them, even if we are not aware of doing so. However, we do it constantly, day in and day out: when we use our cars or bicycles, when we dress in certain ways (belonging to a specific social status), when we drink or eat, when we walk and when we communicate. Communication, a category designers often use as a kind of neutral or even enthusiastic term, is a very good example of the restrictions designed by design. The Latin origin of the word explains what everybody should know: communication derives from *com* meaning together, from *moenia* meaning wall, and from *ire* meaning to walk. Hence, the term 'communication' exactly explains that it relates to all those who are walking inside the same walls (of a city or other community), and the word precisely states that communication is always exclusive as only those who know the signs and follow the rules are part of the community. Guaranteed by communication design.

This also means that even in a social situation that seems to offer some kind of diversity, there is regulation and control – and the agent of control is design. It is impossible to escape, or to deny, the existence of regulations because anti-regulation also needs regulations, or is hijacked by very many rules. Within the perspective just described, design has acted as a service, and the designer has been seen as a servant of industry, capital and the authorities.

This is exactly how companies and governments saw design in the early days: only as a service. In the era of industrialisation, products were of poor quality (because there was no longer a direct connection between customers and producers as had been the case before and the market had become anonymous). Therefore, a new form of creativity was needed that would improve product quality or acceptance. This gave rise to the arts & crafts movement in the second part of the 19th century, a forerunner of design that would encourage the professional development of what we call design today. Through this movement, it became obvious that there was a need for design services, but, at the same time, there was a rather limited view of design: it was not about inventing and constructing all kinds of products, but only about making products more usable and attractive.

However, the relationship between master (traditionally the authorities and the capital) and slave (design) is more complicated, because, by working for the master, the slave quickly and somehow secretly starts to learn the masters' methods, categories and qualities. As that includes the opportunity, or indeed necessity, to emancipate oneself, the slave learns to fight against the master.

And that was exactly what happened in the context of design during the last 150 or so years: design has become one of the powerful and essential factors in the economy and also in social life. Design no longer has to follow and to formulate the rules and regulations prescribed by companies and other authorities: it can invent them itself.

Nevertheless, this still means to construct both normality and information, to give rules and regulations visible and tangible forms that enable us to follow them easily. Maybe one could say that design has invented more interesting or even more humane rules and regulations, but to invent rules still means to control behaviour, understanding, social conditions, and the ways we live our lives. Design has changed, but it has not improved within the concept of a more humane or social situation.

Even worse perhaps: as design is no longer just the master ́s voice, it might now help to better conceal the existence of controlling concepts, and, by so doing, it could be even more authoritarian. At least, it is quite obvious that hardly anyone in design talks about or criticises the so-called 'normal'.

Unnormal and Disinformation

There is no reason to be pessimistic. But, if one wants to argue about social design and about design for activism, we first of all have to understand what is political and what is social. Everything else will only end up in euphoric nonsense (at best accompanied by catharsis). Hopefully, the above reflections on the problem of normality and information might help.

Maybe it needs one more idea at least: talking about normality (and information) only moves across the surface – and this is far removed from the intellectual and academic attitude of trying to grasp what one believes to be important, which is what is regarded as depth. This kind of people (forced by academic institutions and by gestures of intellectualism) always want to know what is behind something, e.g. what is behind a painting. And they do not like the serious and only true answer: the wall. Time to recall an expression by the philosopher Ernst Bloch: "the banality of depth", and also a statement by the composer Feruccio Busoni: "Depth gains broadness and tries to reach this by heaviness". Indeed – and this is not only true for design – we have to observe, to analyse and to work with the surface. That is: with what is called normal.

Any serious political analysis has to describe the power, brutality and authoritarian dimension of the normal. Political and social activism, therefore, has to find ways of explaining the normal to people as not normal, as something that is designed. And everything that is designed is not fixed, but can be and has to be changed. Therefore, radical design offers open possibilities for social life.

It is not so difficult to demonstrate the power of the (designed) normal and, by so doing, to experience the quality of changing normality. Just take three of those red and white, or black and yellow, traffic cones, put them in the centre of a one-way street in your city, near to where another street branches off – and you will see that all cars will turn into the other street (even taxis and the police). Or, have four of five people wear one of those orange or red jackets that official traffic regulators usually wear and you will be able to stop or disrupt both car and pedestrian traffic. Put a "closed" sign on a door and nobody will touch it. More complicated, but not too difficult either, is changing the electronic displays at tram stops – very effective, as the people standing on the platform, waiting and looking at the displays, will suddenly start talking to each other, they will laugh or will be embarrassed and will definitely have a different experience of time. Do some legal hacking like, for example, the design agency *Mindshare Denmark* did: they wanted to change the common image of "beautiful women" into realistic pictures of female beauty. You will notice that this can encourage people to change.

Ask somebody who has just finished talking loudly into their smartphone (as many people do): Excuse me, but who is this Peter you called lazy and stupid? Or use anagrams and palindromes (e.g. "dogma – I am god" or "Red Dot – Der Tod") to broaden the horizon of words and, by so doing, question words and phrases and put them into new perspectives. Don't follow instructions, forget your GPS and Google maps and enjoy getting lost, just follow another person and explore new areas. Buy something in a supermarket, but give the money to a homeless person in the street and not to the supermarket. Play the sound of a river in a pedestrian zone or have the scent of beautiful flowers waft through a public toilet. Change the surface of stairs or handles. Debunk stupid racist arguments and expose the idiocy of those blaming and pursuing refugees. Demystify capitalism and the capitalist normality. And try to love confusion and blur.

All of the aforementioned is, of course, deeply related to design. Analyse the many fakes in the history of the natural sciences and also in the humanities and observe the effects of these fakes. You could regard those activities as deriving from design and as productive design.

This kind of activism has sometimes been adopted by far-right, racist or even terrorist movements and people. In some countries 'trumping up' has almost become a standard practice used by politicians and by people employing petty bourgeois actions. Mr Trump likes to produce fakes, in Germany the AfD (officially *Alternative for Deutschland*, de facto *Away from Democracy*) is based on similar nonsense, and too many elected governments in Europe and other parts of the world are following similar stupidities. They live from fake news, ideologies and other lies.

Of course, this could be depressing for all those trying to shake up normality with the goal of emancipation. But this image is wrong because those nationalists, racists and simple capitalists who preach authoritarian relics still believe, and try to make everybody else believe, that those rules and attitudes are normal. They attempt to convince people of this normality with the aim of secretly controlling them.

As Kurt Schwitters explained nearly 100 years ago: not the protest against normality is chaotic, normality is. Of course, when protesting against norms, normality and the normal, we have to be careful to understand the empirical situation, our critique of the normal must be very precise and we have to use design in its complexity, use its incredible competences for real, serious and joyful and analytical confrontation in order to explain the nonsense of the normal, to explain this as experiences and to open up the structures, enabling people to understand and to criticise that which is regarded as given, but which could be and has to be changed.

There is no reason for pessimism: design offers the chance of optimism, supported by many examples of qualified protest by design. The most convincing example for this can be found when observing people interacting with 'the normal' because, in many of these interactions, people change the rules and regulations, but most of the time, they are not aware of this. Just think of how often people change or extend the function of objects, signs or services when using them. In everyday life, people don't always use chairs for sitting: they use them as coatracks or ladders. Newspapers are not only read: they are used to protect people from the rain or to kill flies. The list could go on. These things do not happen intentionally and they are not some kind of official protest – but people act like this and we should tell them what they are really doing by this non-intentional design.

No doubt, there are also many brilliant examples for smart protests that use and confuse normality. Probably the most convincing one within the last few years was the *Umbrella Movement* in Hong Kong: the activists blocked the main street in the centre of Hong Kong Island, bringing to a halt all the normal traffic and movement in the city. The activists also used normal materials in a kind of non-intentional design to build barricades or to construct stairs across the railings separating the two lanes of the street. They not only cleaned the nearby public toilets (totally opposed to the nature of normal use) but also put perfume, shampoo and lotion in the rooms so that the public toilets could be used as a kind of nice bathroom. There were study corners, the possibility to exhibit printouts from the Internet, a stage with microphones for spontaneous talks and public discussions – and the many activists just lived there, had breakfast, lunch and dinner and listened to music. They simply changed the normal in order to be able to live there.

One more explanation of the specific qualities of intentional misunderstandings and mistakes, showing the quality of design in confusing the normal: *"While you were weaving compliments, something useful could have happened."* (J.W.v.Goethe)

ARTISTIC STRATEGIES IN POLITICS AND POLITICAL STRATEGIES IN ART

Chantal Mouffe

How to envisage artistic strategies in politics and political strategies in art? This is the question that a variety of artists, theorists and activists had been addressing during the 24/7 discourse camp organized in the context of the 2012 Steirischer Herbst. It is clear that posing such a question supposes discarding the view that artists and cultural workers cannot play any more a critical role in society because they have become a necessary part of capitalist production. According to such a view the production of symbols is now a central goal of capitalism and, through the development of the creative industries, individuals have become totally subjugated to the control of capital. Not only consumers but also cultural producers have been transformed in passive functions of the capitalist system. They are prisoners of the culture industry dominated by the media and entertainments corporations. Were this to be true, there would of course be no point in examining the possible modalities of aesthetic resistance. I think that we can therefore take for granted that the participants in this marathon would reject this pessimistic diagnostic. It is likely that most of them, while acknowledging the profound transformations brought about by the current post-fordist stage of capitalism, will argue that those new forms of production allow for novel types of resistances to which artistic practices could make a decisive contribution. It is when it comes to envisaging the forms that those resistances should take that we will find important divergences. To examine the nature of those divergences could therefore help us to clarify the stakes of our encounter.

I think that one of the main disagreements that we will face concerns the spaces in which resistances should be deployed and the type of relation to be established with the institutions. Should critical artistic practices engage with current institutions with the aim of transforming them or should they desert them altogether? An influential approach advocates what can be called a strategy of 'withdrawal'. It claims that the institutions of the art world have become complicit with capitalism and that they cannot provide any more a site for critical artistic practices. Under post-fordist conditions, artists working inside the system are totally instrumentalized and, transformed into businessmen; they are bound to contribute to the reproduction of the system. Resistances are still possible, but they can only be located outside the institutions.

It is interesting to note that this position, which is characteristic of a variety of people influenced by the Autonomist tradition, acknowledges the growth of the culture industry already pointed out by Adorno and Horkeimer, but interprets it in a very different way. As is well known, Adorno and Horkeimer saw the development of the culture industry as the moment when the fordist mode of production finally managed to enter the field of culture. For them this evolution represented a further stage in the commodification and subjugation of society to the requisites of capitalist production. Adorno saw art as the only place where autonomy was still possible. It is this possibility that the pessimistic view mentioned at the beginning declares as having now been eliminated by the advances of the commodification process.

Post-operaist theorists, for their part, see the transition from fordism to post-fordism in a very different way. Paolo Virno for instance, asserts that culture industries have played an important role in the process of transition between fordism and post-fordism (Virno 2004). It is where new practices of productions emerged which led to the overcoming of fordism. They represent, he says, the matrix of post-fordism. Indeed, with the development of immaterial labour in advanced capitalism, the labour process has become performative and it mobilizes the most universal requisites of the species: perception, language, memory and feelings. Contemporary production is now 'virtuosic' and productive labor in its totality appropriates the special characteristics of the performing artist. This transformation opens the way for new forms of social relations in which art and work exist in new configurations. Under post-fordist conditions, the objective of critical artistic practices should be to contribute to the development of the new social relations which are made possible by the transformation of the work process. Their main task is the production of new subjectivities and the elaboration of new worlds that would create the conditions for the self-organization of the multitude.

Such a view of the role of artistic practices goes together with a conception of radical politics formulated in terms of 'exodus'. This strategy of exodus comes in different versions, according to way the future of the multitude is envisaged, but they all assert that the traditional structures of power organized around the national state and representative democracy have today become irrelevant and that they will progressively disappear. Hence the belief that the multitude can ignore the existing power structures and concentrate its efforts in constructing alternative social forms outside the state power network. Any collaboration with the traditional channels of politics like parties and trade unions are to be avoided. The majoritarian model of society, organized around a state needs to be abandoned in favour of another model of organization presented as more universal. It has the form of a unity provided by common places of the mind, cognitive-linguistic habits and the general intellect.

Next to this strategy of 'withdrawal from institutions', there is another strategy which is the one that I want to advocate, a strategy of 'engagement with institutions'. This strategy is informed by a theoretical approach that brings to the fore the discursive character of the social and reveals how it is through a multiplicity of discursive practices that 'our world' is constructed, a construction that is always the result of a particular hegemony.[5] This theoretical approach reveals that society is always politically instituted and that what is called 'the social' is the realm of sedimented political practices, practices that conceal the originary acts of their contingent political institution. As the temporary and precarious articulation of contingent practices, every order is the expression of a particular structure of power relations. What is at a given moment accepted as the 'natural order' is always the result of sedimented hegemonic practices. Things could always have been otherwise and every order is predicated on the exclusion of other possibilities. This is why it is always susceptible of being challenged by counter-hegemonic practices that will attempt to disarticulate it so as to establish a different hegemony.

I submit that this approach is particularly fruitful to apprehend the relations between art and politics and for visualizing artistic strategies in politics and political strategies in art because it highlights the fact that the hegemonic confrontation is not limited to the traditional political institutions but that it also takes place in the multiplicity of places where hegemony is constructed, i.e the domain of what is usually called 'civil society'. This is where, as Antonio Gramsci has argued, a particular conception of the world is established and a specific understanding of reality is defined, what he refers to as the 'common sense', providing the terrain in which specific forms of subjectivity are constructed. Gramsci also emphasized the centrality of cultural and artistic practices in the formation and diffusion of this 'common sense', highlighting the decisive role played by those practices in the reproduction or disarticulation of a given hegemony.

From the standpoint of the hegemonic approach, artistic practices have a necessary relation to politics because they either contribute to the reproduction of the 'common sense' that secures a given hegemony or to its challenging. Critical artistic practices are those that, in a variety of ways, play a part in the process of disarticulation/rearticulation which characterizes a counter-hegemonic politics. This counter-hegemonic politics aims at targeting the institutions which secure the dominant hegemony in order to bring about profound transformations in the way they function. This strategy of 'war of position' (Gramsci) is composed of a diversity of practices and interventions operating in a multiplicity of spaces: economic, legal, political and cultural. The domain of culture plays a crucial role in this war of position because, as we have seen, this is one of the terrains where the 'common sense' is built and subjectivities are constructed. In the present conjuncture, with the decisive role played by the culture industries in the capitalist process of reproduction, the cultural and artistic terrain has become of strategic importance. Artistic and cultural production is indeed vital for capital valorization. This is due to the increasing reliance of post-fordist capitalism on semiotic techniques in order to create the modes of subjectivation which are necessary for its reproduction. As Foucault pointed out, in modern production, the control of the souls is crucial in governing affects and passions. The forms of exploitation characteristic of the

---

5   For a presentation of this approach, see for instance: *Hegemony and Socialist Strategy. Towards a Radical Democratic Politics* (Laclau/Mouffe 2001).

times when manual labor was dominant have been replaced by new ones which constantly call for the creation of new needs and incessant desires for the acquisition of goods. To maintain its hegemony, the capitalist system needs to permanently mobilize people's desires and shape their identities and the cultural terrain, with its various institutions, occupies a key position in this process. We find here a very different strategy to the one of 'withdrawal from institutions' advocated by the first conception that we examined. Critical artistic practices do not contribute to the counter-hegemonic struggle by deserting the institutional terrain but by engaging with it, with the aim of fostering dissent and creating a multiplicity of agonistic spaces where the dominant consensus is challenged and where new modes of identification are made available.

I want to make clear that I am not arguing here in favour of a purely institutional conception of politics or for a relegation of critical artistic practices to the traditional domain of the art world, but for an articulation of different modes of intervention in a multiplicity of places. There exists a great variety of ways of bringing about agonistic spaces and they can emerge both inside and outside institutions. The hegemonic approach envisages radical politics as an articulation of parliamentary with extra-parliamentary struggles and aims at establishing a synergy between parties and social movements. In the specific domain of artistic practices, such an approach encourages a diversity of interventions, inside and outside the traditional world of art. Challenging the view that institutions cannot be transformed and that resistances can only develop and be successful outside them, it stresses the necessity of combining political strategies in art and artistic strategies in politics. In our post-political times where the dominant discourse tries to occlude the very possibility of an alternative to the current order, all the practices that can contribute to the subversion and destabilization of the hegemonic neo-liberal consensus are welcome. Museums, for instance, can under certain conditions provide spaces for an agonistic confrontation and it is a mistake to believe that artists who choose to work with them cannot play a critical role and that they are automatically recuperated by the system.

I strongly believe that in examining the relation between art and politics, it is necessary to adopt a pluralistic perspective. While asserting the continuing validity of traditional artistic forms, the approach that I advocate also acknowledges the significance of the various forms of artistic activism which have recently flourished. By putting aesthetic means at the service of political activism, this 'artivism' can be seen as a counter-hegemonic move against the capitalist appropriation of aesthetics in order to secure its valorization process. In its manifold manifestations, 'artivism' can certainly help in subverting the post-political common sense and in the creation of new subjectivities. For instance, various modes of artivist intervention influenced by the Situationist strategy of 'detournement' like the Yes Men are very effective in disrupting the smooth image that corporate capitalism is trying to impose, bringing to the fore its repressive character. This is only one example among many and we certainly had the opportunity during the marathon to examine a number of other artivist practices and to discuss their connection with the different Occupy movements.

This leads me to what will probably constitute another moot point in our discussions. As I have just made clear, according to the hegemonic approach artistic strategies in politics and political strategies in art are both legitimate and important. They can play a decisive role in fomenting an agonistic contestation and contribute to the emergence of new subjectivities. However it also asserts that critical artistic practices, in whatever form they are conceived, are no substitute for political practices and that they will never be able, on their own, to bring about a new hegemonic order. In the construction of this new order, the strictly political moment cannot be avoided. The success of radical politics requires new political subjectivities, but this only represents one dimension, vital as it is, in the war of position. Many other steps need to be taken for it to be successful in establishing a new hegemony and the long march through the political institutions cannot be averted.

This essay is a revised version of an article first published in the "Reader in Progress" for the 'Truth is concrete – 24/7 marathon camp on artistic strategies in politics and political strategies in art (Graz, 21/09 – 28/09/2012) and another one published in Steirischer Herbst, Florian Malzacher (Eds.) (2014): Truth Is Concrete – A Handbook for Artistic Strategies in Real Politics. Sternberg Press, Berlin.

References

Laclau, Ernesto / Mouffe, Chantal (2001): *Hegemony and Socialist Strategy. Towards a Radical Democratic Politics*, Verso, 2001.

Virno, Paolo (2004): *A Grammar of the Multitude.* Semiotext(e), Cambridge: MIT Press.

DESIGN AND DEMOCRACY

Gui Bonsiepe

I shall present a few thoughts about the relation between democracy and design, about the relation between critical humanism and operational humanism. This issue leads to the question of the role of technology and industrialization as a procedure for democratizing the consumption of goods and services, and finally to the ambivalent role of esthetics as the domain of freedom and manipulation.

The main theme of my lecture is thus the relation between design – in the sense of projecting – and autonomy. My reflections are open-ended and do not pretend to give quick and immediate answers. The university – still – offers a space to pursue these questions that will not generally be addressed in professional practice with its pressures and contingencies.

Taking a look at the present design discourse one notes a surprising – and I would say alarming – absence of questioning design activities. Concepts like branding, competitiveness, globalization, comparative advantages, life-style design, differentiation, strategic design, fun design, emotion design, experience design, and smart design prevail in design magazines and the – all too few – books about design. Sometimes one gets the impression that a designer aspiring to two minutes of fame feels obliged to invent a new label for setting herself or himself apart from the rest of what professional service offers. I leave aside coffee table books on design that abound in pictures and exempt the reader from intellectual efforts. The issue of design and democracy doesn't enjoy popularity – apart from a few laudable exceptions.

If we look at the social history of the meaning of the term »design« we note on the one side a popularization, that is a horizontal extension, and on the other side a contraction, that is a vertical reduction. The architectural critic Witold Rybczynski recently commented on this phenomenon: *"Not so long ago, the term »designer« described someone like Eliot Noyes, who was responsible for the IBM Selectric typewriter in the 1960s, or Henry Dreyfuss, whose clients included Lockheed Aircraft and Bell Telephone Company ... or Dieter Rams, who created a range of austere-looking, but very practical products for the German company Braun. Today, »designer« is more likely to bring to mind Ralph Lauren or Giorgio Armani, that is, a fashion designer. While fashion designers usually start as couturiers, they – or at least their names – are often associated with a wide variety of consumer products, including cosmetics, perfume, luggage, home furnishings, even house paint. As a result, »design« is popularly identified with packaging: the housing of a computer monitor, the barrel of a pen, a frame for eyeglasses."* (Rybczynski 2005)

More and more design moved away from the idea of "intelligent problem solving" (James Dyson) and drew nearer to the ephemeral, fashionable and quickly obsolete, to formal-aesthetic play, to the boutiquization of the universe of products of everyday life. For this reason design today is often identified with expensive, exquisite, not particularly practical, funny and formally pushed, colorful objects. The hypertrophy of fashion aspects is accompanied and increased by the media with their voracious appetite for novelties. Design has become thus a media event – and we have a considerable number of publications that serve as resonance boxes for this process. Even design centers are exposed to the complicity of the media running the risk of failing to reach their original objective: to make a difference between design as intelligent problem solving and styling. After all it is a question of a renaissance of the tradition of the Good Design Movement, but with different foci and interests. The advocates of Good Design pursued socio-pedagogical objectives, the Life Style Centers of today pursue exclusively commercial and marketing aims to provide orientation for consumption patterns of a new – or not that new – social segment of global character, that can be labeled with the phrase: "We made it".

The world of everyday products and messages, of material and semiotic artifacts has met – with rare exceptions – in cultural discourse (and this includes the academic discourse) a climate of benign indifference that has its roots in classical culture in the medieval age when the first universities in the Occident were founded. This academic tradition did not take note of the domain of design (in the sense of project) in any of its disciplines. However, in the process of industrialization one could no longer close ones eyes to technology and technical artifacts that more and more made their presence felt in everyday life. But the leading ideal continued to be cognitive character in the form of the creation of new knowledge. Never design achieved to establish itself as parallel leading ideal. This fact explains the difficulties of integrating design education in the institutions of higher learning with their own traditions and criteria of excellence. This becomes evident in doctoral programs in design that favor the production of discursive results and don't concede projects the same value or recognition as the production of texts. The sciences approach reality from the perspective of cognition, of what can be known, whereas the design disciplines approach reality from the perspective of projectability, of what can be designed. These are different perspectives, and it may be hoped that in the future they will transmute into complementary perspectives. So far design has tried to build bridges to the domain of the sciences, but not vice versa. We can speculate that in the future design may become a basic discipline for all scientific areas. But this Copernican turn in the university system might take generations if not centuries. Only the creation of radically new universities can shorten this process. But the decision space of government institutions is limited due to the weight of academic traditions and due to the bureaucratization with emphasis on formal procedures of approbation (title fetishism). Therefore the new university will probably be created outside of established structures.

Relating design activities to the sciences should not be misinterpreted as a claim of a scientific design or as an attempt to transform design into a science. It would be foolish to design an ashtray with scientific knowledge. But it would not be foolish – and even mandatory – to tap scientific knowledge when designing a milk package with a minimal ecological footprint. It is no longer feasible to limit the notion of design to design disciplines such as architecture, industrial design or communication design because scientists are also designing. When a group of agricultural scientists develops a new sweet from the carob bean that contains important vitamins for school children, we have a clear example of a design activity.[1]

Now I want to focus on the central issue of my lecture: the relation between democracy and design. Indeed during the last years the notion of democracy has been exposed to a process of wear and tear so that it is advisable to use it with care. When looking at the international scene we cannot avoid stating that in the name of democracy colonialist invasions, bombardments, genocides, ethnical cleaning operations, torture, and breaking international laws have been – and are – committed, almost with impunity, at least for the moment. The invoice for this lack of humanity is not known. Future generations will probably have to carry the burden. With democracy these operations have nothing in common.

According to the neoliberal understanding, democracy is synonymous with the predominance of the market as an exclusive and almost sanctified institution for governing all relations within and between societies. So we face questions: How can the notion of democracy be recovered? How can the notion of democracy gain credibility again? How one can avoid the risk of being exposed to the arrogant and condescending attitude of the centers of power that consider democracy as nothing more than a tranquilizer for public opinion in order to continue undisturbed with business as usual?

I am using a simple interpretation of the term »democracy« in the sense of participation so that dominated citizens transform themselves into subjects opening a space for self-determination, and that means a space for a project of one's own accord. Formulated differently: democracy reaches farther than the formal right to vote, similarly the notion of freedom reaches farther than the possibility to chose between a hundred varieties of cellular telephones or a flight to Orlando to visit the Epcot Center or to Paris to look at paintings in the Louvre.

I favor a substantial, and thus less formal, concept of democracy as the reduction of heteronomy, i.e. domination by external forces. It is no secret that this interpretation fits into the tradition of the Enlightenment that has been criticized so intensively by amongst others Jean-Francois Lyotard when he announced the end of the grand narratives. I do not agree with this approach or other postmodern variants. Without a utopian element, another world is not possible and would remain the expression of a pious ethereal wish without concrete consequences. Without a utopian ingredient, residual though it may be, heteronomy cannot be reduced.

---

1   http://www.clarin.com/diario/2005/05/09/sociedad/s-03101.htm Crean un nuevo alimento para escolares en base a algarroba. Monday, 09.05.2005

For this reason the renunciation of the project of enlightenment seems to me the expression of a quietist, if not conservative attitude – an attitude of surrender that no designer should be tempted to cherish.

In order to illustrate the necessity to reduce heteronomy I am using a contribution from a linguist, a specialist in comparative literature – Edward Said, who died last year. He characterizes in an exemplary manner the essence of humanism, of a humanist attitude. As a philologue he limits the humanist attitude to the domain of language and history: *"Humanism is the exertion of one's faculties in language in order to understand, reinterpret, and grapple with the products of language in history, other languages and other histories"* (Said 2003). But we can extend this interpretation to other areas too. Certainly the intentions of the author will not be bent when transferring his characterization of humanism – with corresponding adjustments – to design. Design humanism would be the exercise of design activities in order to interpret the needs of social groups and to develop viable emancipatory proposals in the form of material and semiotic artifacts. Why emancipatory? Because humanism implies the reduction of domination. In the field of design it means to focus also on the excluded, the discriminated, and economically less favored groups as they are called in economist jargon, which amounts to the majority of the population of this planet. I want to make it clear that I don't propagate a universalistic attitude according to the pattern of design for the world. Also I want to make it clear that this claim should not be interpreted as the expression of a naive idealism, supposedly out of touch with reality. On the contrary, each profession should face this uncomfortable question, not only the profession of designers. It would be an error to take this claim as the expression of a normative request of how a designer – exposed to the pressure of the market and the antinomies between reality and what could be reality – should act today. The intention is more modest, that is to foster a critical consciousness when facing the enormous imbalance between the centers of power and the people submitted to these powers. Because the imbalance is deeply undemocratic insofar as it negates participation. It treats human beings as mere instances in the process of objectivization (Verdinglichung) and commodification.

Here we come to the role of the market and the role of design in the market. In a recently published book, the economist Kenneth Galbraith analyses the function of the concept of the market that according to him is nothing more than a smokescreen for not talking openly about capitalism – a term that not in all social classes and in all countries enjoys a high rating on the popularity scale. Galbraith inserts design in the context of techniques of corporations for gaining and consolidating power: *"Product innovation and modification is a major economic function, and no significant manufacturer introduces a new product without cultivating the consumer demand for it. Or forgoes efforts to influence and sustain the demand for an existing product. Here enters the world of advertising and salesmanship, of television, of consumer manipulation. Thus an impairment of consumer and market sovereignty. In the real world, the producing firm and the industry go far to set the prices and establish the demand, employing to this end monopoly, oligopoly, product design and differentiation, advertising, other sales and trade promotion"* (Galbraith 2004).

Galbraith criticizes the use of the term »market« as an anonymous and impersonal institution and insists instead on talking about corporate power. Against this use of design – after all a tool for domination – stands the intent not to remain fixed exclusively on the aspects of power and of the anonymous market. In this contradiction design practice is unfolding and resisting a harmonizing discourse that is camouflaging the contradictions. One can deny the contradictions, but one cannot bypass them.

The issue of manipulation has a long tradition in design discourse, especially in advertising. I remember a popular book that at its time provoked a wide resonance, *The Hidden Persuaders* by Vance Packard (1957). But one should be on one's guard against a critique with declamaratory character that merely denounces. More differentiation is required. Manipulation and design share one point of contact: appearance. We design, amongst others and certainly not only, appearances. For this reason I once characterized the designer as a strategist of appearances, that is phenomena that we perceive through our senses, above all visual senses, but also tactile and auditory senses. Appearances lead us to the issue of aesthetics – an ambivalent concept. On the one side aesthetics represents the domain of freedom, of play – and some authors claim that we are only free when we play; on the other side aesthetics opens the access to manipulation, that is the increase of outer directed behavior. When designing products and semiotic artifacts we want to seduce, that is foster a positive – or according to context, negative – predisposition towards a product and sign combination. Depending on intentions design leans more to one pole or the other, more to autonomy or more to heteronomy.

At this point I want to insert a few reflections on technology. The term technology in general is understood as the universe of artifacts and procedures for producing merchandises with which companies fill the stage of everyday practice. Technology implies hardware and software – and software implies the notion of design as a facet of technology that cannot be dispensed with. Here in Latin America we face the problem of technology policy and industrialization policy. Research on these issues reveals interesting details about progress and set-backs. But these seem to me to favor a reductionist interpretation of technology. Only in exceptional cases texts mention the question of what is done with technology. The question for the design of products remains unanswered. This presents a weak point without wanting to underestimate the efforts by historians. But one cannot defend them against the reproach of being blind to the dimension of design, the dimension of projects, or at least of facing this dimension with indifference. The motives for industrialization include the wish to diversify exports and not to remain an exporting economy of commodities without added value. But behind this plausible argument is hidden another generally not explicitly formulated motif. I am referring to the idea that apart from the growth of the GNP, industrialization is the only possibility for democratizing consumption to provide for a broad sector of the population access to the world of products and services in the different areas of everyday life: health, housing, education, sports, transport, work to mention only a few.

However to mention today the role of government in promoting industrialization can appear almost as an offense of good manners. The role of public intervention has been demonized with one exception, paying the debt of a bankrupt privatized service. In that case public resources are welcome, thus reinforcing the idea that politics is the appropriation of public goods for private purposes. But when the history of industrialization and technology of this subcontinent will once be written, one shall see with clarity that the role of government has been decisive, though the detractors of the public sector with their bellicose voices have belittled its function and contributions. If we look at the recent history of Argentina – a country that until a few years ago followed in subservient manner the impositions of the International Monetary Fund and that in a moment of delirium enthusiastically praised its »carnal relationships« with the leading military and economic power – then we see that this country didn't fare very well with this policy of relentless privatization and reduction of government presence. This process plunged a great part of the population into a situation of poverty unknown until then, and led to an income concentration with the corresponding bipolarization of the society divided in two groups: the excluded and the included. Privatization in this context is synonymous with de-democratization because the victims of this process have never been asked whether they approved the credits and sales of public property that led the country into bankruptcy. Relentless privatization and reduction of the role of government, the unconditional opening of the economy for imports initiated a process of de-industrialization of Argentina, thus destroying the foundations for productive work, including work for industrial designers.

The industrialization policies in various countries in which I have participated, above all Chile, Argentina and Brazil concentrated exclusively on hardware, leaving the communication and information industries untouched. Today the constellation has changed radically. An updated industrialization policy would need to include the information sector of the economy, for which graphic design and information design can provide essential contributions. Here new problems show up that confront designers with cognitive demands that in design education programs generally are not taken into consideration. The expanding process of digitalization fostered a design current which claims that today the important design questions are essentially of symbolic character. As second argument for the semanticization of products – and thus for semantization of the designer's work – miniaturization is mentioned, made possible by printed circuits and cheap chips. These do not allow us to see how the products are working – functions become invisible. Therefore the designer's task would consist in rendering these invisible functions visible. Though it would be blind to deny the communication and symbolic aspects of products, their role should not be overvalued as some authors do. Between the alternative to put a nail into a wall with a hammer or the symbolic value of a hammer, the choice is clear. The material base of products with their visual, tactile and auditive conformation provides the firm base for the designer's work.

With concern, one can observe the growth of a generation of designers that obsessively focuses on symbolic aspects of products and their equivalents in the market – branding and self branding – and that doesn't know anymore how to classify joints. The search for a balance between the instrumental/operational aspects of technical objects and their semantic aspects constitutes the core of the designer's work, without privileging one or the other domain. As the historian Raimonda Riccini writes: *"The polarity between the instrumental and symbolic dimension, between internal structure and external structure is a typical property of artifacts, insofar as they are tools and simultaneously carriers of values and meanings. Designers face the task to mediate between these two polarities, by designing the form of products as result of an interaction with the sociotechnical process"* (Riccini 2005).

It is revealing that Riccini does not speak of the form of products and their interaction with functions, that is the affordances, but that she alludes to sociotechnical development. In this way she avoids the outdated debate about form and function. The once secure foundations for arriving at the configuration of products have been dissolved today – if ever they existed. It would be naive to presuppose the existence of a canon of deterministic rules. He who defends such a canon, commits the error of essentializing Platonic forms. At the same time it would be equally naive to claim an limitless fickleness of forms that would arise from demiurgic actions of a handful of creatively inspired designers. We face here a paradox. To design means to deal with paradoxes and contradictions. In a society plagued by contradictions design too is affected them. It might be convenient to remember the dictum of Walter Benjamin that there is no document of civilization that is not at the same time a document of barbarism.

This is a slightly abbreviated translation of the Spanish speech given at the Metropolitan University of Technology, Santiago de Chile, June 2005. First published in Design Issues, 2006.

References

Galbraith, John Kenneth (2004): *The Economics of Innocent Fraud*. Houghton Mifflin Company: Boston, pg 7.

Riccini, Raimonda (2005): »Design e teorie degli oggetti«. *il verri*, n° 27 - febbraio 2005, 48-57.

Rybczynski, Witold (2005): »How Things Work«. New York Review of Books, vol LII, number 10, june 9, 49-51.

Said, Edward W. (2003): *Humanism and Democratic Criticism*. Columbia University Press, New York, pg 28.

II. SPACES AND THINGS

DISOBEDIENT OBJECTS

Gavin Grindon

The vogue for exhibitions on 'activist art', from *Of Direct Action Considered as One of the Fine Arts* at MACBA in 2000, through *The Interventionists* at Mass MoCA in 2005, to the 2009 Istanbul Biennale and 2012 Berlin Biennale, has involved both the creation of space and visibility for social movement cultures (specifically autonomous social movements, which have been the dominant global movement form of organisation in this period), but it has also entailed an enclosure and recuperation of those cultures. This ambiguous art-institutional turn towards 'activism' raises the question of how art produced within social movement cultures can be written about productively, given that the institutions and institutional roles which traditionally support art writing of various kinds are often at odds with social movement cultures' relations of production and circulation. In attempting to address methods and perspectives combining artistic labour and political participation, my focus is not on the area of performance or dialogue but on objects, the most neglected and apparently problematic category for such work. Objects might seem at a particular inanimate remove from issues of political participation and agency, and most readily reified (which after all means turned into objects) and decontextualised. Formally, music and performance emerging from social movements have received perhaps the most attention from writers, curators and filmmakers, whereas the material objects of movements have most often fallen beyond their remit. But for these reasons such objects are particularly revealing.

There are many ways art and design practices can be politically active. But I am not primarily concerned with the institutional frames of the sometimes-isolated gestures of either 'critical design' or even programmes of 'interventionist' participatory art. Likewise 'activist art' and more recently 'design activism' are established terms referring alternately to a broad range of artists' practices or to socially responsible professional design (Antonelli 2008; Smith 2007; Thorpe 2012). I do not wish to denigrate such practices, and it is true that there are many kinds of 'activism', but at the same time the broad use of the term 'activism' has also functioned as an enclosure of cultural value, authenticity and impact on the part of professional artists, critics, designers, corporations, and even NGOs. Rather, it seems imperative to step back from some of these existing frameworks, and begin with the actually existing but often unacknowledged grassroots cultures of social movements, in order to contextualize the many overlapping current debates on art, design, participation and social change.

What Are Disobedient Objects?

By Disobedient Objects I intend the objects of art and design produced by grassroots activist social movements. The context of movements, their theory and practice, is the primary context for a grounded understanding of activist art, so often misframed purely by more abstract, internal artworld debates in theory and aesthetics.

The perspective I adopt here is that of social art history, specifically of an art history from below. In their history of the revolutionary Atlantic of the seventeenth and eighteenth centuries, the historians Peter Linebaugh and Marcus Rediker observe that for the classically educated architects of the Atlantic economy, Hercules represented power and order. They saw in his mythical labours their own epic imperial ambitions and aggressive economic enclosure of the world. Accordingly, they placed his image on coins, buildings and the finely crafted objects of their domestic lives, and images of him can be found multiplied across paintings, sculptures and ceramics in Western museum collections. Hercules' second labour was to destroy the Hydra of Lerna, in whose image leaders of state and industry saw an antithetical figure of resistance and 'disorder'. It was an unruly monster, part whirlwind, part woman, part snake. When Hercules sliced off one of its heads, two more sprung up in its place. Eventually he killed it and, dipping arrows into the slain beast's gall, harnessed its power for himself and his future triumphs: *"From the beginning of English colonial expansion in the early seventeenth century through the metropolitan industrialization of the early nineteenth, rulers referred to the Hercules-hydra myth to describe the difficulty of imposing order on increasingly global systems of labor. They variously designated dispossessed commoners, transported felons, indentured servants, religious radicals, pirates, urban laborers, soldiers, sailors, and African slaves as the numerous, ever-changing heads of the monster. But the heads, though originally brought into productive combination by their Herculean rulers, soon developed among themselves new forms of cooperation against those rulers, from mutinies and strikes to riots and insurrections and revolution"* (Linebaugh/ Rediker 2001, 3–4).

For Linebaugh and Rediker, the Hydra suggests, in silhouette, the lost history of the multi-ethnic classes essential to the making of the modern world. Historians like them have tried to look at history from below, instead of from the perspective of 'great men' and the agency of state and capital. History is inevitably a matter of selective inclusion. This is equally true of the objects of art and design history, whose canon and collections are most often shaped by a market of wealthy collectors, even as some critical artists, curators and historians have attempted to intervene within the field. Turning to disobedient objects means looking for the objects that open up histories of making from below, often well outside the institutional history of fine art or design. These objects disclose hidden moments in which, even if only in brief flashes, we find the possibility that things might be otherwise: that, in fact, the world may also be made from below, by collective, organized disobedience against the world as it is. But history from below can be difficult to perceive. Its protagonists are barely documented, and we can only tell so much by turning things like silver vases inside out in order to reveal them in negative relief. The art, design and material culture of movements have gone mostly uncollected, unpreserved, excluded from their place in the making of history. Indeed, the image of the heroic worker, which became familiar on labour movement banners soon after the colonial Hercules imagery, itself relied on re-appropriating the image of Hercules as a powerful labouring body, the hydra becoming the constrictions of capitalism, later often pictured as chains to be smashed. Culture, understood (in one narrow sense) as the objects and images we should know about and value – our history of art and design – is also often told from above. This essay is one for the Hydra. Seeing through the Hydra's eyes is often a matter of historical perspective. Social movements, whether focused on feminism, anti-capitalism, global justice or other issues, are at the centre of the struggles that have won many of the rights and liberties we now enjoy.[1] They establish new ways of seeing the world and relating to each other that are often later taken for granted. Social movements are one of the primary engines producing our culture and politics, and this is no less true when it comes to art and design.

Disobedient objects have a history as long as social struggle itself. Ordinary people have always used them to exert 'counterpower' (Gee 2011). Objects have played a key role in social change alongside performance, music and the visual arts. The imagination and creativity of making within social movements has played a key role in achieving social change, upending the terms of public debates and directly influencing more familiar commercial art and design. The role of material culture in social movement is a mostly untold story. There have been many exhibitions of political prints, and there have been exhibitions of movement histories, mostly in social history museums, which included objects but did not focus specifically on them and their making. Likewise, writing on movement cultures has focused on print, performance or music, but less often on object-making.

Social movements, though they may appear chaotic, are one of the principal sites where culture grows. The most common lazy stereotypes, easy to find in certain newspapers, of movements as insensible, unthinking, or inevitably violent, draw on even older classist, racist and sexist Victorian tropes of the flighty, swinish multitude or childlike, colonial savage, which have their roots in a bourgeois fear of the urban poor and 'Oriental' culture.[2] Little better is the notion of movement cultures as mechanisms of blunt political demands (as in the crudely statist notion

---

1   'Social movement' is a sociological term for the organizations behind what is commonly called 'protest' or 'direct action'. Sociologists still debate its exact definition and bounds, but essentially it encapsulates large informal and non-institutional groups of people concentrating on political and social issues.

2   On this social abjection in a contemporary context, see *Revolting Subjects: Social Abjection and Resistance in Neoliberal Britain* (Tyler 2014).

of 'propaganda'). McPhee and Greenwald's phrasing of 'social movement cultures' consciously identifies them as a site of culture and value (See McPhee/Greenwald 2010; on this stereotyping, see Tyler 2014). Movement cultures are the zero-point of political art and design, but tend to be alternatively ignored or problematically recuperated by art and design institutions.

Institutions have an understanding of what constitutes good art and design based on criteria of aesthetic excellence that are rooted in self-perpetuating professional infrastructures and ideas of connoisseurship. The Victoria and Albert Museum (hence V&A), which hosted the 2014-15 *Disobedient Objects* exhibition from which this discussion emerges, for example, has mostly collected commodity objects of elite production and consumption – which are also primarily objects of private consumption. An exception is the collection of prints and posters. The multiple, cheap and distributed nature of the poster meant that even in its most finely designed form, it was integrated into everyday public life. From the late nineteenth century, museums began collecting posters, precisely because their public context suggested an exciting modern medium. A form that has commonly been used by activists (especially from the late 1960s) was therefore already an established museum object-type. So it is as prints and posters that movement cultures have most easily slipped under the doors of museums. But what of the presence and visibility of other kinds of disobedient objects?

Even closely framing the slippery term 'activism' on social movements risks erasing differences: the relative strengths and weaknesses of different politics, or variations in the power, privilege and access found in different movements. It might suggest a narrow typology of objects made by 'activists', an identity that does not always appropriately describe the forms of subjectivity involved in non-Western social movements. It is also essential to acknowledge the politics of the everyday, where social change is made before or beyond the composition of a recognizably 'activist' subjectivity (See in this regard, X 2000).

One might take the position that disobedient objects might also include objects of the right (perhaps for 'balance'). Here, a radical history from below departs from the methods of a liberal capitalist sociology whose language it sometimes appropriates, making 'social movements' stand for agents of struggle against domination rather than an othering disciplinary definition of any contestatory extra-institutional organisation. This position neglects two aspects of the composition of radical autonomous movements. Firstly, the organisation of autonomous movements, and thus their modes of cultural production, tend to involve democratic participation, collectivity, co-authorship, consensus and solidarity. Organisations that foster instead strict hierarchies, strong leadership, fixity and exclusivity, while harking back to an imagined past, produce incomparably different cultures by different means. They tend first of all not to foster radical cultural experiment with objects such as graffiti robots or inflatable cobblestones. Secondly, the categorisation of these as 'left' or 'right' wing objects draws on a rigid geometric scheme originates in the seating arrangements of the 1789 French National Assembly. This is insufficiently nuanced to capture the diversity of movement cultures. Rather, they appear in varying, complexly composed movements, in which liberation movements may also be nationalist; or deploy traditional, even religious, values or oppose ostensibly 'left' communist states.

At the same time, 'disobedient objects' doesn't attempt to define a discipline. The term is intended as an evocative proposition or an invitation rather than a typology or closed concept. It centres on the object-based tactics and strategies that movements adopt to succeed. Its edges remain open to questions. What other forms of agency do these objects involve? Can we identify material points where disobedience begins, or turns into something else? Are some politics unable to produce objects?

We Want Bread, But Roses Too
[Attributed to Lawrence Textile Strikers, 1921]

There is no protest aesthetic. Political movement is always a matter of being emotionally moved, but each movement has its own aesthetic composition. By 'aesthetic composition' we intend something close to Raymond Williams' 'structure or feeling', but emphasizing affect and aesthetics not only as a determined structure (whether emergent or otherwise) but also as bound to agency and processes of political and class composition (Williams 1973; see also Gould 2009).

Accordingly, the objects emerging from these cultures are not unified by style or type. They can be monuments, full of symbolic historical accumulation, or small, quotidian and domestic. Though they are often playful and humorous, they can also be simultaneously traumatic, traversed by antagonism and conflict. Their makers commonly experience pressure from governments and private economic interests, in the form of police harassment, violence, spying, imprisonment, even assassination.

The question of the value of these objects, not least in terms of beauty and aesthetic fineness, is starkly posed when these objects are placed in a museum such as the V&A. Placed beside the V&A's examples of fine craft, movement objects might seem to fail in comparative judgements of aesthetic quality. But a failure to pass can be a form of disobedience in its own right, not least in questioning the narrow grounds of 'quality'. Fine making often belongs to privileged social conditions involving time, institutional training, normalization and patronage. It is bound to discipline and governance. As a result, fine objects are themselves mostly failures in the task of making change. Disobedient objects explore what Halberstam calls the queer art of failure (Halberstam 2011). They may be simple in means, but they are rich in ends. Working (in the words of Critical Art Ensemble) by any medium necessary, often under conditions of duress and scarcity, they tend to foreground promiscuous resourcefulness, ingenuity and timely intervention. This is not to balance aesthetic quality against social significance, but to begin to rethink aesthetic value itself. As Duncombe and Lambert argue: *"Political art [...] is engaged in the world. The world is messy. It has lots of moving parts. This material is impossible to fully control or master [...]*

Whereas compromise for the traditional artist means diluting their vision, compromise for the political artist is the very essence of democratic engagement" (Duncombe/Lambert 2012).

The Bread and Puppets Theatre has since the 1960s been central to introducing puppetry to social movements in the United States. Through the pathos of its archetypal papier-mâché puppets and *Cheap Art Manifesto*, it negates stereotypes about social movement making as crude or naive because the objects are produced quickly, under pressure and with limited resources. Rather, movement-makers are skilful artists, craftspeople and technologists producing considered, practical responses to complex problems, which have proven both effective and aesthetically powerful.

> "I pondered all these things, and how men fight and lose the battle, and the thing that they fought for comes about in spite of their defeat, and when it comes turns out not to be what they meant, and other men have to fight for what they meant under another name."
> (William Morris, *A Dream of John Ball*, 1888)

The strange, sometimes ambivalent, or bitter victories of movements complicate any assessment of successful design in their objects. Some disobedient objects might seem like 'hope in the dark', in Rebecca Solnit's phrase, unlikely to achieve any change (Solnit 2005). But their acts of composing things otherwise, in defiance of all that is wrong around them, are beautiful failures that throw teleological definitions of success into question. Moreover, all successful movements are made up of very large numbers of people carrying out small, seemingly utopian experiments without seeing or even necessarily knowing of each other; having no idea of the sometimes unlikely opportunities their acts might create; not necessarily realising they are already sewing the fabric of historical change.

While the organizations that produce disobedient objects might have little cultural visibility to begin with, social movements are *instituent* – they aim to institute new ways of living, laws and social organizations. As William Morris observed, social movements often find themselves woven into unexpected new contexts that obscure their origins. Or as David Graeber puts it: *"What reformers have to understand is that they're never going to get anywhere without radicals and revolutionaries to betray"* (Graeber 2013). In Bolivia, the Katarista movements of the 1970s revived the Wiphala flag symbolizing Qullasuyu, their quadrant of the Inca empire, as part of their rural, indigenous and anti-colonial politics. The rainbow flag of forty-nine squares recalls pre-Columbian designs and became widespread in indigenous mobilizations in the 1990s. But between 2007 and 2009, when a new constitution refounded the country, the Wiphala flag's resonances altered as it became an official state flag, draped on government buildings and stitched to the uniforms of police and soldiers.[3] If governments sometimes claim credit for movement victories and

---

3   I am grateful to Carwil Bjork-James for his expertise on the role of Wiphalas in social movements. See http://woborders.wordpress.com, accessed 10 December 2013.

appropriate their established cultures, businesses more often do so with their cultural innovations. Today's proliferation of rentable public bicycles in cities began in Amsterdam with a collection of 1960s anarchist-artists called the Provos, who left white bicycles in public for anyone to use and then leave for others. The police confiscated them, saying that people might steal them (some Provos responded by stealing police bikes and leaving these in public painted white, too). Their white bike plan eventually led to government-supported bicycle programmes, since adopted by other city governments around the world. Similarly, the problematic labelling of the recent Arab Spring as the 'Twitter revolution' belies another genealogy: Twitter itself was inspired by an activist media project, the Institute for Applied Autonomy's TXTMob, launched (alongside the Ruckus Society's RNC Text Alert Service) to circumvent mass media and network demonstrators during the 2004 Republican National Convention in New York. These initiatives were in turn inspired by early experiments with mobile phones and text messaging by European movements in the 1990s, especially Reclaim the Streets in Britain.

Making Trouble: Swarm Design and Ecologies of Agency

Disobedient objects are most commonly everyday objects, appropriated and turned to a new purpose, from the wooden shoe of the saboteur (from *sabot*, French for wooden shoe) thrown into a factory machine to the shoe thrown at President Bush by an Iraqi journalist during a press conference with the words, *"This is a farewell kiss from the Iraqi people, you dog"*.[4] Collective appropriation can be found in the noisemaking pots and pans first used in Chile's *cacerolazos* in the 1970s, in which the archetypal objects of domestic design sounded a counter-public sphere, or the mass jingling of keys, which unlocked the air of public space during the 1989 Czech Velvet Revolution. Likewise, in Latin America, a traditional tool by which farmers earned their income, embedded in various local popular traditions, has also long held a powerful symbolic role in protests: the machete. In 1959 Fidel Castro announced the machete as the symbol of the Cuban revolution, echoing the use of ploughs, sickles and hammers in European and Russian socialist iconography. The machete's symbolic function is supported by its long history as a weapon for poor farmers and freed slaves in wars of independence. Still in practical use, machetes are often carried symbolically in demonstrations rather than depicted graphically. By 2012, they could be seen in student demonstrations in Mexico paired with Guy Fawkes masks.

---

4   Ayatollah Ahmad Jannati called for the shoes, 'more valuable than crowns' (see e.g., *The Nation*, 6 November 2014, http://nation.com.pk/international/20-Dec-2008/Iranian-cleric-Jannati-dubs-Muntazer-act-shoe-intifada, accessed 5 November 2014), to be placed in an Iraqi museum, but they were destroyed by United States security forces. The journalist, Muntazer al-Zaidi, was sentenced to three years in an Iraqi prison, of which he served nine months. See al-Zaidi, Muntazer, 'Why I threw the shoe', *The Guardian*, 17 September 2009, http://www.theguardian.com/commentisfree/2009/sep/17/why-i-threw-shoe-bush, accessed 5 November 2014.

But disobedient objects are about making as much as breaking. Disobedience can involve DIY hacking and alteration, and also the design of whole new ways to disobey. The re-use of easily accessible objects, like the shipping barrels comprising nineteenth-century barricades (from *barrique*, French for barrel), implicate these objects in unfinished dialectics of social struggle and make them one means of the global circulation of struggles. For example, wooden pallets, the structural foundation of one unit load, were produced by the mid-twentieth-century standardization of international container shipping. They were brought about by efficiency drives rooted in de-skilling aimed at breaking the power of unionized longshoremen's labour. But these mass-produced wooden frames, designed for disciplining labour and circulating commodities, became, around the world, a shared infrastructural basis for the first 1970s tree-sits in New Zealand; furniture and barricade elements in 1970s Kabouter squats, or those of Okupa in Spain; and more recently the base of 123 Occupy's designs to support the protest-units of Occupy Wall Street tents.

Disobedient objects are not mere props. Or rather, as disability scholars have observed, democracy is prosthetic. The system of voting, for example, has always been propped up by objects, from the Chartists' call for the democratizing impairment of secret ballots, where paper cards replace voices, to the push-button electronic voting machines introduced in India in the 1980s, which facilitated voting for illiterate citizens. Social movements, too, have their own props, and they can fall down without them. (Even though, in British ecological movements, the key material infrastructures of protest events are referred to, self-depreciatingly, as 'activist tat'.) Though I have avoided the term, we might think of these as 'activist objects' in the sense that they are active, bound up with the agency of social change. The objects do not possess agency in themselves, but make change as part of ecologies composed also of other objects, music, performing bodies, technology, laws, organizations and effects. A weaker, less resource-rich power can triumph through asymmetrical innovation, and since the 1980s the strategic advantages of smallness and mobility have increased. So while disobedient objects are often appropriated, they also often appropriate their context of existing architecture or situations, unlocking them to reframe a situation or produce new relationships. As many have argued, the best response to a powerful enemy can be a more powerful story. Eclectic Electric Collective's inflatable cobblestones thrown at the police playfully destabilize relations between police and protestors, while the book bloc implicates the police in a dance with demonstrators. The police's attempt to control the streets using violence is reframed as control of the story of austerity, itself an attack on access to education. The holes wrought in the shields by the police's truncheons are part of their provenance, a certifying signature of their unwitting co-authorship.

While their social and geographical contexts vary widely, disobedient objects share common modes of production, lines of communication and influence. History from below entails multiplicity, and we focus on the interweaving of different historical moments. These objects don't move from producer to market in a circulation of commodities, as in Marx's scheme of Money-Commodity-Money[5], but are one means of a circulation of struggles (perhaps, Movement-Object-Movement). Making a new world is always an experiment, but it doesn't happen in an isolated laboratory. The objects involved are prototypes that exist in the wild, to be modified and reworked to meet the needs of different times and places. They have a distributed collective authorship, involving multiple re-appropriations and re-workings as movements learn from each other and develop each other's tactics, or solve similar problems with parallel approaches.

Tripods

Tripods, objects that augment the body's ability to blockade, are an archetypal example of this swarm design. On 26 March 1974, loggers arrived in the village of Reni in Uttarakhand in northern India. Female villagers, after trying to reason with them, explaining that they relied on the trees for their livelihood, were threatened with guns. In response, they extended Ghandian methods to *chipko*: hugging the trees in a bodily blockade. Their successes in forest conservation became a strategic rallying point for the nascent ecological movement. In 1978 in New Zealand, as part of anti-logging protests that led to the foundation of Pureora Forest Park, activists extended such blockades by moving out of easy reach, building platforms using wooden pallets high up in the trees to blockade the felling with 'tree-sits', a tactic also adopted in Australia's Terrania Creek in 1979 (in what became national park land, including the picturesque Protesters Falls), and in the US in 1985 to prevent logging in Willamette National Forest, Oregon. As the tactic spread, tree surgery businesses or industrial rope access firms were sometimes hired in the United States and Britain to assist police and bailiffs in extracting protesters from trees. But protesters out-designed the authorities once again. In 1989, during huge anti-logging blockades in Coolangubra State Forest, Australia, activists raised a three-legged tripod about six metres high that blocked the single logging road into the forest: a tree-sit without a tree. The first tripod was a metal scaffold, pulled into place by a vehicle, but others there and at the parallel Chaelundi forest blockades used wooden logs. One person sat atop the tripod, so that removing any of its legs would cause him or her to fall and be injured. Some of these forests later became national parks. The North East Forest Alliance's 1991 Intercontinental Deluxe Guide to Blockading spread tripod (and lock-on) designs to the UK and US (some individual activists travelled between Australian, American and British actions, too). In the US, wooden tripods first appeared in 1992 blockades protecting the Cove Mallard wilderness. In Britain, the tripod was adopted by Reclaim the Streets, where urban activists with strong ties to earlier British tree-sits scavenged steel scaffolding poles to make tripods. In an urban context they constituted 'intelligent barricades' that closed a road to cars but left it open for pedestrians and bicycles.

---

5   For an introduction to the idea of a 'circulation of struggles', see Witherford (1999).

Beginning on Angel High Street, London, in 1994, these tripods made Reclaim the Streets parties possible. The design spread through the how-to guide Road Raging. Bipod and even unipod designs, alongside complex multi-tripod architectural arrangements using overlapping legs, sometimes in response to the development of specialized police removal units, proliferated in the United States, Asia-Pacific and Europe. Groups invested in lighter, more quickly erected aluminium (and even bamboo) poles over steel scaffolding. From the 2006 British Climate Camp protests, the tripod became a graphic icon of protest and was sometimes erected at camp entrances for purely symbolic reasons.

This ecology of agency also involves different contexts and power relations, traversing and transforming these objects. The role of the law is perhaps the clearest example. The state, in a paradox of sovereignty, attempts to define what is legal and an acceptable form of protest against it. Many modern forms of action, such as unions or strikes, were once illegal and required either secrecy or open lawbreaking. Recently in Britain new laws redefining 'public order', as well as cuts to legal aid and investment of public money in the surveillance and disruption of peaceful movements, have curtailed the right to protest. Objects are intimately involved in this negotiation of what constitutes the space of 'legitimate' protest. The pocket-sized 'bust cards' first developed by US and UK black and queer communities, detailing legal rights and advice in case of arrest, are now commonplaces in public demonstrations as democratic protest is increasingly criminalised. In the US during the 2000s, the sticks that support a dancing puppet were reclassified as 'potential weapons', perhaps explaining a move to inflatables by some groups. In Britain, the 1994 Criminal Justice Act, Section 60, made wearing a mask at a protest (for example, in objection to police data-gathering teams) an offence. In 2012, United Arab Emirates police announced people should not wear Guy Fawkes masks, as 'objects deemed to instigate unrest are illegal', while their import into Bahrain was banned in 2013. The Molotov cocktail, which first appeared during the Spanish Civil War and later in Finnish resistance to Soviet invasion in the 1930s, entailed a semi-permanent change in the conceptual status of mass-produced glass bottles as unproblematic everyday objects. In Belfast during the early 1990s, art students carrying milk bottles (in which they used to wash their paintbrushes) were often stopped as potential terrorists because – for the state – their artists' tools had become irrevocably associated with more insurgent appropriation. Here, too, we must include the many imaginary disobedient objects that have been conjured by the police, and fed to the media, which have at various points served as a pretext for curtailing protests. Despite their potent psychological associations these objects never surfaced at protests and would have little practical reason for doing so – from condoms filled with urine at the Seattle 1999 WTO protests to 'rioters armed with samurai swords and machetes' at the London 2001 May Day protests.[6]

Sometimes, the media's imaginative framing of objects is embraced by or otherwise becomes definitive for movements, from the fictional 'bra burning' in reports on the

---

6   Graeber (2014); 'Armed Police on May Day Riot Alert', *Observer*, 22 April 2001.

1968 Miss America protests to the coinage of the term 'black bloc' by the German press in the 1980s to describe the dress of some Autonomen (Dow 2003).

The Master's Tools Will Never Dismantle the Master's House.
[Audre Lorde, *Sister Outsider*, 1984]

Context is everything. We should be wary of any uncritical affirmation of the power of making, 'creative' activism or transversal innovation in the context of the neo-liberal relations of the 'creative industries'. Rather, the contradiction remains open: to produce any value at all, capital relies on the same capacity to be creative that is always also escaping and refusing. This creativity can come from mobilising traditions and religious or spiritual values as much as experimental novelty, for example, in the dense iconography of British labour union banner, Indonesian group Taring Padi's 'protest puppets' adaptation of the traditions of *wayang* puppet theatre, the carved Maori *pouwhenua* (pre-European land-marker post), made for carrying at the head of the 1975 Maori land rights march and subsequent protests, or the avatar of the Goddess of Good Governance protecting street hawkers in Sewa Nagar market in Delhi, who, in her many arms, holds a video camera to film the police.

Many more playful or creative disobedient objects only function in specific social-democratic contexts, in which governments, even if in increasingly limited ways, recognize people as subjects with a right of resistance to speak and act politically. Without such acknowledgement – most often the case for movements composed of people of colour and indigenous communities – struggles for rights and freedoms sometimes necessarily take different forms, from urban self-defence to rural or desert guerrilla warfare. Their objects necessarily become improvised objects of physical force, often outmatched by but dialectically bound to the violence and oppression they resist; from 'fards', single-shot guns made by blacksmiths from scrap water pipes, used by neighbourhood protection groups in the poorest areas of the 2011 Egyptian revolution, to 'technicals', the improvised battle vehicles engineered by anti-Gaddafi rebels during the 2011 Libyan revolution. Even among other movements, the diversity of tactics has often been key to their success, which includes objects of militant community defence or property destruction; such as the appropriation of a Lucozade bottle as a weapon among 1980s British antifascists confronting neo-nazis; or the role of 'tree spiking' in the success of American forest protection campaigns (Bari 1994).

Undisciplined Knowledge

"I jumped up and said 'Arm me – I'll kill a white dude right now!' The whole [Black Panther] meeting got quiet. They called me to the front of the room, and the brother who was running the meeting looked at me for a minute, and then reached into the desk drawer. My heart was pounding. I was like, 'Oh my god, he's going to give me a big-ass gun!' And he handed me a stack of books ... I said, 'Excuse me, sir, I thought you were going to arm me?' He said, 'I just did.'"

(Jamal Joseph, interview in *Time* magazine, 9 February 2012)

Disobedient objects also lead us to think about how movements produce new forms of knowledge and strategy that help us see from below. While they may find footholds in various disciplines, they also draw from popular global and local traditions of making, outside professional art and design. Some of these are evoked by the many how-to publications which instruct their readers on the design of disobedience: the barricade diagrams of Auguste Blanqui's 1866 *Instructions for an Insurrection*; Bread and Puppet Theatre's *68 Ways to Make Really Big Puppets*; Dave Foreman's *Ecodefense: A Field Guide to Monkeywrenching*; *The Squatter's Handbook*; *The Activist Tat Collective Recipe Book* for camps and convergences, or the recent collection *Beautiful Trouble*. These objects embody knowledge and skills. They are not formed from nowhere. We might consider the section of Marx's *Grundrisse*, in which he argues that the fixed capital of factory machines materially embodies the 'general intellect' of workers: their aggregate social skill and knowledge (Marx 1973). This might prompt us to wonder what other anti-capitalist machines the general intellect might imagine and embody itself in. We might think of the objects and performances of social movements as just such machines, embodying knowledge otherwise. There is certainly a mutiny of professional knowledge, including fine art and design, in these objects. But they are also moulded by the collective, informal, experiential knowledge of local laws around protest, of how to negotiate with police, of political meeting and street protest dynamics. Additionally, they spring from a base in leisure and domestic skills that become political tools, from camping to knitting and sewing.[7] Behind the design of tripods stand other changes in leisure and education, for example, the growth of climbing as a sporting activity and the growth of indoors walls in the 1980s, often appearing first in university gyms. Such knowledges are one example of what Harney and Moten call 'the undercommons'. Its appearance in the museum echoes its role in the university. To document them without betraying them here is to attempt to appropriate the academy (or the museum) as a means of amplification, transmission and reflection.

"It cannot be denied that the university is a place of refuge and it cannot be accepted that the university is a place of enlightenment. In the face of these conditions one can only sneak into the university and steal what one can. To abuse its hospitality, to spite its mission, to join its refugee colony, its gypsy encampment, to be in but not of – this is the path of the subversive intellectual in the modern university" (Harney/Moten 2013, 26).

This position 'within and against' an institution emerges principally from careful

---

7   *"One of the paternalistic ideas I have often heard from academics is that cutting edge political thinking takes place in the academy. I have found the opposite to be true - that it takes place outside of the academy where it is not hampered by institutional requirements, such as the focus on individual scholarship [or] the need to develop special vocabularies and grand theory in order to be taken seriously"* (Wolfe 1997).

attention to these objects and their own instituent power (Raunig 2005). It isn't just about antagonism, although that is important. Rather, it implies a 'with and for'. As a project's spaces of autonomy develop, less time might be spent in antagonism than in co-research towards a collective project, composing the many 'yeses' behind the 'noes'. In attending to these objects one must return, in one sense, to a quite traditional idea of the etymological roots of a curator as one who cares. 'Care' is here used not in the sense of bureaucratic administration or discipline, but as an ethics of solidarity, mutual aid, even love (Hardt 2012; Heckert 2010). Caring for these objects involves becoming with and for them, listening to them and understanding how their making is bound to a making of history that is both neglected and incomplete.

Unfinished Objects

"The posters produced by the ATELIER POPULAIRE are weapons in the service of the struggle and are an inseparable part of it. Their rightful place is in the centres of conflict, that is to say, in the streets and on the walls of the factories. To use them for decorative purposes, to display them in bourgeois places of culture or to consider them as objects of aesthetic interest, is to impair both their function and their effect. This is why the ATELIER POPULAIRE has always refused to put them on sale. Even to keep them as historical evidence of a certain stage in the struggle is a betrayal, for the struggle itself is of such primary importance that the position of an 'outside' observer is a fiction which inevitably plays into the hands of the ruling class. That is why these works should not be taken as the final outcome of an experience, but as an inducement for finding, through contact with the masses, new levels of action, both on the cultural and the political plane."
Atelier Populaire statement, 1968

Swarm-designed objects are necessarily rough, raw things, whose edges are open to further modification and appropriation. Only their contexts of use make them whole, and this makes these objects unfinished in another, more teleological, sense. Documented or exhibited, rather than being 'dead' like a butterfly enclosed in a case, disobedient objects are unfinished, like a political sticker never stuck, its hope and rage still held fast to its laminate backing. Their aura is that of an unfulfilled promise. But this incompleteness needn't be a melancholy sign of failure so much as one of possibility.

A suffragette tea set promoting votes for women is a comfortable object to contemplate to the extent that a consensus has formed about the struggle that produced it – what happened, who won and what that means. The jeopardy, trauma and grief encapsulated in many contemporary disobedient objects, however, is raw and ongoing in ways that may make them uncomfortable or disturbing. They embody uncomfortable truths about the present and destabilize the official line of politicians and media organizations. They are full of uncertainty – and the empowering and terrifying idea that our own actions (and inaction) could make a difference.

The Atelier Populaire's critique, though totalizing, is well-founded. Social movements, in contesting our ways of seeing and acting, find themselves beset by a long and recent history of misrepresentation, in which they are ignored or maligned by mass media while simultaneously being appropriated for their vitality and authenticity. Museums are not immune to this process of caricature. Visiting the Political Art Documentation and Distribution archive at MoMA in New York, two independent researchers found a collection of undocumented American Indian movement posters, with a Post-It note inside their archive drawer that read, 'not cool enough to catalog' (Sholette 2011, 88; Jordan 2010). Other groups, such as the Laboratory of Insurrectionary Imagination or the various Occupy movements, have found themselves invited – as content – to participate in museum programmes. The museum then often attempts to contain or stifle the same organizing vitality that originally attracted it when it becomes apparent that it might trouble the museum's sponsorship or labour relations.[8] The Atelier Populaire's resistance to institutionalization intersects with the anecdote quoted earlier from a Black Panther meeting, which suggests that reflection can be as important as action. But the terms of that reflection are crucial, and this problem of representation must be the primary concern when re-presenting social movement objects. When objects such as these have appeared in museums, they have usually been presented as ephemera, displayed not for close attention in their own right so much as incidental objects that were present while important social change was happening. More rarely, they have appeared as fetishes, valorised as 'edgy' or 'vital' cultural capital and thus commodified in ways counter to the political goals they were made to achieve. These two conditions, ephemera and fetish, are principal dangers.

This essentially methodological discussion on how we might begin to approach activist art by grounding it in social movement cultures has been accompanied by a practical experiment in an exhibition of the same name in a major cultural institution. Whatever our emotional reaction or identification with these unfinished objects, we mostly encounter them for only a brief moment, and even then always mediated by other objects and social relations: perhaps inches from, or touching, our bodies in a crowd, held by (or holding up) our friends or comrades, in news footage of people who could be us, in photographs of days growing distant, or suddenly reappearing in a courtroom. The exhibition or academic documentation of these objects is, in fact, one moment when you might actually spend time with them, right in front of you, able to slowly examine them. How does this moment (where the objects are placed in historical, and relative, contexts) relate to these other moments, its use by activists, newspaper photographers, and so on? The undercommons test the claim

---

8   One other non-public site which I and my co-curator did not pursue in attempting to exhibit these objects was the undisclosed holdings of movement objects seized or stolen by the state, though we found traces of these ghost archives in stories of an undocumented confiscated protest banner used as mocking decoration in a British police station, the Chinese government's alleged longstanding archive of objects handed in or left on the street after demonstrations, or the Occupy Wall Street barriers that reappeared outside the police chief's office on their anniversary, as reported in 'Whodunit at Police Headquarters: Occupy Accuses Police', *New York Times*, 17 November 2012.

of a museum or university to really be a 'public' space of participation. Invited to a dance with the institution that Brian Holmes calls a game of liar's poker (Holmes 2007), presenting disobedient objects in institutional contexts sets a wager on what the institution does to disobedient objects and what they do to the institution, as well as – crucially – what else this might institute beyond it. The process of writing or exhibiting is one of institutional critique, but it may also be a process of counter-institution. Disobedient objects were not made, for example, with a museum in mind. Nor do they rely on the museum to legitimate them – but this does not mean that they have nothing to gain from appearing there. That an exhibition can provide space to consider, away from the rush of a political action or the hyperbole of mass media, was demonstrated at the ARTPLAY design space in Moscow during the demonstrations (or 'fair election' rallies) against Putin's election as president in 2012. Recognizing that a new style of public protest was emerging in Russia, exemplified by individualized and often witty handmade placards, ARTPLAY invited protestors to lend their placards to the gallery for a short period during which they staged an exhibition, entitled *You don't even represent us / You can't even imagine us.* Afterwards, many of the placards were collected by their makers and carried in further demonstrations. The 'makeshift gas mask guide from the V&A exhibition, based on a design used in the 2013 occupation of Istanbul's Gezi park, was shared on blogs and twitter during the exhibition in 2014 with the #Ferguson hashtag, following the heavy teargasing of protests in Ferguson, Missouri, over the police shooting of an unarmed teenager. Protestors there made the mask from this design to protect and care for each other. Masks using the V&A design were made and used on an even wider scale during the 2014 Hong Kong pro-democracy protests. The visibility of the museum as a place for looking amplified and projected this general intellect around mask-making in solidarity, from one undercommons to another (Bell 2014). Inflatable 'carbon bubbles' made during museum workshops have appeared in the streets during the 2014 climate justice marches in New York and London. Engaging with the unfinished struggles of which activist art is a part, as a historian or curator, is not only an abstract question of methodology or representation, or of critique (institutional or otherwise) but one of strategy. Strategy implicates the position of the writer as participant, and such a critical perspective must include a reflection on one's own participation, privilege and responsibility.

This chapter is a revised version of the essay entitled "Disobedient Objects" (first published in Flood/Grindon 2014).

References

Antonelli, Paoloa et al. (ed.) (2008): *Design for the Elastic Mind.* Thames & Hudson.

Bari, Judi (1994): The Secret History of Tree Spiking, in *Timber Wars,* Courage: Monroe, Maine, 264–282.

Bell, Alice (2014): The Global Network of DIY Tear Gas Masks, http://www.howwegettonext.com/Article/VEQ_cTUAADEAjFQ3/the-global-network-of-diy-tear-gas-masks and *Designing Protest*, BBC Radio 4, 25 November 2014, http://www.bbc.co.uk/programmes/b04ps6py, accessed 1 December 2014.

Dow, Bonnie J. (2003): Feminism, Miss America, and Media Mythology, in: *Rhetoric & Public Affairs* 6/1 (2003), 127–49.

Duncombe, Stephen / Lambert, Steve (2012): 'An Open Letter to Critics Writing About Political Art'; *Center for Artistic Activism*, 20 October 2012, at http://artisticactivism.org/2012/10/an-open-letter-tocritics- writing-about-political-art/, accessed 10 December 2013.

Flood, Catherine / Grindon, Gavin (Eds.) (2014): *Disobedient Object*s. London: V&A Publications.

Gee, Tim (2011): *Counterpower: Making Change Happen*. London: World Changing; Edition Unstated edition.

Gould, Deborah (2009): *Moving Politics*. Universtiy of Chicago Press.

Graeber, David (2013): online question and answer sesison on reddit, 28 January 2013, 16:58 UTC, reply to 'effigies', http://www.reddit.com/r/IAmA/comments/17fi6l/i_am_david_graeber_an_anthropologist_activist/, accessed 5 November 2014.

Graeber, David (2014): 'On the Phenomenology of Giant Puppets', *Disobedient Objects*, exh. Cat. V&A, London.

Halberstam, Judith Jack (2011): *The Queer Art of Failure*. Durham: Duke University Press.

Hardt, Michael (2012): The Procedures of Love, Documenta Series 068 [Documenta 13] of *100 Notizen – 100 Gedanken/ 100 Notes, 100 Thoughts*, Kassel.

Harney, Stefano / Moten, Fred (2013): *The Undercommons: Fugitive Planning and Black Study*. London: Autonomedia.

Heckert, Jamie (2010): Listening, Caring, Becoming: Anarchism as an Ethics of Direct Relationships, in Benjamin Franks and Matthew Wilson (eds), *Anarchism and Moral Philosophy*, London, Basingstoke: Palgrave, 186–207.

Holmes, Brian (2007): 'Liar's Poker', Unleashing the Collective Phantoms. New York: Autonomedia.

Linebaugh, Peter and Marcus Rediker (2001): *The Many-Headed Hydra: Sailors, Slaves, Commoners, and the Hidden History of the Revolutionary Atlantic*. Boston: Beacon Press.

Jordan, John (2010): On Refusing to Pretend to do Politics in a Museum, in *Art Monthly* 334 (March, 2010), p.35, available online at http://www.artmonthly.co.uk/magazine/site/article/on-refusing-to-pretend-to-do-politics-in-a-museum-by-john-jordan-2010, accessed 5 November 2014.

Marx, Karl (1973): *Grundrisse: Outlines of the Critique of Political Economy*, trans. Martin Nicolaus, London, 690–712.

McPhee, Josh, and Dara Greenwald (2010): *Signs of Change: Social Movement Cultures 1960s to Now*. Edinburgh: AK Press.

Raunig, Gerald (2005): Instituent Practices: Fleeing, Instituting, Transforming. *Art and Contemporary Critical Practice: Reinventing Institutional Critique*, ed. Gene Ray and Gerald Raunig. London: MayFlyBooks/Ephemera.

Sholette, Gregory (2011): Not Cool Enough to Catalog: Social Movement Culture and its Phantom Archive, in *Peace Press Graphics 1967-1987: Art in the Pursuit of Social Change*, exh. Cat. CSU Long Beach University Art Museum, Long Beach, 87–96.

Smith, Cynthia (2007): *Design for the Other 90%*. The University of Chicago Press.

Solnit, Rebecca (2005): *Hope in the Dark: The Untold History of People Power*. Edinburgh: Canongate.

Thorpe, Ann (2012): *Architecture and Design versus Consumerism: How Design Activism Confronts Growth*. Taylor & Francis.

Tyler, Imogen (2014): *Revolting Subjects: Social Abjection and Resistance in Neoliberal Britain*. London: Zed Books.

Williams, Raymond (1973): *The Country and the City*. Oxford University Press (2011).

Witherford, Nick Dyer (1999): *Cyber-Marx: Cycles and Circuits of Struggle in High-Technology Capitalism*. Chicago: University of Illinois.

Wolfe, Maxine (1997): 'Inside/ Outside the Academy: The Politics of Knowledge in Queer Communities', invited roundtable presentation, *Forms of Desire. The Seventh Annual Queer Graduate Studies Conference*, 3–5 April 1997, CUNY Graduate School, www.actupny.org/documents/academia.html, accessed December 2013.

X, Andrew (2000): 'Give Up Activism', *Do or Die* 9, pp.160–6 (originally published in London as part of the pamphlet *Reflections on June 18ᵗʰ*, 1999).

DEMO:POLIS
THE RIGHT TO PUBLIC SPACE

Barbara Hoidn

Democracy and public space are two inextricably linked concepts. A democratic society without public space is inconceivable, unviable, and implausible. In a democracy, the right to public space is equivalent to the policy makers' and politicians' obligation of transparency, the state's guarantee of unobstructed access to information for all, the individual's right to expression of opinion and participation, to active and politically mature forms of cooperation, and also the striving for a balance of individual and collective interests. However, the originally positive connotation of the term "public" as the counterpart of "private" or "not publicly accessible" has steadily eroded. When the protected status of the private realm in a democratic state is disputed, "public" can even transmute into a threatening scenario.

Ever since the existence of state-organized and -approved data theft has been uncovered, and against the backdrop of populist campaigns by financially powerful politicians, who with the support of their own media channels buy publicity or suspend democratic rights, there has emerged a justified concern that citizens have been degraded to the state of "vitreous" puppet voters under constant suspicion.

The World Wide Web's social networks and virtual global communities bring together people with apparently similar needs and desires to form selectively public groups with distinct rules, which are then, quite incidentally, relabeled as mere target groups and cashed in on. No one is safe from unauthorized intrusion in the name of the people. Data and private content is copied, gathered, and exploited.

Individuals' rights to public space and its protection as a neutral zone, as personal free space in the best sense of the word, whether on the internet or in the real world, is threatened and, apparently, must be permanently renegotiated. Democracy becomes a matter of trust between citizens and the representatives of the state.

How do contemporary planners, architects, politicians, and artists currently assess the significance of public space for democratic development of cities? Does the aspect of public space even play a substantial role in urban planning at all? How well-suited are the existing spaces for the social tasks and challenges that lie ahead? What kind of atmosphere does an urban society, a nation mediate through its public spaces? Who formulates demands and registers claims, who finances renovation when what is available no longer functions or must be modernized? How dominant are partial interests and who assures that balance is achieved? The power source for the perpetuation of democratic communities lies in a permanent redefinition and further development of the concept of public space, in changing protagonists testing the limits and appropriating space; from this emerges an ability to withstand authoritarian and dictatorial encroachments.

The right to demonstrate – a visible expression of democracy

The German reunification succeeded because of relentless protests in the public space. Paradoxically, the ensuing rivalry of ideas and systems will most likely ultimately culminate in the total destruction of the central public symbolic sites in the former capital of the GDR between Alexanderplatz and the already destroyed former Foreign Ministry building.

Throughout the world, people carry out political upheavals, heated protests, silent demonstrations, courageous announcements of solidarity, and spontaneous rebellions at central symbolic sites. Demonstration is the most fundamental form of expression of political will. In our era of modern media, global attention can be captured in real time. Only in this way can messages or notes of protest be spread throughout the world, plausibly and genuinely, even in remote places and often at substantial risk. People become involved and take on the hardships of political activism. Political fatigue is not discernible. Public space is made, directly and fundamentally. The most recent protests of students allover the US following the 2018 mass shooting in Parkland, Florida, ignited encouraging solidarity through a snowball system activism. The student leaders are determined to begin a long lasting march against the American gun lobby.

They draw energy from the successes of global Hashtag movements such as #JeSuisCharlie, #Bataclan and most recently the silence breakers #MeToo creating a powerful political momentum with enormous public impact.

Art interventions as a reminder of personal civil rights and liberties

Refined forms of politicization of public space arose in reaction to the historical event of the German reunification. Symbols and commentary were implanted in the public space. A multitude of individual, part planned, part spontaneous, clever, poetic, contemplative art projects and interventions in the urban landscape shaped Berlin in the years after the fall of the wall and became a powerful spoken and visual subtext of an increasingly illegible urban layout of the formerly divided city.

From retracing the now demolished Berlin wall to the photographic posters at the former border crossing Check Point Charlie or Wilhelmstraße, the book-burning memorial at Bebelplatz, the "stumbling stones," the details along the waterfront promenade on those stretches of the River Spree that once constituted the border, and the discussions surrounding the competition for the Holocaust Memorial – recognizable in all this is the will to give back meaning to the sites through concrete information in the urban space and to allow the past to remain visible in the future.

The concept of art interventions in public space was elevated to a new level by works as the memorial signs in the Bayerische Viertel in Berlin Schöneberg or the work *Bus Stop* for the Holocaust Memorial competition. The subtle yet poetic achievement of Berlin artists Stih and Schnock – who are, themselves, permanently and contentiously rooted in the conceptual and visual world of Berlin – was to firmly anchor these artistic works in the places of historical events, pairing them with factual information, and thus avoiding the exalted atmosphere of many a memorial site. The invisible is made visible again. A place becomes a home, also in an uncomfortable sense. Art mingles with the people, as it were, in their everyday life.

The naughty comments by artist Banksy displayed in the public realm are addressing in a similar, yet broader sense the eventual erosion of individual rights, of freedom of expression and strict safety measures in the name of the public while oppressing the individual.

Social artworks overcome clichés

Art interventions such as these, in turn, inspire other projects, which from the start are conceived as interactive social artworks or interventions. They often demand active participation or point out dysfunctional, paradoxical, or simply contrary conditions, as, for example, the different appropriations of space by urban gardening activists or the impromptu *diners en blanc,* for which hundreds of people gather at short notice at an agreed-upon site to dine together in the middle of the street.

It is the peaceful playfulness of these events and the interactive dialogue with a larger anonymous public that aims at reestablishing trust and confidence in the sustainability of the contemporary city. A new social contract!

But there are also the quiet projects that skirt the topics of hedonistic life in the metropolises around the world. The seemingly improvised projects by students at the School of Architecture in Talca, Chile, can be named as examples. They managed to restore to the city of Talca sites of public life, projects that are characterized by dignity and respect, first after the end of the Pinochet dictatorship and once again after the widespread destruction caused by an apocalyptic earthquake in February 2010.

Public space equals trust in democracy

Current projects in Latin America, in particular, reveal the need to protect public space and the vulnerability of the collective city when safety is not guaranteed and drug cartels, violent gangs, and social grievances cause the public dimension to dwindle. When people's trust in the security of public spaces dissolves or they gradually stay away, it marks the beginning of the end of communal life and a disproportionately greater loss than merely a deserted place where they roll up the sidewalks in the evening. What better place in Germany to study the urgency of this phenomenon than in the rural regions with sparse population density where young people are forced to meet in informal places like the remaining benches of bus stops or at service stations for lack of other, more animated spaces.

What it means when civil trust in the protective role of public space and its administration becomes frail can be observed in the decay of the proud central space of Berlin Alexanderplatz or through the recent occupation of the central Tiergarten Park in Berlin by homeless refugees, prostitutes and drug dealers with all its consequences for crime by opportunity. The widely established public confidence in the public realm was staked on administrative ease and loss of a sense of reality for the most recent urban challenges.

Public space with no trade-off?

As a positive outcome of contemporary urban tourism and the capitalization of cities as property investments, official channels in many places have launched ambitious programs for the improvement of public space, the creation of squares, parks, and landscapes, or for an inventive repurposing of decommissioned industrial facilities. The most renowned example is certainly the High Line in Manhattan's former Meat Packing District, but also the recreational facilities initiated by the 1989-99 IBA (International Building Exhibition) Emscher Park on decommissioned industrial properties in the Ruhr area.

The price for these significant investments is often enough to equip the gentrified public parlors and parks with surveillance cameras and free WLAN for greater security, but also to better locate individuals and an easy connection to appropriate apps, which make using the city and its commercial offers child's play. Especially in those global metropolises that have come under extreme pressure due to financial speculation, such as London, Paris, and New York, startling developments along these lines are taking place.

The price for a prominent and attractive space is now a higher security risk.

Nonetheless, these multi-million-dollar projects, such as Brooklyn Bridge Park in New York City, are the positive flipside of the new commercialization of the city with regularly held events and festivals in the urban space, which many residents see as an imposition. Games and entertainment for a traveling audience have become a fundamental income source for communities and have begun to oust everyday public life to other neighborhoods or zones. In Berlin, for example, central sites are basically rented out all year round. Berlin has a multitude of open space, parks, and urban axes, which are adored by the Zeitgeist, and has therefore set new standards in the category of mass events, from the Love Parade to the cordial "summer fairy tale" with the public screenings of matches during the Soccer World Championships in 2006, flat marathon courses through a seemingly never-ending city center, soccer stadiums that can be adapted to many purposes, and fashion shows on former airport grounds, along with a steadfast tolerance of the beer bottles carried by partygoers in the Berlin subways and commuter rails running 24/7.

The finite resource of memorable urban spaces and thereby urban stages must be regularly expanded, as the creative scene steadily produces and needs new imagery. Residents thus also turn to other sites. Riverbanks and parks as formerly ancillary urban recreational areas are discovered and utilized for relaxation and enjoyment. New rituals arise and become solidified in the repeated use of such areas. Funding, as well as the permission for use, is hard-earned. Tempelhofer Feld is a prime example of this. That which is not used, or no longer used, will soon lie fallow again.

Democracy and form - democracy in transition

The Greek cities created at the drawing board of urban planner Hippodamus first gave the Attic democracy its form. The city layout consisted of separate egalitarian lots, which were structured by a network of streets on a rectangular grid, with special, communally maintained gathering places, such as the natural harbor and the marketplace, excluded from it. The public facilities, such as temple, stoa, stadium, and theater, were conceived as geometrically pure solitary structures and implanted in the city layout. The more public spaces a city had to show for itself, the higher it ranked in the polis network. The form of public buildings and the actions carried out by the people therein created an inextricable bond, mutually influencing one another. Public space only gained its complex meaning and form through formal rituals and communal use. The space was completed only through its usage. Exceptional sites were thus created that are still visited and marveled at today.

Democracy as client, what does that mean for public space nowadays? Who is responsible, who feels responsible, and how do comprehensive planning principles emerge? Who formulates them?

In the early years of the German Federal Republic, the commitment to democracy was translated almost naïvely into a simplistic architectural expression. According to the German architectural avant-garde's credo, structures had to be transparent, or else they weren't democratic. The structures of the Bonn Republic embody this attitude. The corresponding public space, however, was diffuse, defined rather by ambitious speech bubbles than actually to be experienced. Forums, agoras, amphitheaters, stadiums, and, most of all, pedestrian zones and urban landscapes were created.

But also emerging were, and still are, space-devouring suburban agglomerations of single-family homes, at best grouped into urban landscapes without any claim to collective public spaces. The public space, the "residential environment" on the periphery of cities is a clunky concept void of content. Strip malls attached themselves to these areas and, following the American model, became a replacement for public space in the suburbs. Those who can pay the entry fee are welcome.

The gradual appropriation of sidewalks in the city by food stands and ice cream parlors might have been timid and seasonal, but in any case, it was not officially planned or anticipated. The same applies to the gradual change of appearance and revitalization of depopulated city centers through the influx of Turkish guest workers and other European and non-European population groups. German tradition, however – shaped by seasonal events such as the Oktoberfest, wine festivals, Christmas markets, carnival, and church festivals – continues to define public life. Yet, the transition to a more international understanding became visible especially in the cities. Undesirable neighborhoods in close proximity to the railway stations led the way.

Youth culture with major open-air music events and festivals or political happenings changed and eased the relationship between state authority and subject. In the 1960s, authorities confronted the informal appropriation of spaces with increasing equanimity. The peace movement, squatters, and terrorist threats by the RAF, however, once again put strain on the situation in the 1970s. Mistrust between citizens and state increased. But civil disobedience as a means to demand more democracy had already become an integral part of the debate. University campuses as breeding grounds of democratic will and rebellion gained greatly in importance. Social changes occurring at the universities was representative for society at large. Again, all of these changes were unplanned and thus not politically foreseen or approved. Evil to those who evil think of the fact that new university complexes in the 1970ies were generally built in isolated areas remote from the city center.

Arising as new public spaces were mainly streets, in line with a car-friendly restructuring of the city for an increasingly motorized population. At the same time, Italy's distinctive, intact, and lively city centers became sites of desire for Germans raised in purpose-oriented cities.

Tightly packed hotels and vacation-home complexes for mass tourism sprang up along the Italian and Spanish coastlines and on the Mediterranean islands, which once again, especially enticed tourists from Germany. The social behavior and atmosphere in the public spaces defined by vacationers have become legendary. Heinrich Klotz offered a beautiful memorial to this development in 1977 with the book of essays, *Die röhrenden Hirsche der Architektur*.

The cautious redesigning of Barcelona's city center in preparation for the Olympic Games in 1992 inspired a number of cities to follow its example. With a meticulously planned program for the upgrading of public spaces, the extreme density of the gothic city center was lowered, practically "aired out." Interventions in public space were supported throughout the entire city, giving rise to an unparalleled dense network of small squares, alleys, and streets. The interventions were often unnoticeable at first glance, as they assimilated through a selection of specific surfaces and proportions: a higher-quality surface here, a tree planted there, along with a bench, there a fountain, and first and foremost, art! Tradition and future complement one another symbiotically. Through the relocation of the harbor, which facilitated the connection of the city promenade Rambla to the Mediterranean, and the creation of a city beach in front of the former harbor district Barceloneta, the combination of unique athletic event and regular urban renovation became a highpoint of design-based and farsighted urban development. Without the high qualitative demands of the local authorities, the reinvention of Barcelona would not have been possible. They showed visionary power and the courage to be extravagant. The planners focused, first of all, on the quality of life for the citizens of Barcelona, the success of businesses and industry, and only then on the streams of tourists.

The municipal administration of Berlin is currently facing the major challenge of developing core urban areas: the Kulturforum, the Rathausforum between Alexanderplatz and Humboldtforum, the Spreeknie including the Bürgerforum, and Tempelhofer Feld. Quo vadis, Berlin? And how public will these spaces become?

The latest cynical anecdote for a core area in Berlin was written by billionaire Nicolas Berggruen, son of the art collector Heinz Berggruen, who specializes amongst other activities on the acquisition of landmark buildings. He bought most of the few public pavilion buildings along Karl-Marx Allee in order to eventually turn all of them into private VIP event locations.

Public space supports social peace and democratic values

Based on information from the UN, 60 million people throughout the world were considered forcibly displaced by the end of 2015. Ten years ago that number was 37.5 million. That is an irrevocable fact. How will Europe, how will Germany, and how, ultimately, will cities deal with this? How will new population groups orient themselves? Are there spaces accessible to everyone, where casual encounters can occur, where people can learn about their new home, and pick up on normative patterns? Where can one make the claim of belonging?

According to most recent data collected for Berlin, since 2012 the city is growing steadily by 40,000-50,000 inhabitants per year. The incoming people are from all social levels and nationalities, from low to high labor skills, with no or average income. Public space is fiercely contested. The political dimension has become an essential one.

Of course, it is also necessary to mention that public space is in no way accessible to all, access is not granted to everyone in the same way, and discrimination can take place here. Repeated racially motivated police actions in the US draw attention to this, as do the *banlieues* in Paris, which have again and again gone up in flames over the years. Pegida[1] demonstrations in Germany increasingly resemble mob rallies and zero in on feelings of insecurity and exclusion. Democracy is politically radicalized here. In times like these, is permission to openly carry weapons, as has now been granted in Texas, the right signal?

London used to open its museums free of charge and developing the shores of the Thames as a huge, appealing public space. People could spend time here and

---

1   German nationalist, far-right movement.

enjoy themselves without horrendous consumption expenditures, and they were not discriminated against in terms of access to the most important educational and cultural facilities. Unfortunately this policy was recently retracted. In class-conscious London this was just as much a contribution to social peace as, for example, the freely accessible Copacabana in Rio de Janeiro with the annual free concert by the Rolling Stones and other megastars held on the beach there, which confirms the farsighted and versatile planning by Roberto Burle Marx and the then-young Republic of Brazil.

Without exaggerating, it can be noted that regarding the topic of immigration, the difference between countryside and city has also become a public stress test for the willingness to welcome and encounter others. In areas where public space has already been devoured by ravenous shopping malls, insecurity prevails, together with a lack of informal and free opportunities to meet up in familiar, stable roles and neighborhoods. Social contact requires action and constant practice, rather than passive, supposedly bustling crowds in shopping centers, which can hardly be reached on foot.

It is in the small towns and de-populated regions all over Europe where the right wing demagogues dominate the public spaces, virtually and physically.

The variety of measures and services offered by unpaid helpers and volunteers constitute an urgently required public space. Arising here is an entirely new caliber of public life without precedent and, in any case, no assistance or mandate from the administration. The stability of the German society at the moment of crisis in 2015, when the peak of the immigration wave was reached was definitely reassuring, yet it should not be forgotten that the right wing movement grows steadily since the 1990s when quantitatively similar immigrations waves from Eastern Europe and Africa had to be dealt with and asylum camps were set on fire for the first time.

Outlook

The discussion surrounding the composition of public space and its significance for contemporary urban society has just begun. Publicness has to be tolerated. It is obvious that quality and function of public spaces must be taken seriously as distinct and independent dimensions in urban planning.

As the seventy-year history of democracy in Germany proves: public spaces change in unforeseen ways and through their constant use. City planners must be alert and evaluate, as Jane Jacobs once did. Public space is a reflection of successful politics and its approval of responsible citizens. Behavioral patterns that are encountered, are copied. When there are none, a void remains. For that reason, taking a position is called for, now more than ever before. We must not forget the images of the shoes on Paris' Place de la République in November 2015 – representative of the demonstrations that were called off for security reasons, due to the terror risk during the climate summit. We need more than abstract demands of politics and administration for more protective measures. We must design a future.

Projects that use and spatially realize the population's proposals and willingness to help are to be concretized as integration measures. Language acquisition and access to educational facilities and information technology are the primary instruments and next steps to generating a shared public life. Politics can easily and purposefully decide upon corresponding infrastructural projects for kindergartens, schools, and vocational schools, which can be implemented by administration. Proportionate housing contingents in new building projects can be secured for migrants as a start but in the long run it means to build in general more small and affordable apartments for a larger segment of the population than currently available. Investments have to flow into public transportation infrastructure, since investments in the commuting systems are investments for the less affluent to secure their ongoing participation in urban community. One must simply exercise a will and cease the shrill slogans.

Either Western democracies, their citizens, and the vocal proponents of Western values prove capable of sustaining Western values in public spaces and mediating them through appropriate role models and patterns of behavior, or the lights will slowly go out in "Dunkeldeutschland"[2] and elsewhere. We are confronted with tangible, concrete problems that cannot be made taboo or put aside with a smile, but instead, must be solved pragmatically – problems which, approached without a charity attitude, will unfurl economic benefits.

In the irreversible transformation process of becoming the immigration country Germany, within a unified democratic continent called Europe, that is part of a "free" world, violence, racism, and right-wing hate speech against personal civil rights and liberties, and human dignity, are unacceptable and counterproductive.

Some understand this sooner, some later, some never. That, too, is a part of democracy.

References

Jacobs, Jane (1961): *Death and Life of Great American Cities*, Random House.

---

2 Dunkeldeutschland is a slang expression describing the high percentage of right wing voters in some areas of Germany. "Dunkel" has various meanings in German such as gloomy, murky, obscure, dark.

TEAR GAS DESIGN AND DISSENT

Anna Feigenbaum

A saleswoman sits at a meeting table, a bright wool sweater draped over her shoulders, hair dyed an unnatural orange. She stands out among the sea of business-suited men. The only other women in the room are dressed in white, handing out purple lanyards and exhibition floor plans to police representatives, military buyers and international dignitaries. All around the room these men chat over champagne, popping breath mints branded with security company logos. The middle-aged woman is alone, surrounded by glass display cabinets. Each holds row after row of cartridges and casings. Orange caps, blue caps, yellow caps – each signifies a different size and strength of smoke or bang or bullet. Above the woman, advertising banners make claims in bold colors: *Innovation. Preferred Supplier. Safe is Smart.*

This is Milipol, Europe's largest internal security expo. Operating since 1984, Milipol is one of the longest-running and most established trade shows in the industry. The 2015 Expo, hosted just days after the Paris bombings took 130 lives, featured 949 exhibitors, drew 24,056 visitors, and hosted 115 official delegations from 77 countries.[1] Each of the exhibition stalls is a compact display unit. Branded backgrounds depict police and military in action. There are live demos of micro-drones and unloaded guns to play with. The display cases are stocked full of riot control of all shapes and shades. Mannequins wear the latest fashion in protective gear. A Chinese exhibitor features a riot cop clad in spiked body armor. Even the boudoir corset on display is made of heavy-duty bulletproof rubber. This is today's riot-control industrial complex, a design show for world leaders in state repression.

Exhibitions like Milipol take place all around the world, from Israel to India, Qatar to Canada. They form part of a growing internal security sector, predicted to expand by 20 per cent by 2020. Investment researchers at Markets and Markets explained in 2013, *"The prevailing uncertain economic circumstances, the complex political situation, and the deteriorating security condition across the globe have given rise to popular unrest and protests."*[2] Unlike other parts of the economy that are hit hard by social

---

1   This essay draws from participant observation research conducted at Milipol in 2013 and 2015. Milipol, "Milipol Paris 2015: High Attendance of Homeland Security Professionals at the 2015 Edition," press release, November 26, 2015.

2   "Global on-lethal Wepaons Market report 2018," *iBusiness Wire*, November 26, 2013.

unrest, the riot-control industrial complex profits off political upheaval. The Arab Spring uprisings in 2011, followed by mass demonstrations across Europe, the United States, Canada, Chile, and later Turkey, Ukraine, Brazil, and Hong Kong, have generated purchase orders for millions of tear-gas canisters and related riot-control products.

Meanwhile, supplies to East Africa, Thailand, Indonesia, and the Indian subcontinent also grow as struggles for democracy, the effects of climate change, and economic austerity fuel conflict in these regions. In the west, Britain's withdrawal from the European Union, Trump's election as US president, the refugee crisis in Europe, and the rise of the far right provide excellent marketing opportunities. Experts in the riot-control industry carefully track outbreaks of resistance to inform both sellers and buyers of where there are profits to pursue. Their sales force travels the world. Tear gas, internationally accepted as the most humane technology for social control, is a top seller. Carrying a stamp of approval from Western democracies, it travels into other nations with colonial-era promises of "civilizing" their police forces.

Cruel Design

Behind these humanitarian promises of safety is a toxic gas, a chemical weapon designed to attack the senses simultaneously, producing both physical and psychological trauma. In medical terms, tear gas operates on multiple sites of the body at once, primarily affecting the mucous membranes and respiratory system. It can cause excessive tearing, burning, blurred vision, redness, runny nose, burning of the nostrils and mouth, difficulty swallowing, drooling, chest tightness, coughing, a choking sensation, wheezing, shortness of breath, skin burns, rashes, nausea, and vomiting. Tear gas has also been linked to miscarriages and long-term tissue and respiratory damage (Centers for Disease Control and Prevention 2003; Hill et al. 2000; Atkinson/Sollom 2012). This is what researcher and curator Gavin Grindon recently termed 'cruel design,' referring to those objects whose research and development is driven by an objective to cause human harm and suffering.

While in photographs tear gas looks like a cloud of smoke, it actually operates as moisture that sticks to and covers everything it touches – the skin, the soil, the surrounding architecture. The toxicity level of each type of tear gas is determined from the ratio of toxins released per square meter. This means that only a certain number of canisters are meant to be set off in any given space – the smaller the space and the more gas is released, the more toxic it becomes. Protocols for firing tear gas attempt to standardize the distance from which grenades are fired at crowds, accounting for the direction and strength of the wind as well as the locations of barriers and structures that might trap the chemical substance in the air. Firing tear gas into an enclosed space significantly elevates the risk of serious injury and death from inhalation, while invoking trauma and anxiety in choking people in poorly ventilated spaces where there are no clear exits.

Tear gas causes harm in two other important ways. First, tear gas is stored and fired through canisters or grenades that are often made out of aluminum, plastic, or other combustible materials. A major cause of injuries from tear gas is the canisters themselves striking people, particularly on the head. Since the earliest "peacetime" uses of tear gas, there has been a steady stream of reports of lost eyes, cranial damage, and deaths due to direct hits from tear-gas canisters. Many of the grenade launchers and rifles used to fire tear gas were originally designed and promoted for use as short-range firearms. Early models were called "tear-gas guns," and today's euphemistically named "multi-launchers" were the "tear-gas machine gun" of the early twentieth century. The most famous of these was made by Manville Manufacturers, the company responsible for bringing the "street-sweeping" Manville machine gun to the market in the Prohibition-era United States.

Another way that tear-gas canisters or grenades cause harm is through their pyrotechnic devices or flammable components. For the tear-gas chemical compound to heat and disperse, other substances must be present. The use of these incendiary forms of tear gas has caused damaging and sometimes lethal fires in homes, vehicles, and agricultural fields. Recent reports on SWAT team raids in the United States document these fire hazards. For instance, in April 2011, a Virginia SWAT team sent a Defense Tech triple chaser grenade (which separates into three parts) inside a trailer using a bomb-squad robot. The house immediately went up in flames, leaving its residents homeless. In other cases, a substance like alcohol mixed in with the tear-gas compound might be flammable, or the propellant in a spray, such as butane. Tear gas can also mix with household items to cause fires, as reported by fire inspectors in Vallejo, California, in 2012 after a SWAT raid caused sixty thousand dollars' worth of damage to a home and killed two dogs (Owens 2012; Burchyns 2012). Public pressure has forced many companies to stop manufacturing tear gases that contain flammable components; however, there is no comprehensive national or international set of regulations to monitor or enforce this.

Of course, as with all weapons, there are different scales of violence used in deployments of tear gas. If I toss a CS grenade on the ground in front of a crowd where there are clear exit points (as protocol suggests), it is less likely that someone will die than if I lob that same grenade into a car or a prison cell or a subway station. Likewise, if I shoot you in the foot you are less likely to die than if I shoot you in the head. However, this does not mean that the bullet shot into the foot is a "humanitarian agent" and the head bullet is a violent weapon. Unlike other objects that are not normally weapons but can be weaponized (for example, baseball bats or frying pans), tear gas has no alternative, "normal," or everyday use. And – contrary to what Fox News anchor Megyn Kelly told Bill O'Reilly in 2011 – pepper spray is not "a food product, essentially." It is, in fact, 1.3 million heat units hotter than the hottest pepper you could eat. As this essay will discuss in detail, tear gas was designed as a poison that causes physical and psychological pain. For the past hundred years it has been modernized to be both more effective and more efficient.

Less Lethal Deaths

On February 14, 2011, two weeks into the Arab Spring uprisings, people in the tiny Gulf state of Bahrain called for their own day of action. Peaceful pro-democracy demonstrators flocked to the streets. Young people, Sunni and Shia, gathered at the capital city of Manama's Pearl Roundabout, many carrying Bahraini flags. They called for a new constitution that would end the royal family's rule. As they marched, the government retaliated with a violent crackdown. Rubber bullets flew and tear gas saturated the streets. The police killed two protesters that day. The BBC reported that the Saudi and US governments might soon intervene.

As the protests continued, the police shot tear gas into cars, homes, and mosques. Hundreds went to the hospital with head trauma, lost eyes, miscarriages, and respiratory failure. Bahraini civilians and independent journalists used social media to distribute and circulate images of canisters bearing the logos of the US companies Federal Laboratories and Combined Systems Inc., along with Brazilian exports from Condor Non-Lethal Technologies. The *New York Times* wrote of "systematic and disproportionate use of tear gas" in Bahrain, drawing international attention (Gladstone 2012). Amnesty International condemned its use and Physicians for Human Rights released a report after the first eighteen months of protests that documented thirty-four tear gas related deaths (Physicians for Human Rights 2012). Among the victims were babies, children, and the elderly (Amnesty International 2012).

Since 2011, tear gas remains the international weapon of choice for riot control. Sales projections are still up, with business booming in the Middle East and markets growing in Africa and South Asia. Hundreds more around the world have died from its effects. People have lost eyes and limbs. They have suffered brain damage, third-degree burns, respiratory problems, and miscarriages. Their animals and their crops have been poisoned.

Disobedient Design

As tear gas goes off around the world, it is met with evermore-innovative practices of resistance and resilience. Facing tear gas, people create, adapt, and share techniques for combatting and surviving tear gas. Caring for each other, they transform this weapon into a collectivizing tool. Aided by social media and mobile technologies, protesters transnationally circulate relief remedies, gas mask designs, and grenade throwback techniques. Displaying what social movement researcher Gavin Grindon has called "grassroots cultural diplomacy," these tips are tweeted from Greece to New York, from Palestine to Ferguson, from Egypt to Hong Kong.

In places like Bahrain and Palestine, widespread and even daily use of tear gas has made this chemical weapon a part of life. As a way of exhibiting and collectively processing this trauma, people sometimes transform tear-gas canisters into other objects. Acts of anger, grief, and memorializing emerge as artistic practices. For example, in Bahrain, people designed a throne made out of tear-gas canisters to signify their royal family's role in the suppression of democracy protests. In Palestine, tear-gas canisters have been used as Christmas tree ornaments to send a holiday message to the United States about the role of its tear gas and arms manufacturers in the violence of the Occupied Territories. In 2013, images of a Palestinian garden made out of plants potted in empty tear-gas shells went viral, picked up by mainstream media outlets as an image of hope and quiet resistance. Yet, as Elias Nawawieh pointed out in *+972* magazine, absent from the news stories, Twitter photos, and Facebook posts was the grave built as the garden's centerpiece. It bears a translucent photo of Bassem Abu Rahmah, who was killed by the IDF in 2009 after being shot in the chest at close range by a tear gas grenade.

In 2013, Occupy Gezi in Turkey became a site of innovation, a place where people designed, adopted and adapted novel modes of resistance and resilience to tear gas. There was Ceyda Sungur, the woman in the red dress, pepper-sprayed at close range and turned into a movement icon. There were dancing ballerinas in whirling, brightly colored skirts that contrasted against the harshness of the full-cover gas masks they wore as they spun around. Penguins wore gas masks to symbolize the media's failure to cover police violence. Christian Gubar writes that *"As both political commodities and stage props, goggles and gas masks were embraced for their eerie theatricality, speaking volumes to the grotesque banality of living under billows of noxious gas."* (Gruber 2013, 31)

But these objects were as much about material reality as symbolism. Protesters in Gezi borrowed, translated, and reproduced instructions for making a gas mask out of a plastic bottle, and for using Maalox and other household ingredients as remedies for the painful effects of tear gas. Talcid Man appeared after a rumor spread that Talcid (a liquid medicine to relieve stomach inflammation) could help ease the effects of pepper spray. He emerged on site distributing the medicine as an embodied, mobile care unit, and became a symbol of the movement's resilience and generosity, depicted in stencils and sketches that circulated far beyond the occupied park.

In the gas-flooded streets, a variety of shops, sidewalk stands, ground-level flats and even a hotel became makeshift medical field stations, providing remedies and treatments to protesters. At these sites, health workers and those with basic first-aid skills converged. These medical volunteers often have a clearer and more accurate understanding of the real-world impact of "less lethals" than scientists running tests in sterile laboratories. It is here, under the tarpaulins of protest architecture and in the pop-up clinics, amid the chaos these weapons intentionally provoke, that the bruises and bleeding, the choking and vomiting, the inability to breathe, the concussions, and the paralysis are immediately felt.

At the site of protest, pain is not a toxicity count or a threshold percentage. "Less lethal" is no longer a technical term but a vision of how much torment a body can take, of how close someone can come to death without dying. Measured in human experience, the medical field stations of protests can make visible the reality of riot control. Their ways of seeing and knowing medical injury can move us beyond the flames and smoke of media screens. They can provide far more accurate and detailed on-the-ground accounts than hospital records can. Their testimony can be mobilized to challenge the clinical tests produced by military-paid scientists.

From canister sculptures to the ad hoc architectures of these street medic field sites, all around the world people come together to enact such strategic and creative acts of resistance against the tear gas. But while resilience can keep movements moving, corporate and government accountability for the use of tear gas is hard to come by. Shielded from public view, sealed in secret files, and buried behind the paywalls of export databases, tear-gas sales continue to grow, largely unregulated. With deals made in five-star hotels and exhibition meeting rooms, exposing or inhibiting the sale of tear gas is a daunting task. But even the best PR tactics and corporate cover-ups cannot always outsmart the passion and knowledge of everyday people. Whether at the local, grassroots level or as part of Amnesty International, people are conducting investigative research, leaking documents, sneaking inside arms fairs, and holding sit-ins, die-ins, and kiss-ins to protest against riot control.

The Riot ID Project

In an effort to offer further tactics for increasing corporate and government accountability for tear gas use, in 2015 the RiotID project took shape, inspired by the protests that swept the world in 2011. During the Arab Spring uprisings in Egypt, protestors started a blog identifying the tear gas canisters that turned up on their streets. The *Tear Gas ID* site recorded details such as source information, links to company websites, and close-up images of canisters. The bloggers used Twitter (@tg_id) and the hashtag #teargasID to aggregate information and create chains of accountability. Similarly, when police and National Guard took over the streets of Ferguson, Missouri, journalists and activists on the ground worked to catalogue and identify riot-control weapons and linked this information to that collected in Egypt and Palestine.

Drawing from these projects and our work with journalists in Ferguson, in the summer of 2015, the civic media research team of which I am a part at Bournemouth University partnered with the NGOs Bahrain Watch and Omega Research Foundation, as well as graphic designers at Minute Works, to launch the RiotID project. RiotID (riotid.com) is a civic media project designed to help people identify, monitor, and record the use of riot-control agents against civilians. Making accurate identifications of less lethal weapons can help people medically respond to the effects of exposure and injury, monitor human rights violations, challenge abuses, and identify the manufacturers and countries of origin of the devices.

The main resource that #RiotID uses is a pocket guide for documenting and identifying less lethal weapons that has been translated into seven languages. The ID process has two steps. First, people on location document the riot-control technologies. The #RiotID book provides techniques for recording and documenting all the information needed to do an identification. This includes photographing the device from all angles and recording all numeric and text information on the sides, top, and bottom of the device. Step two is using the documented features of the weapon to figure out what it is, as well as the supplier and country of origin. We designed a diagram that uses shapes, sizes, and details to help identify different kinds of less lethal impact and chemical munitions. Once a device is narrowed down to its size (i.e., 12-gauge, 37mm, 56mm) and type (flashbang, OC, baton round), it is easier to identify the manufacturer, as different companies make and specialize in different products. For help with identifications, people can tweet their photos to @riotID or use the hashtag #riotID. The RiotID team draw on their expert knowledge to help match photographs of weapons being used on the street and where they come from.

Since RiotID launched in August 2015, we have identified expired canisters being used in Uganda, Zambia, and Mexico. Expired tear gas is unsafe and can be volatile. As tear gas is a toxic chemical waste product, it must be properly disposed of after expiration. In Saint Louis, our identifications exposed the misuse of barricade-penetrating munitions. We also worked with migrant solidarity activists in Calais, France, to help identify and monitor riot-control used in refugee camps there. Incorporating concerns over security and social media into the project, we are now teaming up with Eyewitness Media to utilize their secure documentation app. We are also responding to requests for more introductory information on tear gases and impact munitions. Working with young people, we have also designed infographics that answer basic questions about what these riot-control weapons do.

Conclusion

Tear gas is an object designed to torment people, to break their spirits, to cause physical and psychological damage. No amount of corporate public relations or safety guidelines can hide that foundational truth of chemical design. Tear gas is a weapon that polices the atmosphere and pollutes the very air we breathe. It turns the square, the march, the public assembly into a toxic space, taking away what is so often the last communication channel people have left to use. If the right to gather, to speak out, is to mean anything, then we must also have the right to do so in air we can breathe.

This text is adapted from excerpts in "Tear Gas: From the Battlefields of WWI to the Streets of Today" (Verso 2017).

References

Amnesty International (2012): "Bahrain's use of tear gas against protesters increasingly deadly", press release, January 26, 2012.

Atkinson, Holly G. / Sollom, Richard (2012): "Weaponizing Tear Gas". Physicians for Human Rights.

http://physiciansforhumanrights.org/library/reports/weaponizing-tear-gas.html.

Burchyns, Tony (2012): "Report: Vallejo SWAT Tear Gas Rounds Likely Ignited 'Accidental' House Fire". *Vallejo Times-Herald*, April 16, 2012.

Centers for Disease Control and Prevention (2003): "Facts about Riot Control Agents" http://www.bt.cdc.gov/agent/riotcontrol/pdf/riotcontrol_factsheet.pdf

Gladstone, Rick (2012): "Bahrain Is Criticized for Its 'Torrent' of Tear Gas Use". *New York Times,* August 1, 2012.

Gruber, Christiane (2013): "The Visual Emergence of the Occupy Gezi Movement" in *Resistance Everywhere: The Gezi Protests and Dissident Visions of Turkey*, edited by Anthony Alessandrini, Nazan Üstündağ, and Emrah Yildiz. Boston: Tadween Publishing.

Hill, A.R. / Silverberg, N.B. / Mayorga, D. and H.E. Baldwin (2000): "Medical Hazards of the Tear Gas CS: A Case of Persistent, Multisystem, Hypersensitivity Reaction and Review of the Literature," *Medicine 79*(4), 2000: 234–40.

Owens, Michael (2011): "Despite Warnings, Tenn. Officers Start Home Fire With Pyrotechnic Grenade". *Bristol Herald-Courier*, May 19, 2011.

Physicians for Human Rights (2012): "Tear Gas or Lethal Gas? Bahrain's Death Toll Mounts to 34", March 16, 2012.

THE CORE UTOPIAN CITY
ON ACTIVIST PRACTICES IN AND BEYOND TAHRIR

Mikala Hyldig Dal

Media-archaeologists of the future might mark 2011 as the year of transition from a locally disparate politics of dissent to a global protest culture. What we have been witnessing this past decade could be the emergence of a new visual regime in which geographical distinctions are dissolved into networked singularity.

The following essay is sparked by my observations of rapid changes in Cairo's public space during three years of daily passage through the city in the wake of the January25 revolution. During this time I was researching iconography in Egypt's political transformation(s) and teaching art and design at the German University in Cairo (GUC) and the American University in Cairo (AUC) in New Cairo City. I will discuss art and design practices as integral to the political struggle that made *midan Tahrir* a global icon of civil dissent. I will also suggest that the history we touch upon is still *in a state of becoming*.

The aesthetics at play in the simultaneously unfolding Arab uprisings resonated in protest movements in Turkey, North America and Europe by introducing a new form of political engagement. A new sensitized field of experience that testifies to a shift in the location of politics and unsettled the balance of existing power structures.

Considering political action as an integral form of experience engaged in a process of shared *worlding*,[1] the place of politics always relates to public space[2] and the interrelation of a plurality of human bodies in this (Butler 2015). How did the experiential field activated by the movements of 2011 feel like? How was it formed and formatted, which were the architectural designs, visual codes and modes of togetherness that defined its axis? In the ruptures of 2011, can we trace the outlines of a social sculpture in which artistic practice is integral to political participation?[3]

---

1   I use the expression *worlding* inspired by Donna Haraway's sense of a writerly, creative mode of world-engagement by means of expressive immersion.

2   *Thoughts on Politics and Revolution* Hannah Arendt interviewed by Adalbert Reif for The New York Review of Books, 1971 (From the section *Bodies in Alliance and the Politics on the street*, first published in 2011)

3   *"Only on condition of a radical widening of definitions will it be possible for art and activities related to art [to] provide evidence that art is now the only evolutionary-revolutionary power. Only art is capable of dismantling the repressive effects of a senile social system that continues to totter along the deathline: to dismantle in order to build 'A SOCIAL ORGANISM AS A WORK OF ART'... EVERY HUMAN BEING IS AN ARTIST who – from his state of freedom – the position of freedom that he experiences at first-hand – learns to*

"The core utopian city" was a nickname given to midan Tahrir by protestors who turned the heavily trafficked roundabout in downtown Cairo into a place for living.[4] The place came to host a cluster of tents that offered shelter during nightly sit-ins. It contained a people's kitchen and provided treatment for medical emergencies. It also embraced a speakers' corner, a public video archive, a stage for music and theatre performances, a painting work-shop – and an everchanging image gallery of photographic prints and graphical posters promoting new political groupings, commemorating victims of regime violence and invoking social engagement. The images created in this space spread out to murals throughout the dense architecture of the capital and, via online media, entered the global imaginary.

Image galleries, theatre-stages and artisan workshops are formats that we know from art and design contexts. In 2011 they became defining of the social texture that laboured the global political transformation(s). I will suggest that we can unify the theories of political philosopher Hannah Arendt and art-historian Jaques Rancière in reflecting on the *core utopian city* of *Tahrir*.

For Hannah Arendt political action occurs when public space is activated as a *space of appearance* in which "being and appearing coincide". The space of appearance comes into existence when individuals gather to express, negotiate and realize their visions of communal life. It is in this process that individuals become citizens and their shared space becomes a polis. It is a tentative space that *happens* rather than a topos to which we can ascribe an a-priori existence; when citizens seize to gather in a mode of joint action the space of appearance seizes to exist (Arendt 1958; Arendt 1978). In this space *"I appear to others as others appear to me ... men exist not merely like other living or inanimate things, but to make their appearance explicitly"* (Arendt 1958, 198f.).

As a space defined by visibility it is deeply connected to the problem of representation. Among the political desires most intimately connected with the early revolutionary movement was that of a re-thinking of society from a top-down hierarchical structure, in which the majority of the population possessed no representation nor any means of gaining one,[5] to a more just society, integrating a multitude of voices. In 2011 people came together to discuss and formulate the changes necessary to create this society. In Egypt people, simply by gathering, defied a decade-long ban on public assembly, and in this exceptional act, paradoxically, put an end to the military's seemingly permanent "state of exception".[6]

In reclaiming public space activists overcame prevailing gender, class, religious and ethnic divides. Performative visual strategies, that ranged from the explicitly

determine the other positions of the TOTAL ART WORK OF THE FUTURE SOCIAL ORDER." Joseph Beuys: Public Dialogues with Willoughby Sharp, 1974, video 120 min.

4   See for instance Eliane Ursula Ettmueller's *Egyptian Letters* blog, entry from March 7th 2011 www.egyptianletters.blogspot.de/2011/03/what-comes-after-fall-of-system.html

5   Before the rise of web based media platforms and common access to image recording and distribution techniques in Egypt matters of representation were dominated by state-controlled media.

6   Until the protesters of 2011 changed the status quo the state of emergency had been imposed continuously since 1981.

theatrical to the deeply immersive, were central to the subversion of autocratic power structures. Painters and moviemakers became iconic figures for the resistance.

Whereas Arendt pays little attention to the artistic components at work in the process of *becoming* visible Jaques Rancière's line of thought places the visual manifestations of the discourse at the very core of the political project: *"The distribution of the sensible ... defines what is visible or not in a common space, endowed with a common language, etc. There is thus an 'aesthetics' at the core of politics ... It is a delimitation of spaces and times, of the visible and the invisible, of speech and noise, that simultaneously determines the place and the stakes of politics as a form of experience. Politics revolves around what is seen and what can be said about it, around who has the ability to see and the talent to speak, around the properties of spaces and the possibilities of time"* (Rancière 2004, 57).

It is in the testing and probing of communicative formats that the political becomes experiential and it is in the performative visuality that emerges from the process that we can sense the kind of society the political struggle is directed towards. For a time the citizens of the core utopian city of Tahrir embodied the ideals of the larger polis they aspired to create. We might think of Tahrir in its early incarnation as a miniature-format model for a new society *in the becoming*.

From the Womb of Tahrir

The protest movements images were created, shared and published in a way that made the notion of singular authorship seem obsolete; in a process that resonated Roland Barthes's "Death of the Author" a new type of witness-bearing emerged. Citizen journalism arose and the global file sharing system Youtube became, for the first time, politicized (Snowdon 2014). During the past years image recording technologies and world-wide-web access have become common goods to large parts of the world population. In this net-worked context local signs permeate into global lexica, and visual vocabularies approximate; in the sphere of visuality geography has become arbitrary for those who are connected. Signs such as the Anonymous mask, the protesting dancer and logos of social media platforms oscillated between demonstrators in Cairo, New York and Istanbul.

The common ability to produce, screen and distribute vast amounts of images has brought forth an increased awareness both of visuality as a political tool and of the power of one's own image. Many protestors were intertwined in reproductive image circuits in which they were simultaneously recording and being recorded. On Tahrir and in other places there was an instantaneous feedback between the event itself and its medial representation: Via online streaming protestors could watch themselves protesting in real time (Dal 2014a). "Tahrir Cinema" was formed by the independent filmmaker collective *Mosireen* that travelled the country to organize public screenings of footage documenting regime violence.

Image making was perceived as an active tool of resistance, a counter-tactic to the brute force of machine guns. Artist Lara Baladi recounts: *'in the whole region during the Arab uprisings, the act of photographing became not only an act of seeing and recording; it was also fully participatory. At the core of the Egyptian uprising, photographing was a political act, equal in importance to demonstrating. It constituted civil disobedience and defiance of the regime'* (Baladi 2013).

Many activists signed their protest-banners in both Arabic and English: Holding their texts close to their bodies they provided pre-made image captions to foreign journalists. From the extended skin of these protesting bodies cascades of text grew onto house walls, street blockades, shop windows, scribbles in the dust on public monuments;[7] text passages crept onto the linen surface of the tent-city architecture where they intermingled with photo-collages of national symbols and documentary photos of revolutionaries broken bodies (Dal 2014b, 232–238, 258).

The young designer, Mona Diab, who assisted my research at GUC, collected photographs from the media tent on Tahrir in March 2011; some show protesters lying flat on their backs with protest signs attached to their upper bodies. A man, with a primitive gas mask pulled up onto his forehead and crotches at his sides, uses his protest-banner as a garment, the shape of his words follow the lines of his body: *"I would wear a burial gown for your love Egypt – Down with the regime. Signed: A disabled person".*[8]

This space was one for making explicit claims, it was in ever so many ways a space of appearing, and it allowed marginalised groups to take control over their own representation. Arendt connects three central concepts to this political space: *plurality, action* and *natality*. In Arendt´s terminology *Plurality* is intrinsic to the human condition and at the essence of the political: Being human means evolving from and partaking in the community of an integrative body of other human beings. Our singularity as individuals constitute the shared basis of experience that binds us together as a species.[9]

We might conceive of *Action* as inter-action in consequence of the pluralistic nature of human society. Action is the material manifestation of freedom of thought. It is action that produces and commemorates political bodies and as such it is action that forms the basis of historical narration and witness-bearing (Arendt 1958, 7f.). *Natality* is at the root of *world-making*; a promise of novelty inherent to the birth of an individual as well as in the emergence of new societies. The concept of Natality is intimately related to the instance of the revolution as *"revolutions are the only political events which confront us directly and inevitably with the problem of beginning"* (Arendt 1963, 21).

As it relies on continuous action to persist we might consider the modus operandi

---

7   I reflect on the interplay between writing and architecture in the essay 'Writing the City: Notes on Urban Transformations in Cairo' in *Egyptians During the Transition Period* published by the Danish Egyptian Dialogue Institute in Cairo 2017.

8   The photos were collected by Mona Khaled Diab, my research assistant from the German University Cairo, and accredited to Mohammed Saad (Dal 2014b, 60f.).

9   Plurality is defined by *"the fact that men, not Man, live on the earth and inhabit the world"*; *"Plurality is the condition of human action because we are all the same, that is, human, in such a way that nobody is ever the same as anyone else who ever lived, lives, or will live."* (Arendt 1958, 7f.).

of the space of appearance as one of perpetual birth. It was the metaphor of birth that gave rise to the new collectivity on Tahrir. *Mulid* traditionally refers to festivities surrounding the birth(day) of religious or historical figures but in 2011 it was channeled into celebrations of the birth of Tahrir as a social space.`It quickly became clear that the celebratory mulid-like energy that installed itself on the midan would become one of the most effective didactic experiences for millions of Egyptians alongside a whole spectrum of creative tactics of mass protest, all of which effectively transformed traditional ritual into inciting a mode of revolt'* (Keraitim/Mehrez 2012). Protestors would deescalate violent aggressions by collectively and repeatedly chanting "Selmya, Selmya" (peaceful, peaceful); through the predominantly pacifist mode of engagement among the demonstrators the *mulid*-energy grew. When activated the space of appearance generates *Power,* in Arendt's terminology a pluralistic, horizontally-oriented, essentially democratic energy that stands in opposition to the military's hierarchical use of *Force.* In Arendt's line of thought we can place autocratic dispersals of public gatherings outside the realm of politics, and consider them as mere executions of *Force.*

During the budding democratization processes 2011-2013 the aspiring presidential candidate Azza Kamal, described her candidacy as "Born from the Womb of the Midan" (c.f. Dal 2014b, 38). An unprecedented number of political candidates from all social spheres filled up public space with election ephemera: Posters, flyers and banners, many integrating scenes from Tahrir, created a paper skin on top of the city's concrete skeleton (ibid., 126–158).

Amado Fadni, Nadja Mounier and Hamdy Reda were among the activists that intervened in the election process with participatory graphic design projects. Fadni and Reda designed posters in which anonymous citizens figured as presidential candidates. Reda interviewed inhabitants of the populous, low-infrastructural area Ard El-Lewa about their visions for a new state of politics and printed the collected statements on posters throughout the city. Fadni created posters that functioned as empty framings for passers-by to write their visions for a new society into. Over the course of time each of these posters became unique copies, records of various dynamic re/editing processes (fig 1). Mounier inserted different versions of her own body image into election-formatted posters as a means of addressing patriarchal gender norms that were also at play in the electoral process (c.f. Meier-Menzel 2014).

Abla Mohamed, a design student at the GUC, was able to vote for the first time. She experienced the event as a process of growth that related directly to her body. Her photo-series *Growth (fingernail)* traces how ink stains from the voting process left marks on her body. She observes how the remains are encapsulated in her fingernail and juxtaposes the process with newspaper clippings of unfolding political events (fig 2).

Figure 1: "If I was president". Photo by Amado Fadni.

Figure 2: "Growth". Photo by Abla Mohamed.

Dancer on a bull's spine

The bodily experience of being embedded in a process of societal transformation resonates in Salma Abdel Salam´s dance pieces: *"As a dancer, the 2011 Egyptian revolution presented an event of such magnitude that it instigated in me an incredible urge to move"* Salam recalls. It brought about a desire to engage with dance as *"a tool of malleability and political possibility, and a revolutionary tactic that presupposes the convergence of space and subjects in creating new collectivities through the utility of bodies and physical gestures in space"* (Salam 2016).

In *Bodies in Alliance and the Politics of the Street* Judith Butler considers the 2011 protest movements in and beyond the terms of the Arendtian space of appearance and locates the power generated here in the in-between space of active bodies: *"No one body establishes the space of appearance, but this action, this performative exercise happens only 'between' bodies, in a space that constitutes the gap between my own body and another's. In this way, my body does not act alone, when it acts politically. Indeed, the action emerged from the 'between.'"* (Butler 2011). Like Butler, Arendt asserts that politic is not something one can conduct alone. It relies on bodies coming together in a mode of joint voicing. It relies on vocalization and physical proximity. And in a networked reality it thrives on the sharing and multiplication of icons produced from within this hub of interconnected bodies.

The "Green Revolution" in Iran 2009 contained prototypes of many of the activistic formats that unfolded in the 2011 movements. Inspired by the Iranian movement curator Ashkan Sepahvand stresses the transformative power of bodies acting in unification: *"When bodies come together, TRANSFORMATION happens. This is a body-politic, not as biopolitical critique, or as a recourse to a 'performativity' of bodies. I am thinking of the body as an aggregate composition, a configuration of movements and processes that articulate conflict and negotiate the circulation, exchange, and expenditure of excess energy. In this sense, 'politics' is a coming-together to be in a state of differentiation and dissensus, bodies enacting a choreography towards a rhythmic unfolding of the surplus they each individually generate."*[10]

Sepahvand presents us with the thought experiment of a dance performance that takes place in a museum. The performance is so powerful that it displaces and ruptures the building: *"An explosion rips through the foyer of the museum; the action is denounced as an act of terrorism, yet the artist, and the art-world-apparatus supporting him, insist that no, this was a concrete demonstration of a radical technique the Dervishes had expertly developed"* (Sepahvand 2015).

Sepahvand's story resonates both the subversive power of radical art engagement, as experienced on Tahrir, and regime denunciations of a number of artists as

---

10   *Superconversations Day 60: Ashkan Sepahvand responds to Anton Vidokle, "The Communist Revolution was Caused by the Sun: A Partial Script for a Short Film", E-Flux 2015* https://conversations.e-flux.com/t/superconversations-day-60-ashkan-sepahvand-responds-to-anton-vidokle-the-communist-revolution-was-caused-by-the-sun-a-partial-script-for-a-short-film/2165

quasi-terrorists.[11] It also speaks to how the overarching embeddedness of artistic practices in political movements since 2009 has influenced curatorial practices in the institutionalized art world. The Berlin Biennale 2012 and the Kassel-Athens Documenta in 2017 can be seen as expressions of this interchange. What these types of exhibition initiatives lack in terms of fulfilling their stressed political agendas might be the presence of bodies that act collectively and intertwined in eruptive momenta of dissent.

The dancer, as a figure of creative political potency, is among the shared symbols of the 2011 movements. In the Adbusters poster for Occupy Wall Street a contemporary dancer gracefully balances on top of Arturo Di Modica´s sculpture charging bull. In Gezi park in Istanbul a ballerina and a pink-skirted dervish dancer performed to the crowd, both wearing gas masks. In Mohamed Mahmoud street around the corner from Tahrir fights intensified; so did the volume of street art testimonies. A mural by Shaza Khaled and Aliaa El Tayeba depicts a ballerina and a masked protestor in a joint choreography; they appear as mirrored instances of the same movement. The murals and the flexible, malleable bodies they derive from reflect the deleuzian smooth space of an unfixed society.

Joy was found and felt both on Tahrir, in the Occupy Movements and on Taksim Square. Hannah Arendt also noted its presence when reading the personal correspondences of the "founding fathers" of the American revolution (Arendt 1963): Discovering oneself as an agent of active and communal world-making brings with it pleasure as well as danger. In my case it was when I emerged in the small but intense and intimate nightlife of Cairo that I would meet many of the activists that defined the protest movements struggle. There might be a subversive political potential inherent to the act of celebrating in itself; a life energy that intuitively resists the subjugation to authoritarian power structures. The prohibition of dancing, intoxication and public displays of affection in many dictatorial regimes indicate as much. If we follow Salam's invitation to consider society as a developing dance choreography we might think of resistance as an *unlearning* of conditioned restrictions of movement, and a rediscovery of our bodies as agents of a smooth space and unlimited potentiality.

Hannah Arendt asks: *'What is a revolution? The word does not tell us, it tells us, if anything, the opposite of what we understand by it. Still, it is of great importance to understand how revolutions came about. Revolution, astronomical term, revolvere, describes the eternal recurrence of the heavenly bodies, their swinging back to a pre-established point ... The term was used in political language in the seventeenth century, and meant the exact opposite of a "revolution,", namely a restoration. And this is important, because all the first revolutionaries had in mind was restoration.'* (Arendt 1963). In this line of thought the popular movements of 2011 can be understood as attempts to restore the freedom of thought and action that define our *Natality*, as individuals and as collectives.

---

11   See for instance: www.freemuse.org/news/egypt-finnish-and-egyptian-street-artists-labeled-terrorists-for-graffiti-art-project/ and: www.observers.france24.com/en/20160516-comedian-egypt-charged-terrorism-arrested

Spaces of dis/appearance

It was specifically at the eyes, and by extension at the power of the visual agency of the protestors, that the regime directed one of its most morbid forms of attack. So-called eye-snipers were dispatched to rob demonstrators of eye-vision using bird-shots in order to blind, rather than to kill (See Dal 2014a; c.f. Hamdy 2017).

The reinstatement of military rule in 2013 was preceded by another kind of visual attack: Military propaganda highjacked many of the icons produced by the revolutionary movement, notably the icon of Tahrir Square itself (Dal 2014). Following this attack on vision public space has become again drastically delimited: Emergency law has been reinstated and police patrols secure and maintain the emptiness of the midan. Midan Tahrir has been effectively transformed from an Arendtian space of appearance to a Foucauldian "space of surveillance".

Architect Mohammad El Shahed notes that it lies in the nature of any autocracy to avert the rise of truly public spaces because these are physical manifestations of democracy.[12] The deconstruction of Tahrir mirrors the destruction of Bahrain's Pearl Roundabout, and the dislocation of Myanmar´s entire capital into a desert area with no city centre, no confined public space, and *"no place to make a visual – let alone political – impression".*[13] And it echoes in the violent dispersal of demonstrations against capitalist exploitation worldwide.

Yet as Hannah Arendt reminds us *"the Polis, properly speaking, is not the city-state in its physical location; it is the organization of the people as it arises out of acting and speaking together, and its true space lies between people living together for this purpose, no matter where they happen to be"* (Arendt 1958).

In The Soul of Tahrir: Poetics of a Revolution Sanders and Visonà describe the body of the revolution as the people, the midan as its heart, and poetics as its soul. *"This soul knew no bounds, in neither space nor time"* (Sanders/Visonà 2012). The poetics and the poiesis at play in the core utopian city brought about a distribution of the sensible that is not, and cannot be erased as little as the burning of a book can erase the memory of its content in the minds of those who read it. The birth of Tahrir as a social space has left us not just with visions and visual testimonies but also with memories of a society in becoming. A society in which art, as Ranciére pleads, gives us more than the spectacle, more than something dedicated to the delight of passive spectators, because it acts in favor of a society where everybody is active (Rancière 2008).

---

12 *"Like all autocracies, the Mubarak government understood the power of a true public square, of a place where citizens meet, mingle, promenade, gather, protest, perform and share ideas; it understood that a true midan - Arabic for public square - is a physical manifestation of democracy."* (El Shahid 2014).

13 Siddharth Varadarajan: Dictatorship by Cartography, blog entry. www.svaradarajan.blogspot.de/2007/02/dictatorship-by-cartography-geometry.html

Through the intervention of graphic designers, painters and performers, activist groups and individual artists, the urban landscape of Cairo has testified to a deeply motivated desire to shape, structure and imagine our collective living space. The creative energy that brought about the toppling of one autocratic regime might yet tilt another. The movement that opened up public space to a participatory renegotiation of society inspires hope of a transformation still to come.

We see traces of this in the interconnected utopian core cities that emerged on a global level in 2011, by means of new visual languages and modes of togetherness tested by activists. With their bodies, with their vision and with their ability to connect.

References

Arendt, Hannah (1958): *The human condition.* Chicago, University of Chicago Press.

Arendt, Hannah (1963): *On Revolution.* New York: The Viking Press.

Arendt, Hannah (1978): *The life of the mind.* San Diego, Harcourt Inc.

Baladi Lara (2013): When Seeing Is Belonging: The Photography of Tahrir Square. *Creative Times Report,* retrieved 16 September 2013. www.creativetimereports.org/2013/09/16/lara-baladi-photography-of-tahrir-square/

Butler, Judith (2011): Bodies in Alliance and the Politics of the Street, *eipcp,* www.eipcp.net/transversal/1011/butler/en

Butler, Judith (2015): *Notes Toward A Performative Theory of Assembly,* Harvard, Harvard University Press.

Dal, Mikala H. (2014a): Eye-snipers –The iconoclastic practice of Tahrir. In: Seismopolite Journal of Art and Politics, vol. 7, 2014. www.seismopolite.com/eye-snipers-the-iconoclastic-practice-of-tahrir.

Dal, Mikala H. (Ed.) (2014b): *Cairo Images of Transition.* Bielefeld: Transcript

Hamdy, Sherine (2017): All Eyes on Egypt: Islam and the Medical Use of Dead Bodies Amidst Cairo's Political Unrest. In Antonius C. G. M. Robben (Ed.): *Death, Mourning, and Burial: A Cross-Cultural Reader,* Hoboken, John Wiley & Sons.

Keraitim, Sara / Mehrez, Samia (2012): Mulid al-Tahrir: Semiotics of a Revolution. In: Samia Mehrez (Ed.): *Translating Egypt's Revolution: The Language of Tahrir,* Cairo: AUC Press. p 25–68.

Meier-Menzel (2014): Visual Election Campaigning in Egypt. In: Mikala Hyldig-Dal (Ed.) (2014): *Cairo Images of Transition.* Bielefeld: Transcript, 79–87.

Rancière, Jacques (2004): *The Politics of Aesthetics: The Distribution of the Sensible.* London: Bloomsbury.

Rancière, Jacques (2008): Aesthetic Separation, Aesthetic Community: Scenes from the Aesthetic Regime of Art. In: Art & Research, vol. 2, no. 1, 2008. www.artandresearch.org.uk/v2n1/ranciere.html#_ftn1

Salam, S.A. (2016): 'Un/Interrupted Formations – Choreographing Spaces of Gesticulation', www.ibraaz.org/essays/145

Sanders IV, Lewis / Visonà, Mark (2012): The Soul of Tahrir: Poetics of a Revolution. In: Samia Mehrez (Ed.): *Translating Egypt's Revolution: The Language of Tahrir,* Cairo: AUC Press. p 213–248.

El Shahed, Mohammad (2014): Tahrir Square: Social Media, Public Space & Revolution in Egypt. In: Mikala Hyldig-Dal (Ed.) (2014): *Cairo Images of Transition.* Bielefeld: Transcript, 12–14.

Sepahvand, Ashkan (2015): 'Superconversations Day 60: Ashkan Sepahvand responds to Anton Vidokle, "The Communist Revolution was Caused by the Sun: A Partial Script for a Short Film"', www.conversations.e-flux.com/t/superconversations-day-60-ashkan-sepahvand-responds-to-anton-vidokle-the-communist-revolution-was-caused-by-the-sun-a-partial-script-for-a-short-film/2165

Snowdon, Peter (2014): The Revolution Will be Uploaded: Vernacular Video and the Arab Spring. In: *Culture Unbound – Journal of Current Cultural Research*, vol. 6, 2014. www.cultureunbound.ep.liu.se/v6/a21/

III. TOOLS AND STRATEGIES

WHY SO MUCH ART AND ACTIVISM FAILS

(AND WHAT WE CAN DO TO FAIL BETTER)

Stephen Duncombe and Steve Lambert

We've been doing Artistic Activism for a long time and have seen many ways in which it can fail. In fact, you might call us experts at failure because of our personal experience with the subject: we've failed ourselves so many times in so many ways. But failure is important: it's how we learn and develop our craft. Samuel Beckett expresses this well in his play *Worstword Ho*:

Ever tried. Ever failed.
No matter. Try again.
Fail again. Fail better.

If we are going to be creative, and try new things, we are guaranteed to fail, over and over again. The trick is to fail better, and to learn from our mistakes. Here are some of the common mistakes we've watched others make...and made ourselves:

Good Intentions

Most artists and activists working on social and political issues do what they do with the best of intentions. Fueled by passion and compassion, we put ourselves, our ideas and our creativity out into the world. We are good people doing good things. Good results are bound to follow. Right? Wrong. Good intentions don't necessarily lead to good results. Actions resulting from the best of intentions can be ineffectual, misdirected, and even have an unintended detrimental impact. Good intentions are an important first step, but for those good intentions to lead to good results, with any regularity, means rationally evaluating the impact of our actions, and then developing a reasoned plan of how our actions fit together in order to multiply their impact.

When we make good intentions the sole criteria of our success we also turn away from the world and focus on ourselves, not the impact our creations have on other people, power relations, and material conditions. This is fine if your goal is just "working on myself," but when our goal is to work with others to change the world then our attention needs to be turned to the æffect we have on things outside of ourselves and our intentions.

Do you have good intentions? Yes? That's wonderful, we can check that off. Now it is time to think about what good we can do in the world.

Political Expressionism

Artists reading this are probably familiar with the term "Abstract Expressionism." It was an arts movement of the 1950s in which the artist's rage, joy, disgust, or hope was communicated to the world directly through their medium. Jackson Pollock was the poster-boy of Abstract Expressionism: the rebel artist communicating his passion though the paint he dripped, splashed and threw upon on the canvas. *Political* Expressionism is the same principle applied to art and activism. But instead of the artist's personal emotions being expressed it's the person's political passions. The bold act of political self-expression itself becomes the purpose of this work, and the success of the piece is determined by how well it conveys the artist or activist's feelings about the political moment.

But, honestly, who really cares what any single artist or activist thinks or feels? *They*, themselves, might, but that's part of the very problem. Like Good Intentions, Political Expressionism is really more about the artist or activist and less about the issue they want to address or the change they want to create. And, because it's all about the artist and *their* expression, there's little space for participation by others.

The assumption, conscious or not, is that the mere expression of hope or rage will bring about change. Political expressionism is also based upon a misunderstanding: that social change happens and movements ignite because people finally get angry enough. Following this logic, if you express your anger you're doing something noble and necessary. You are sticking it to the Man. Anger and disgust certainly can be motivators. As *The Clash* sang,

Let fury have the hour,
anger can be power.
D'you know that you can use it?

But moving from anger (or hope) to change is a complex process, and the expression of anger can retard action as easily as motivates it. Thinkers as far back as Aristotle have recognized that mere expression can even act as an escape valve for social unrest, a way to blow off steam before returning to work for the Clampdown.

Like good intentions, political expressionism is an understandable and even laudable early step. The burning desire to express your passions can fuel your action; it can get you off the curb and into the street. But nothing concrete happens just because you show the world how angry you are. The question, to tweak *The Clash*, is: H'you going to use it?

Lifestyle

Another variant of Political Expressionism is choosing to live an "authentic" life as an artist or activist. This sounds something like: "I've refused to be part of the system. I am not a banker or a real estate agent! I don't work in advertising or sales! I have chosen to live my life with political and artistic integrity. I am an Artist! I am an Activist! *This* is my political act."

Committing ourselves to creative expression and social transformation *is* political. But we are a means, not the end. It's the things we create, the actions we take, and the results that come from these actions and creations, that have political impact – not our mere self-identification. When we view our lifestyle as our politics, then our actions can become more interested in perpetuating the idealized image of the artist or activist with paint stained jeans and t-shirts with political slogans than creating work that fully engages with the world in which we live. In fact, self-identification as an "authentic" outsider – an incorruptible rebel – can get in the way of understanding and communicating with the everyday people we are trying to reach. Furthermore, this emphasis on an authentic rebel identity also prevents us from taking on roles and personas – think of the suits and ties of the Civil Rights activists, or the top hats and tiaras of the Billionaires For Bush – that may be tactically important. Turning the focus on ourselves and our intentions, our expression, and our identification can lead an artistic activist to turn inward and gauge their success on who they are, rather than their impact on the wider world.

Yes, we need to be able to express ourselves if we are going to be creative, and we need to have good intentions to begin this work, and *we need to indulge ourselves* in order to live happy, creative lives. But all of this focus on ourselves amounts to little in terms of social change if we don't also gauge our success on how we impact others.

Raising Awareness

The impetus behind raising awareness is noble. To expose an uncomfortable or inconvenient truth, to reveal facts about reality – often concerning corporate malfeasance, government corruption, or social injustice – that we believe are hidden, censored or otherwise unknown by the public at large, is certainly a wirth aim. The problem here does not lie in the information itself, or valuing facts and evidence, as any sustainable social transformation must be built upon facts and evidence, it lies with the delusional faith that the mere exposure to facts and statistics, information and The Truth, will magically and automatically result in action and transformation.

We are all subject to this *information delusion*: if people just had the right facts on pollution, inequality, injustice, oppression, whatever, then something is bound to happen. This assumption is based upon several fallacies:

People don't have access to the information. In totalitarian societies, in the pre-Internet age, this was a pretty safe assumption. Today, in much of the world, it is naïve. Most people have more access to more information than they know what to do with. And this might be the very problem: we know too much. With access to too much information we are overwhelmed by infinite possibility and doubt and, paralyzed, we turn away. Lack of information about an issue is surely an obstacle to understanding, analysis and action, but we need to step back and ask ourselves: Where does the lack of information lie? Is it in the minutia of how bad the problem is, and whose fault it is, or is what's missing useful information regarding *what steps one can make to change things for the better?*

The right information just isn't presented in the right form. Designers and artists, in an effort to make cold facts more aesthetically receptive, employ their talents to sculpt and form data into visualizations that present difficult to grasp statistics in complex, beautiful, interactive, charts and diagrams. This can make for interesting (and sometimes dreadful) art and the best examples can draw people in and might actually increase comprehension. All this is good. But too often the art speaks louder than the data, and the aestheticization of information transforms facts into form: something to be appreciated and admired, displayed and contemplated...but not necessarily acted upon.

People will do what we want them to do with the information we are giving them. We often presume that once people have the "right" information they will act in the "right" ways. But people don't just "get" facts that they are given – they need to *make sense* of them: putting them into context and giving them meaning. Unfortunately, living in a consumer society as we do, one of the ways we make sense of information is as just another commodity. Knowledge becomes something we possess, maybe show off at parties, but ultimately put up on a shelf, or use up and throw away. In a society which valorizes consumption, not production, ideas often become things we consume, not act upon. If we want people to do something other than merely consume information as a commodity, then we also need to also provide alternative models of what they can produce with it.

Information is action. College professors (mea culpa) often suffer this particular delusion, propping up their radical credibility while justifying their lack of activity by insisting that their activism happens in the classroom. Here they expose students to the lies they learned in high school history class, or introduce the latest transgressive and subversive theories, trusting that the transference of specialized knowledge itself will lead to some sort of change. This is magical thinking, better suited to alchemy than artistic activism. This idea that the exchange of information is a transformative activity also haunts forms of political activism. This is most apparent amongst conspiracy theorists, who operate as if knowing and sharing the truth about power – mumbling a few words and casting a spell – will cause those structures of power to crumble. Like magic.

Awareness is important. It is also not enough. Raising awareness, to borrow a phrase from the sciences, is a "necessary but not sufficient condition". Ultimately, information needs to empower the people and move them to action. Action without awareness results in an unthinking artistic activism with stupid, and sometimes terrible, consequences. But awareness without action is, perhaps, worse. It results in the appearance of political engagement without any of its result. It is an artistic activism of bad faith.

The Whole World is Watching[1]

We've interviewed scores of talented political artists and we've worked with hundreds of amazing political activists, and the most common criteria they use to gauge the success of their projects is media attention. If the work is covered by the mainstream news or the art press, or commented upon in activist or radical art circles, then it is deemed a great victory. This emphasis on media attention makes a certain sense: the more people hear about our piece, and the more people are exposed to the issues or see our vision, then the more people might be moved to think and act in a different way. Media attention also provides a nice and easy metric for success. We can measure how many times our piece was mentioned, the quality of the coverage, how big an audience it reached, and so on. For these reasons and others, designing pieces with potential media attention in mind is important.

But media is a means, not an end. Literally. *Media* is the plural of the word *medium*, which comes from the Latin for "middle". Media is a means for delivering our ideas or feelings to another person or, in the case of mass media, many other people. It's a conduit; that's all. What really matters is the message and what people do once they receive that message.

Yes, we know that the medium, too, has its own message, blah blah, McLuhan, blah blah blah, but when we forget that media is a means to an end and let the notice of newscasters and Internet bloggers become the Holy Grail, then it's too easy to start creating pieces whose primary function is to capture their attention. Media click bait. And when media attention becomes the primary concern, then aesthetic form and even social content can become secondary. An audience of millions matters little if our piece has no content. If we are "successful" it just means millions of people watching nothing. And if having the whole world watching our piece is really the ultimate goal, then creating pictures of cute cats with funny sayings on them is a surer path to success than artistic activism. Don't get us wrong: We love kittens, but they are *not* the revolution.

---

1   Chant first used by protesters in the 1960s, later picked up by Occupy Wall Street.

Starting a Discussion

Many artists, and even some activists, no matter how political they are, are reluctant to take a stand and have their work convey "a message". Instead, the goal is to stir the pot and begin a dialogue around a topic so audience members, either individually or collectively, can arrive at their own conclusions. The success of the work is determined by whether it prompts a conversation on a particular issue. There's a lot to commend in this approach. In a democracy, decisions should be arrived at through discussion rather than decree, and by opening up space for conversation through our pieces, we are facilitating this critical component of a free and open society. This is the power of the public sphere. Besides, telling people what to think makes for bad art, and ineffective propaganda.

The problem, again, is confusing means and ends. Facilitating a free and open conversation about a topic is great, but is this really the end we are looking for? What do we actually want that conversation to do? What do change do want to come from that conversation? The public sphere is politically important not just as a forum for discussion, but because this forum is a place where new perspectives are created, problems are identified, solutions are formulated and then actions are taken. Otherwise the result is just talk and more talk. This may be a fine activity for a coffee house or a seminar room, but this isn't – by itself – very effective in challenging power or creating change. The *power* of the public sphere doesn't come from the conversation itself, but what happens within that conversation... and what comes after.

God fucks Goats (Or: Shock Value)

There's another problem related to those above. What gets the most media coverage and generates the most conversation? Controversy. Burn a flag! Get naked! Put a crucifix in a vat of urine! Both art and activism have a long history of using shock effect in order to get people talking. It often works. But what do people talk about? Usually the controversy. This is good for the artist or activist's own renown, but it usually doesn't get people talking about the real issues (other than about the right to create such shocking work). Our work should foster *meaningful* dialogue that leads somewhere. Getting everyone to talk about our piece just means everyone is talking about our piece.

A radically new perspective can reorient our fundamental coordinates of reality: a Rancierien "re-distribution of the sensible". And surprise is invaluable for countering expectations that can open up a space for increased cognition and an opportunity for re-thinking. But this is only the case when this new sensibility truly challenges the normative structures of society; when it shocks us out of how we "make sense". Today, however, shock value *is* our sensibility. In a world where Donald Trump can become president of the United States via a steady stream of scandal, provocation and outrage, and a "Sensation" exhibit is sponsored by advertising mogul Charles Saatchi at the Royal Academy of Art in London, controversy constitutes the core of the system. Maybe once, when sober Victorian values held sway, shock value had some transgressive and transformative value, but that time has long passed. Shock value has been devalued, and "shocking pieces" are often not that shocking.

Means as Ends

Many of the common mistakes of art and activism outlined above are not really mistakes at all. There's nothing wrong with expressing your rage, getting media attention, or starting people talking. Good intentions are key, and awareness is important. The mistake lies in means and ends. We often conflate the two. Simply put: ends are where we want to go and means are the steps we take in order to get there. But, of course, nothing is ever that simple because means and ends work in cycles: an end may be a means to an even greater end. Still, in order to be æffective as artistic activists, it is important to know what are our ends and what are the means to get there.

Getting our issue on the evening news, for instance, may be a mark of our success. And it is a success, an end to strive after and celebrate once we've attained it. Yippee! But then we need to stop and think: Is what we really want just news coverage? Or something more? Was getting on the news really an end, or just a means? Here's a broad strokes example of how this questioning might look in practice when we've set our initial sites on attracting the attention of the media for a piece we've done on climate change.

Q: Why do we want media attention?
A: So people are aware of the problem of climate change.

Q: Why do we want people to be aware?
A: So they'll think and feel something about climate change.

Q: Why do we want them to think and feel?
A: So they'll be motivated to do something about climate change.

Q: Why do we want them to do something?
A: Because then there's a chance of having an impact on climate change.

Sure, we want our piece to be picked up and amplified by the media, but by thinking it through we might realize that what we really want is people's action to bring about social and environmental change, and media coverage is just a means – perhaps a necessary one – to this greater end. Once we know this we can plan accordingly: creating pieces that get media attention, but *also* move people to act to bring about change.

In our own practice, and through working with others, we've come up with a technique to avoid many of the common failures we've witnessed (and perpetrated ourselves). It's really, really simple. As you plan your piece and think about what you want it to do, ask yourself this question: *And Then What Do I Hope Happens?*

If I have good intentions. Then what do I hope happens?
If I express myself. Then what do I hope happens?
If I live an authentic life. Then what do I hope happens?
If I make people aware. Then what do I hope happens?
If I start a discussion. Then what do I hope happens?
If I shock people. Then what do I hope happens?
If I [fill in the blank]. Then what do I hope happens?

None of this it to say that there is a "right" goal or a "right" path. Maybe raising awareness or starting a conversation, is the ultimate goal, and, in certain instances, having a conversation about a subject is form of social change itself. (Though we'd still encourage thinking about what we really hope to have happen in and from that conversation [camaraderie? confidence? new subjectivities?] as it may help us create a stronger piece). We often trust that our first gestures will be imbued with grand and magical powers, transporting us great leaps forward, further than we've bothered to plan for or even imagine. Back in reality, taking giant steps is almost guaranteed to lead to missteps. We need to think the steps we take through, methodically. Asking what happens next can help us do this.

But there are no guarantees. All creative work involves risk, and combining art and activism is a very risky proposition. We are bound to fail sometimes when we do it. There's no set of rules or "best practices" to follow. Vladimir Lenin's confidence notwithstanding, there is no one answer to the universal question of *What is to be Done?* In fact, we don't think such a simple response would do justice to the power of art and the myriad ways in which social change happens. Acknowledging this, however, does not allow us to retreat back into magical thinking where we create a piece and: Poof! change happens. If our artistic activism is going to have meaningful impact it's imperative that we think seriously about exactly what we want our work to do, and how we will accomplish this. And we will fail a lot. But hopefully, by learning common pitfalls of artistic activism, we can fail a bit less often, and when we do fail: fail better.

This essay is adapted from our forthcoming book: How to Win! The Art of Activism.

TOOLS FOR THE DESIGN REVOLUTION

Harald Gruendl

In light of the worrying advance of destructive lifestyles rampantly spreading around the world, the theory and practice of design are expressing far too little initiative to take a step forward for positive change and develop appropriate alternatives. In academic circles designers fancy themselves as resistant through the practice of speculative design (cf. Dunne/Raby 2013) or – and this is the bigger group – as obliging vicarious agents, cloaked in stardom, dreaming up lifestyle drugs for an alienated consumer culture. But even with its transcendental effect, the product fetish still has to be cheap. Today democratic design means externalising the costs of its production. First off, the environmental impacts are shifted to poorer regions with little clout in the arena of global politics, where the destructive depletion of resources can be achieved as capitalism-friendly as possible. When there is still handcraft left to be done in the manufacturing process, despite the automation euphoria in the industry, then things are 'Made in' China, India, Vietnam, or wherever else in the world where cheap wages are tagged as economic development support. Technology companies hold ritual annual product presentations – masses where year after year flocks of dependent followers rejuvenate their faith in always improving technology. We work hard in order to afford the renewal of our lifestyles at this speed. And we fear losing the good life, or that our children might later. We have condemned ourselves to be ever-faster, and all the more innovative.

In Europe, where politicians still ceremoniously recite the grand narration of full employment in their democratic institutions, doubts are long widespread. It is a narrative built upon economic growth (cf. Jackson 2009), which is currently leading the world straight to an ecological catastrophe. The planet is already marked by the overuse of its biocapacity. We are living in an age that is exhaustively informed, like never before, about the looming, precarious ecological change. The topic has arrived in mainstream society and regularly graces the front page of daily newspapers. The level of information today is based on scientific knowledge, which has been conferred by an overwhelming majority of the sciences. And nevertheless we stand before a tragedy of the commons (cf. Ostrom 1990), the destruction of the greatest public domain we share – the global climate. A decisive tool in order to avoid destroying or overusing public commons is information about their condition, which can be accessed by all users of the commons (cf. Bollier/Helfrich 2010; Bollier 2014). This important instrument is on hands in the case of the climate change. Emissions are recorded and the data shared around the world (IPCC 2014). The fact that the climate has not yet collapsed altogether is owed not to highly developed technologies, the climate conferences of the United Nations, or a resolute environmentally friendly economic policy but to poor countries that despite their large populations only emit low levels of greenhouse gases. The international community does not sanction such lacking solidarity. Why shouldn't every person on Earth have their fair claim to use the world's resources? Why is it okay that resources are shared in such an unjust way? And this will not change as long as the developed states of the Global North are dominating the political arena. It is a failure of world politics that begins with the little things. We will have to explain to our children why we did not act. We have both the knowledge and the necessary tools to implement it.

When the existing social institutions fail in this respect, it is time for resistance and activism. Design is perfectly suited to support a different political agenda, from propaganda to the articulation of alternative lifestyles. Unfortunately, history is also full of examples where outstanding artistic and socially relevant design promoted the wrong political concepts. It is an easy diagnosis to condemn artists, architects, and designers after the fact for their wrong or lacking ideologies. It is all the more difficult, however, for one to realise that the careless perpetuation of our consumer culture at the cost of other parts of the world is actually a wrongdoing that resides within ourselves. With any right, the global community is proud of diminishing hunger, poverty, and child mortality. But at the same time we are missing out on developing a greater humanist perspective beyond just globalised industrial capitalism. It could very well be that the competition economy is only a transitional model which – once the generated prosperity also becomes fact for the majority – will change into a cooperative economy. Systems sciences call this transition a paradigm shift. Prevailing concepts give way to new ones.

'Attack the Mindset'[1]

The transition to new, more sustainable ideas of design theory and practice goes back to the time before the first oil crisis in the 1970s. The success and growth of today's rich countries in the world are based on the exploitation of cheap energy resources like coal and petroleum. The report by system scientists from the Massachusetts Institute of Technology to the Club of Rome marked the first recognition that the path followed by the rich countries will lead to a collapse of natural resources. 'Limits to growth' (cf. Meadows et al 1972) are often misinterpreted as a prognosis for the future. But in fact they are intended as a warning to a linear thinking consumer society. One property of complex systems is namely that they might not develop

---

1   Quote from an informative video on system theory: Donella H. Meadows, *Sustainable Systems*, lecture presented at the University of Michigan on 18 March 1999, YouTube, https://www.youtube.com/watch?v=HMmChiLZZHg [accessed 5 November 2017].

linearly. We like to watch growth curves and derive short-term economic successes from them. But in the case of commercially-used non-renewable resources the curve rises for a while and then drops drastically. 'Peak oil' is a good example for such a turning point. The oil industry is a system that generates capital from the exploitation of a non-renewable resource. It is a system whose feedback mechanism is controlled, first and foremost, by the profit of the employed capital: The more capital in the system, the higher the production rate, but the greater the decrease of resources. Simply put, it is predatory exploitation. Due to the exponential growth the resource is exploited faster than initially projected. But then there comes a point when the production rate is reduced because of decreasing revenue, and new investments don't pay off anymore – that's the turning point. Market economy, however, leaves this turning point to the profit-driven competition dynamic as opposed to a feedback system, which incorporates environmental impacts into the system. Today we know that we have to leave a great amount of the Earth's remaining resources untouched: Not to keep a bit for our descendants but to prevent the climate from collapsing on the short term.

Throughout her life the system scientist Donella H. Meadows researched effective system interventions for positive change. In her reflections on 'thinking in systems' (Meadows 2008) the co-author of *Limits to Growth* formulated instructions about how we can recognise systems and eventually learn to surmount them. In a list of guidelines for life in a world of systems, some system interventions are given as examples for how design could be employed as an effective medium. On a high system level it is important to comprehend the rhythm of the system and to make the inherent thought models visible. Meadows recommends to metaphorically put the prevailing system on a pedestal, to exhibit it. Activism does just that. Polluted rivers and inhuman work conditions in developing countries hidden behind the globalised 'Made in...' system are revealed. This system intervention is an extremely effective tool, but it is not used enough in order to weaken the existing system's imperviousness to change. It can be a potent instrument for designers who want to actuate change.

'Planet Earth First'[2]

On another system level, prices and green taxes can be simple and effective feedback strategies against the destruction of the environment. Alone the mere readability of electric meters in households can lead to a change in behaviour regarding the use of electricity, just like an increase in energy costs. Why don't we use the means of design to shed light on our own ecological footprint? Experience shows that transparency has a self-regulating effect on systems. Instead of laws stipulating thresholds for environmental degradation, the radical disclosure of environmental pollution could be a far more effective system intervention, which

2   Greenpeace slogan from a protest action during the G20 Summit in Hamburg in 2017.

relies on the self-regulation mechanisms of a solidary and informed society. Making information visible, information design, is an obvious intervention from a design perspective. The more people know about the state of a system, the better they can make informed personal and collective decisions. Design can also draw attention to hidden system correlations and to the effects of our actions. It must be used as a means against alienation and ignorance. The following sections outline different types of system interventions based on the abovementioned perspectives. They are not intended as tips or advice, rather they are field reports which should inspire alternatives to the prevailing system and encourage other designers to take action.

Here Are the Tools. Choose one! Start the Design Revolution!

Found an Alternative Design Institution!

IDRV – Institute of Design Research Vienna was founded twelve years ago as a non-university research institute; a non-profit scientific organisation for investigating design as a means and expression of positive transformation in society. At that time it seemed advantageous to apply academic standards to the research but to avoid subjecting the knowledge transfer to academic rituals. The feedback system in academic research involves – albeit not undisputed – an evaluation of the scientific performance by peers. Knowledge is 'paid' in the currency of credits in peer-reviewed journals. Endless lists of publications are required not only for scientific project funding but also for a successful academic career, which is organised top-down and strictly hierarchical. Universities rise and fall in the rankings, not least, due to these evaluations of performances. The opinions of two colleagues as reviewers decide survival or ruin and about the value of the knowledge. This control mechanism could be easily augmented if the relevance of the knowledge was discussed with a greater number of participants. What was devised as a measure to ensure quality leads all too often to systemic rigidity in methodology and thought. Given its dependency on third party resources from the industry, academic research is increasingly used as a system-serving as opposed to a system-critical knowledge generator. Public funding intended for educational and research institutions quickly becomes private capital for a start-up culture that incorporates it in the profit logic of patents and personal gain. IDRV has always rejected this dynamic and ensured – also in research grants from the industry – that the knowledge is accessible to all. The design practice can also benefit from the establishment of institutions with a non-profit character, such as collaborative models between members of the architectural community, who employ their knowledge and adapted technologies to realise new and open projects in developing countries, which brave the profit orientation and influence of the industry in the construction process and encourage people to build site-specific, self-empowered, environmentally-friendly, and cost-effective architecture with local resources. However, we should not just export this knowledge, rather test and employ it in our immediate surroundings as well.

Write a Book!

The eponymous book *Tools for the Design Revolution* (IDRV 2014)[3] is a compilation of personal experiences, collected and documented in the framework of numerous design interventions. The book medium seemed best-suited for both historical narrative and knowledge transfer. Its visual language cites the radical Global Tools movement in Italy, whose performative knowledge production serves as an important historical reference. It also recalls times when academies and universities employed synergies between artistic and scientific research approaches in their efforts to trigger social transformation. The book demonstrates the role of graphic design in the development of strong statements which cannot be conveyed by the text alone. Double images serve as an emotional gateway to introduce complex contexts. For example, a wilted leaf and a T-shirt that is compostable quickly and concisely explain the system of a biological circular economy, which must become an indispensible basis of the economy in the future. Visual metaphors and irritating images – like a headless doll, representing planned obsolescence – are also useful for a broader understanding of the contents.

Make a Performance!

An artistic action is a temporary form of knowledge transfer. One can learn about it in art history but also from the actionism of environmental organisations. Producing propaganda falls, as such, into the realm of design and can be employed as a creative disruption in our advertising-saturated attention economy culture. Visual demonstration culture is already largely professionalised: Professionally designed banners and posters with standard slogans are held high at workers strikes or political demonstrations. Individual articulation of protest is more and more in the hands of professional slogan writers, who otherwise dream up marketing lines for dog food or deodorant. However, performance can also be a strategy in a communication practice to give knowledge a discursive and open form. A performance is an invitation for discussion and reflection. An effective performance that IDRV has repeated numerous times in workshops and museum contexts focuses on design values which are important for the technical cycle of objects: A Kalashnikov AK-47 is disassembled into all of its individual components.[4] A narrative then unfolds about the distribution of this weapon across all continents, its resilience against environmental factors when in use, its reparability and easy

---

3   The ambitions of the publication are documented in a corresponding paper (Gruendl et al. 2015).
4   The action was first performed in the exhibition 'Made 4 You' at MAK – Museum of Applied Arts | Contemporary Art in Vienna and most recently during a tour through the exhibition 'WEtransFORM' at Neues Museum – State Museum of Art and Design in Nuremburg (see Thun-Hohenstein et al. 2012; Neues Museum 2016). A video documentation of the performance is available under: MAK Vienna, *departure/MAK d>lab.01: Tools for the Design Revolution*, Vimeo, https://vimeo.com/45831748 [accessed 5 November 2017].

assembly, and why it is still being used in combat today despite the introduction of far more efficient weapons. This martial object irritates and contradicts the story about a better world, which definitely will not be achieved with force of arms. Here artistic practice and scientific knowledge about ecodesign fuse into a dense and intensive experience for the audience. The deadly instrument transcends the necessary positive destruction of an exploitative and unsustainable system of the prevailing production paradigm, which only employs ecodesign for greenwashing.

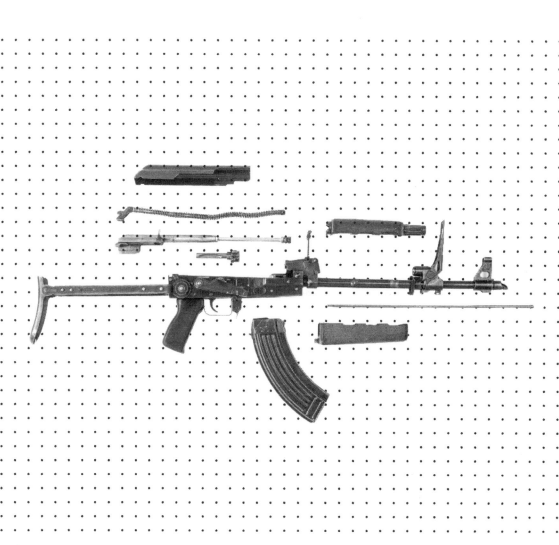

Figure 3: Kalashnikov AK-47. In IDRV workshops, performances, and exhibitions the object represented positive design qualities like durability, resilience, and simple and quick repair.

Pick a Fight with Goliath!

In design activism it is helpful to choose an opponent whom a large number of people have had an everyday experience with and who has a prominent market presence in consumer culture. In order to change the system positively one must draw attention to faults in the system. We have done this, for instance, by thematising aluminium coffee capsules. A global food company propagated the portioned packaging of coffee in shells as a premium product for making coffee. After public malaise about the aluminium packages, even a life cycle assessment report was released, which should evidence that this solution was the most environmentally friendly in comparison to competitors. What the company did not say, however, was that the unnecessary packaging doubles the footprint of coffee-making, regardless whether the packaging is made of aluminium, plastic, or bioplastics. The right conclusion from the analysis would actually be no packaging, not the most environmentally friendly in relative terms. Another commercial strategy was a much-advertised return system with stylish paper collection bags. Consumerist misconduct is simply white-washed. Because aluminium is endlessly recyclable – the endless capsule with a recycling halo. Our enquiries at the Institute of Nonferrous Metallurgy at Montan University in Leoben then shed new light on the reality of aluminium recycling. When you melt 1000 kilograms of mixed scrap aluminium alloys you only salvage 850 kilograms of aluminium. The rest is disposed as slag. With the collection rate of 85% that the company aims for, after just a few rounds of recycling there is just one capsule remaining from ten. Longevity is somewhat different. We drew attention to these facts in performances, videos, and exhibitions. We also made a prototype for a T-shirt with Adbuster-esque variants of the coffee brand's slogan. Given the aggressiveness of such companies, one should, however, be cautious not to give them grounds for legal action, a fact that has delayed dissemination over social media thus far. We hope one day to win this fight, which follows an archetypal pattern of stories and provides people with the real facts. We will also produce explanatory A4 posters which can be hung above capsule coffee machines in company kitchens and similar contexts. The Design Revolution is an Information Revolution.

Lay a Cuckoo's Egg!

The IMM International Furniture Fair in Cologne was the site for an action we conducted together with Köln International School of Design. The fair organisers had opened a new hall and attracted numerous premium manufacturers. We were able to use an unbooked area amidst the designer furniture companies. Under the title 'The Consequences of Design', we exhibited an Italian designer stackable chair. It was placed on a wooden box from the 'Tools for the Design

Revolution' exhibition. The chair had undergone an ecological assessment in a pilot project by a university, so we knew the ingredients needed to realise this design. These were then exhibited in the due scientific character: iron, salt, limestone, gravel, nickel, chrome, a pile of coal, a canister of crude oil, biomass, and finally 550 litres of water in white 10-litre plastic buckets, which ran along the complete length of the fair stand like a white tail. We received a lot of feedback about the intervention – mostly negative. The furniture production community obviously saw the installation as more of an attack than as objective information about a rather successful chair, which can even be separated into the plastic seat and metal frame without tools, thereby facilitating easy material sorting after its use phase. It appears as if we are not willing to view the impacts of design in all objectivity and then think about how we can develop more environmentally friendly objects. The idea was not to single out a manufacturer and make them look bad but to praise the transparency of the design and propagate informing the public as an attitude worthy of imitation. The vehement hostility towards the students who ran the stand was a lesson for all: Companies do not want to know what their furniture are actually made of, namely resources attained under precarious conditions – coal, oil, and radioactive materials. The proposal to the fair to accommodate the successful stand next year with a different theme was unfortunately not accepted. So we'll have to look for another nest for our propaganda.

Make an Exhibition!

The exhibition medium is an effective form for generating and imparting knowledge. The research for the exhibition, personal contact with protagonists, looking up related literature, and then physically staging the exhibits and the acquired knowledge have made a decisive contribution to our own knowledge and attitudes. We also search for project partners who can spread the ideas as widely as possible. For example, an exhibition in the framework of the Vienna Biennale 2017 (cf. Thun-Hohenstein 2017a) at the MAK – Museum of Applied Arts | Contemporary Art, which was developed in cooperation with the Vienna Business Agency and its creative centre 'departure', showcased examples of a paradigm shift in design. More than 50,000 Biennale visitors could gain insights into sustainable design scenarios. These discourses are also migrating more often into the domain of such temporary institutions and no longer take place exclusively at conferences or in academic publications. However, new ways of archiving this knowledge must be found as limited exhibition budgets do not always cover modes of storing knowledge beyond the exhibition duration. Electronic forms of publishing exhibition views, video materials, and related exhibition texts could be an alternative for conserving exhibition knowledge.

Make a University Course!

IDRV was a pioneer in Austria to use Massive Open Online Courses (MOOC). On an international platform, where knowledge from universities from around the world is shared, we could concisely document our discussion event media and also establish a design course on sustainable design strategies.[5] The course, which is based on the *Tools for the Design Revolution* book, had more than 8500 interested subscribers. If one were to have such a large number of design students at a university, there would need to be several generations of design teachers. With contemporary media it is also possible for a small institution in the design sciences niche to make a remarkable contribution to change. Having said that, what was interesting was the discussion about admitting IDRV to the university platform. Despite the academic focus, the argument was originally whether such a small player could generate enough interesting content. Now, after several years, we – the small knowledge provider – have delivered more content than some other design education establishments financed by the public hand, which obviously do not want to share their knowledge. It should actually go without saying that all educational institutions publicise their contributions to generating knowledge and catalyse new forms of knowledge appropriation that take place outside of institutions.

Write a Column![6]

Design is anchored in mass media primarily as a fashionable discipline. Albeit, many challenges in society can also be viewed, articulated, and discussed as design problems. Mass media – even the antiquated daily newspapers and weekly magazines – have a huge impact. Quality media, too, have a quite ambivalent position in the formulation of design problems. Hence, a discussion with open-minded publishers could present an opportunity to make regular commentary from a designer's perspective. Although design is an everyday phenomenon, the political dimension of design is paid little heed. Design is a tool that must be placed in the service of democracy, and free media are tools for democratic knowledge creation. Perhaps it doesn't need to be a column in one of the daily newspapers right off; a contribution from the design practice in a trade journal now and then would also help evolve the discourse, just like a well-considered review of a book in social media.

---

5   The IDRV courses 'Tools for the Design Revolution' are available free of charge on iTunes U, the open education platform by the technology corporation Apple. On iTunes U there is also documentation of the *Circle* discussion series and expert interviews.

6   Since 2013 the author has been a contributor to the 'Design and Architecture' section of the weekly magazine *Spectrum* by the Austrian daily newspaper *Die Presse*. This opportunity arose when he addressed the chief editor with the remark that this section had been publishing architectural critique for years but never design critique.

Fight Fake Idols![7]

Design prizes were originally tools to proclaim the need for good design in the early days of industrial design and to reward it and present it as a precedent. Despite good intentions in the jury criteria, like ecological sustainability, these prizes have mutated into a homage for fashionable and often destructive design objects. How else is it possible, even with this category, that a design team is celebrated for their hypermotorised vehicle with a combustion engine? Is this design attribute not as highly praised as an affirmative design? This commercialisation no longer contributes to the original intention of design prizes. On the contrary, they reward an industry, which is going in the wrong direction, with confidence that they are doing the right thing. Design prizes must return to the service of society. We should applaud what supports positive change and not what digs us deeper in the problems.

Write a Design Manifesto!

On the occasion of the exhibition 'CityFactory: New Work. New Design.' we compiled our main ideas in a 'New Design Manifesto'. The attributes of new design were mapped out from the set context of 'new work' in keeping with the ideas of social philosopher Frithjof Bergmann (cf. Bergmann 2004) and comprised new social work, new creative work, new sustainable work, and new robot work. New work is only informed by paid work in part and supplemented by personal productions and works that we really, really want to do. This scenario served as a basis to generate a new design paradigm to lead us out of the existing system. Above all, the possibilities of working locally with decentralised high-tech fabrication methods create a new perspective for design. Open design, cooperation instead of competition, and environmentally responsible design in a circular economy form a new moral system for design, which now juxtaposes the profit logic of the market with the logic of commons. Through a media cooperation the manifesto could be printed full page in the magazine *form*[8] and in a magazine about sustainable lifestyles.[9] A print version was also taken home by hundreds of exhibition visitors. One could call this strategy activism with an institutional interface.[10]

English version: Peter Blakeney & Christine Schöffler.

---

7   See article about German design prizes (Gruendl 2014).
8   IDRV – Institute of Design Research Vienna, 'New Design Manifesto', *form Design Magazine*, 272 (Jul/Aug 2017), p.131.
9   *BIORAMA, Magazin für nachhaltigen Lebensstil*, 50 (August/September 2017), p. 61.
10   The director of the MAK also wrote a very poignant essay on the occasion of the Vienna Biennale 2017 (Thun-Hohenstein 2017b).

References

Bergmann, Frithjof (2004): *Neue Arbeit, Neue Kultur*. Freiamt im Schwarzwald: Arbor.

Bollier, David (2014): *Think Like a Commoner: A Short Introduction to the Life of the Commons*. Gabriola Island: New Society Publishers.

Bollier, David / Helfrich, Silke (eds.) (2012): *The Wealth of the Commons. A World Beyond Market & State*. Amherst, MA: Levellers.

Dunne, Anthony / Raby, Fiona (2013): *Speculative Everything: Design, Fiction, and Social Dreaming*. Cambridge: MIT Press.

Gruendl, Harald (2014): 'Deutsche Designpreise, Role Models', *form Design Magazine*, 255 (September/October 2014), pp. 88–92.

Gruendl, Harald / Naegele, Christina / Kellhammer, Marco (2015): Tools for the Design Revolution, in *Agents of Alternatives. Re-designing Our Realities*, ed. by Alastair Fuad-Luke, Anja-Liasa Hirschner, and Katharina Moebus. Berlin: Agents of Alternatives, pp. 86–93.

IDRV – Institute of Design Research Vienna (2014): *Tools for the Design Revolution. Design Knowledge for the Future*. Zürich: niggli.

IPCC – The Core Writing Team, Rajendra K. Pachauri, and Leo Meyer (eds.) (2014): Climate Change 2014: Synthesis Report. Contribution of Working Groups I, II and III to the Fifth Assessment Report of the Intergovernmental Panel on Climate Change. Geneva: IPCC.

Jackson, Tim (2009): *Prosperity without Growth: Economics for a Finite Planet*. London: Taylor & Francis, Earthscan.

Meadows, Donella H. (2008): *Thinking in Systems: A Primer*. White River Junction, VT: Chelsea Green Publishing.

Meadows, Donella H. / Meadows, Dennis L. / Randers, Jørgen / Behrens III, William W. (1972): *Limits to Growth*. New York: Universe Books.

Neues Museum – State Museum for Art and Design (ed.) (2016): *WEtransFORM – Art and Design on the Limits to Growth*. Nuremberg: Verlag für Moderne Kunst.

Ostrom, Elinor (1990): *Governing the Commons: The Evolution of Institutions for Collective Action*. Cambridge: Cambridge University Press.

Thun-Hohenstein, Christoph (ed.) (2017a): *Vienna Biennale 2017 Guide – Robots. Work. Our Future*. Vienna: Verlag für Moderne Kunst, 2017.

Thun-Hohenstein, Christoph (2017b): Sense and Sensibility in the Digital Age: Let Us Wake Up and Take Action!, in *Discussing Technology 2017: Digitalisation*, ed. by art:phalanx. Vienna: Amalthea Signum, pp. 124–29.

Thun-Hohenstein, Christoph / Esslinger, Hartmut / Geissler, Thomas (eds.) (2012): *Made 4 You – Design für den Wandel / Design for Change*. Nuremberg: Verlag für Moderne Kunst.

WALL OF WORDS
DIALOGIC ACTIVISM IN COLLECTIVE DESIGN

Cathy Gale

Design is enmeshed in a changing landscape of private and public communications due to the close relationship between the state and the market, social and communication networks. Traditionally valued for their technical skills, which facilitate the function and flow of business, designers operate in an inherently co-operative matrix of makers, thinkers and users. In an exponentially global multi-dimensional practice the cultural and commercial threads of Twitter, Facebook, WhatsApp, Instagram are intertwined with design products and services in a techno-social activity. As widespread access to the (digital) tools of visual communication has increased, global social networks have empowered new possibilities for collective authorship and activism. However, (graphic) design is also entrenched within a neoliberal landscape, which renders the perception of all messages and artefacts subject to suspicions of the designer's corporate involvement, in the eyes of the public: as commerce and culture have merged, cognition of the design's conceptual scope or its potential as an agent of socio-political change has diminished. In 'Power by Design' Rick Poynor (2012) suggests that (graphic) designers have always held less intellectual and political power than their multi-disciplinary skills set supports, in contrast to the disciplines of fine art and architecture. Yet, he also identifies the soft power of designers as *"the ability, through their work, to influence, mold opinion, persuade, change behaviour, initiate and spread visual trends, shape the aesthetic environment, and help to inform the public"* (Poynor 2012, 1).

What I am calling 'soft protest' is introduced in the context of collective design, a unified response to the soft power of contemporary capitalism and the socio-economic crises this has invoked, in a more co-operative and collaborative notion of design activism. The source of power in soft protest is derived from a synergy of diverse voices and expertise in a more socially connected mode of design practice and pedagogy underpinned by critical thinking: acting both within *and* beyond the market. Soft protest exploits the tools and techniques of graphic design in a material critique, which draws on Anthony Dunne and Fiona Raby's broad definition of critical design in *Design Noir: The Secret Life of Electronic Objects*: a design that asks difficult questions about consumer capitalism, industrial visions of technology, the political economy, eco-culture and design's role in these relationships (Dunne/Raby 2001, 58). The micro and macro examples of collective and co-operative organisation included in this essay highlight explicit drivers of socio-economic policy, socio-political modes of architecture, formulations of critical design practice, and paradigm shifts in artistic production and cultural validation.

As a graphic design educator, researcher and practitioner my evaluation of collective practices in design is framed predominantly by taught projects and staff-student research collaborations in the contexts of studio-based education, academic conferences and exhibitions. The design conference frames my evaluation of the manifesto as a pedagogic tool for design activism in academic communities of practice, referring to Etienne Wenger's definition of a social system (Wenger 2010, 1) in which learning is located between the designer and the world, and is characterised by an ongoing negotiation of identity and cultural meaning. The manifesto represents an adaptable model of graphic authorship and collective ideology embodied in material, pictorial or typographic form: a critical deployment of visual rhetoric, which exploits the persuasive methods and media of visual communication, in a proactive discourse with the audience/viewer. The Word As Weapon section features a brief overview of student work produced in a project, which tackles sustainable design in the context of a manifesto and is followed by Wall of Words, which extends the discursive possibilities of visualising design debate framed by a collaborative exhibition at Kingston School of Art in January 2017.

This essay is dialogic in tone, contributing to a co-operative discourse around the role collectives can play in socio-political design activities, rather than presenting a closed argument: it seeks to pose questions rather than offering absolute dialectic positions. The dialogic mode of (design) discourse is defined by Richard Sennett in *Together: The Rituals, Pleasures and Politics of Co-operation* as an open-ended space in which the design process or debate can take unexpected directions while seeking common ground (Sennett 2012, 19). Difference and 'otherness' enhance creative collaboration and build stronger mutual understanding in the iteration of this process. The associated terms collective, collaborative, co-operative and community are examined first in this essay across architecture and (graphic) design, in relation to notions of post-capitalism. What does design activism mean in contemporary education and practice and how can the tools and techniques of the design help facilitate participation in this untapped critical power for the discipline?

Contemporary contexts / commerce and culture

As globalisation has increased, neoliberal reductions in state management and funding have simultaneously led to an explosion of branding and marketing which, in turn, determines the priorities of production, professional practice and education. The conceptual boundaries between commerce and culture have blurred in public discourse, mass media and government policy (in the UK, relating to art and design education). On the one hand designers are tasked with meeting the rapacious demands of consumer capitalism, while simultaneously being urged to address social fragmentation and economic inequalities. Design theorist Guy

Julier argues in 'From Visual Culture to Design Culture' that globalisation has benefitted the advancement of design, yet also acknowledges that contemporary capitalism contributes to unequal relations between producers and consumers (Julier 2006, 69). Experimental Jetset, a small Amsterdam-based graphic design studio are critical of institutions that commission cultural projects for marginalising designers in preference for advertising (hip communication agencies) in a process of shedding 'ideological weight' (Experimental Jetset 2009, 90–91). From a more critical perspective the manipulation of society's needs and wants by multinational corporations and the flow of capital within which western values are embedded can be seen as a form of 'cultural imperialism' (Moline 2012, 123). Not only are designers implicated in the proliferation of consumer goods, contemporary capitalism delimits design's intellectual and ethical scope. Let's consider for a moment how this has affected the political, social and cultural capital of design.

As the educator, writer and theorist Mark Fisher puts it in *Capitalist Realism. Is There No Alternative?*, "capitalism seamlessly occupies the horizons of the thinkable" leading to "a widespread sense that not only is capitalism the only viable political and economic system, but also that it is now impossible even to imagine a coherent alternative to it" (Fisher 2009, 2-8). He describes capitalist realism as, "a pervasive atmosphere, conditioning not only the production of culture but also the regulation of work and education... acting as a kind of invisible barrier constraining thought and action" (ibid., 16). A state of isolated 'precarity' is characterised for the design educator and practitioner by intermittent teaching contracts and ever-inflating studio rents, while for students, 'success anxiety' and debt form reductive pressures delimiting the territory of tertiary education (in the UK). Contemporary labour is increasingly short-term in character, leading to superficial social relationships, lack of emotional investment, reductions of experience and knowledge carried forward by long-term employees (Sennett 2012, 7).

Isolated modes of creativity are sought (and taught) as the most desired route to commercial success and celebrity. In an over-crowded field this competitive impulse is fed by a (UK) design press that promotes and rewards budget size and client status above socio-political or ecological impact, for instance. Through competitions and awards the battle for supremacy pits design individuals (and agencies) against each other, fuelled by a thirst for novelty: a market-led approach, which is problemetised further by gender, race and class bias (Poynor 2012, 1). The notion of individual genius (connected to 'otherness') is partly rooted in the (romanticized) figure of the author or the artist struggling against the odds (often with their own eccentricities and tragedies): a concept that has been transferred, via consumer culture, to commercial design practice. Yet this construction of the designer's identity and the narrative landscape in which he/she plays prescribed roles, disguises the tension between individuality and collectivity: design, studios often showcase the (brand) name of the creator behind whom numerous employees are concealed (Cumulus 2017, 1). In social, political, and cultural terms collectives represent alternative ideological and economic models and "a way to overcome the limitations of isolated practice" (Vaughan 2012, 8).

In *PostCapitalism: A Guide to Our Future,* political journalist Paul Mason describes capitalism as an integrated system of social, economic, demographic, cultural and ideological issues, which enable open markets and private ownership (Mason 2016, xiii). Co-operatives and collaborative business models offer more socially-orientated benefits. But market mechanisms have bled into our private lives and co-opted knowledge and behaviour as commodities. In response Mason proposes collaboration as a co-operative economy to replace a predatory one: a mode of disrupting uneven power relations in which wealth and influence remain with the top few percent where the efforts of those in power are employed in sustaining this status quo. Collective design activism is framed in my essay, not as a 'detached spectatorialism' (Fisher 2012, 6) in which participants are invited to 'comment' or 'like' a protest just as another commodity, but as a dialogic engagement through design practice. This is framed by Harriet Edquist and Laurene Vaughan in *The Design Collective. An Approach to Practice* as a generative creative structure, with the potential to link socio-economic change and political agency (Vaughan 2012). In the next section collective, collaborative and co-operative methods, organisational structures and social contexts will be examined in relation to the processes of studying and practicing (graphic) design.

Collective / collaborative / co-operative

Many designers and illustrators share spaces and resources, whether seeking an alternative to excessive rent in an ad hoc manner, to develop interdisciplinary practices or simply to extend the social network and studio culture encountered and enjoyed at college. This can be understood as a traditional inter-disciplinary framing of 'commons' which Charlotte Hess and Elinor Ostrom describe in *Understanding Knowledge as Commons: From Theory to Practice* as bounded (in the studio), transboundary (the internet) and without clear boundaries (knowledge) (Hess/Ostrom 2007, 4-5). In open-plan warehouses or office spaces creative practitioners build fluid micro-communities as pragmatic systems exploiting the tangential richness of skills and experiences found therein. In this context, the shared studio or communal space might feature "creative interaction, spontaneous brainstorming or critique" as an everyday exchange (Vaughan 2012, 11). Unexpected exchanges of ideas, skills and professional nous can be embraced as a knowledge-commons in an informal co-operative work environment, forming a wealth of professional experience and technical knowledge (saving time and money), defined by Hess and Ostrom as a shared social intellectual resource (Hess/Ostrom 2007, 7-8).

Anthropologist Alberto Melucci (1996) argues in 'The Process of Collective Identity' that collective action is often the result of opportunities and constraints encountered by a group. In design this may comprise lack of funds due to student debt, high costs of studio space and an industry-wide dependence on expensive computer software. The design process requires co-operation from diverse producers and resources involved in bringing a project from initial concept to outcome, but this practical partnership does not necessarily produce a co-operative. In a co-operative *"there are shared intentions, contexts and ownership, underpinned by a willingness to work in conjunction with others"* (Vaughan 2012, 11). Unlike the co-operative the design collective's identity is not fixed but fluid, emerging through the actions and skills set of its members representing a way to overcome or soften the edges of discipline boundaries. The design collective, which may not incorporate joint ownership or responsibility is conceived as a group with shared/common interests, who undertake activities together to achieve common goals. In addition, even though a collective may have many points of interconnection, co-production of ideas and processes, collaboration is not essential (ibid., 10). For Vaughan, to collaborate is *"to work together, especially in a joint [creative, social or] intellectual effort"* (Vaughan 2012, 9), devising a common language through *difference*, in a more reflexive typology of approaches. From a critical perspective, the collective may seek to work with design's core social values, exploiting its capacity to change more than consumer behaviour: embedding technological, social and ethical questions in the process. Collaboration in this context may be sought as a more fruitful exchange between divergent stakeholders and voices in contrast to the more passive service-orientated consumer relationships with which graphic design is often associated.

In an adaptation of Melucci's notion of collective identity the designer is framed as an 'actor' in the discipline's social operations both internally (between co-producers) and externally (with the user/audience, political system, social control) disrupting cultural codes. Collective identity is described as a cognitive tool employed by the designer-actor in a continuous process of adaptability: internally the collective process forms a micro-community of participants acting as a group in a network to 'build a practice of freedom' (Melucci 1996, 2). At a macro level, 2012 was declared the United Nations Year of the Cooperative in recognition of the power to enact more democratic principles, to politically and/or economically empower (women), and in so doing 'build a better world'. Notions of co-operative action and organisation are being proposed to draw attention to and encourage action on urgent global socio-economic and ecological issues, with the intention of facilitating the erstwhile powerless in society to exercise more community-based control over local resources. Member-driven in nature, cooperative enterprises are envisaged by the UN as based on participation, autonomy and independence. In this co-operative structure members own, control and benefit from the businesses or social groups by defining and defending their own goals and benefits. Training and information-sharing ensure that members can contribute effectively to development of their co-operatives thereby sustaining the group's evolving impact and value as a future community resource (United Nations 2012, 1). In the words of the Secretary-General of the United Nations (2007-2016) Ban Ki-moon: *"Cooperatives are a reminder to the international community that it is possible to pursue both economic viability and social responsibility"* (Ki-moon 2012, 1).

The next section considers collective and collaborative practices from hybrid art-and-architecture groups to recent design graduates. The underlying principles and methods employed in these inter-disciplinary contexts are framed as adaptable models to graphic design education and real world applications.

Collective design and social engagement

In recent years, collective housing projects, organized around the principle of exchanging smaller private spaces for larger, shared spaces, have been emerging across the globe – many of them realized through local community groups excluded from conventional power structures. This section will look at moments of cultural and political transformation that have inspired collective practices forming a nexus between gender, socio-environmental housing, and cultural production.

The feminist architecture group, Matrix (set up in 1980) was run as a workers' co-operative with a non-hierarchical management structure and collaborative design methods exploring the socio-political context of the built environment. Their participatory approach sought to make the design process more accessible and engaging for clients and users, underpinned by feminist theory and critique on urban architectural practice. *"We believe that, precisely because women are brought up differently in our society we have different experiences and needs in relation to the built environment which are rarely expressed"* (Dwyer 2007, 45-46). Focusing on the spaces that women use, Matrix became spatial agents and advisors empowering women by involving them on the processes of designing. The writer and feminist Beatrix Campbell argues that second-wave feminism of the 70s and 80s could have had the answers to patriarchal constraints in the workplace: it was a period when, *"feminist ideas became the language of common sense. Then, capitalism begins to liquidate the conditions in which we could affect serious structural change"* halting the possible illumination and transformation of the world that this offered (Williams 2017, 1).

The Muf collective, established in 1996 comprising three women – two architects and an artist – resists notions of the single author, forming a collective organization in which socially engaged art practice is applied as a mechanism of collaboration. Defined by founder-member Melanie Dodd as a creative collaboration by a collection of individuals: *"the deliberate creation of a sufficiently generous atmosphere to make room for different disciplines and personalities, both ours and those of consultants, and friends"* (Dodd 2012, 55-60). In a similar convergence of art and architecture, working in collaboration with a community, *"Assemble champion a working practice that is interdependent and collaborative, seeking to actively involve the public as both participant and collaborator in the on-going realisation of the work"* (Assemble 2017, 1). Established in 2010, this group of 18 designers and architects became the first collective to win the Turner Prize in 2016. A *Guardian* review describes the differences of Assemble's approach to conventional commercial practice: *"Where many architects make themselves into brands and build up their egos both to help sell themselves better and because they want to, Assemble's members are genuinely collaborative, both with each other"* and with members of the public (Moore 2015, 1). Their collective action is *"less about creating a finished object than it is about the series of actions by which a space is designed, built and inhabited"* (ibid.). The cultural validation associated with the Turner Prize may represent a paradigm shift from individual genius to collective process. An emergent cultural authority in the collective can be traced back to curator and art critic Nicolas Bourriaud's notion of the 'altermodern' in which displacement, fragmentation and collective authorship form a new cultural framework for the arts. Altermodernism is defined by a multitude of possibilities, otherness and a 'constellation of ideas' (Bourriaud 2009, 2-5).

The term 'design community' is a commonly used generic term covering a broad spectrum of practitioners and educators but very little connects its participants beyond an umbrella term for the discipline at large. Although graphic designers often work in teams there are very few collectives based in this discipline, cross- and trans-disciplinary collectives comprising graphic designers working with other subjects representing more multi-dimensional modes of collective practice are more frequently formed. An Eindhoven-based collective of recent graduates represents a rare example of the design discipline adopting a similar focus on the *process* of design*ing* rather than only presenting finished outcomes. In devising a collaborative exhibition, 'Envisions in Eindhoven', the Envisions Collective sought to make their work more understandable and approachable to the public by exploiting design tools and visual rhetoric. In this way they created *"a climate for interaction and exchange... triggering a dialogue between designers, clients and manufacturers who are encouraged to approach each process as a collaborator"* (Bourton 2016, 1). Here, the unfinished nature of the work features as a catalyst for discourse: a dialogic community-based approach comparable to the working methods of Muf.

One advantage of graphic design's commodity value as a subject of degree-level study is the growing network of trained practitioners and researchers with access to design tools and techniques, many of whom are looking beyond design's service-orientated roles to more socio-political intentions. Through the proliferation of competitions, conferences and the expansion of accessible digital software a sector of society is emerging that is (more or less) actively employed in the facilitation of consumer culture but also engaged in socio-political discourse and action unimpeded by geographic location.

Word as Weapon: Manifesto as a Mode of Design Activism

Events and conferences established by design research groups such as the Design Research Society (DRS), the Design History Society (DHS), the International Council of Graphic Design Associations (Ico-d), Alliance Graphique Internationale (AGI) or the International Association of Universities and Colleges of Art, Design and Media (Cumulus) represent some of the few opportunities for designers to meet, share ideas and identify common ground. In this section, my case study 'Word As Weapon: The Manifesto As A Catalyst For Design Activism' (Gale 2013) focuses on the manifesto as a pedagogic tool and co-operative action. Developed in a community of design students and shared with a community of educators and practitioners the 'Word As Weapon' case study sought to test the role of design mechanisms and aesthetics, as principles of persuasive communication, in a material critique. The DHS 'Design Activism and Social Change' conference framed the discursive aims of my paper with an invitation to contributions from creative practices that invoke social, political and environmental agency, embracing marginal, non-profit or politically engaged design theories, articulations and actions (Julier 2011, 1). I will briefly give an overview of how the articulation of strongly-held beliefs or approaches to creative practice in a manifesto, coalesces individual practitioners in a unified context – as a statement of intent, or provocation.

Historically the manifesto has set out to reduce confusion, consolidate opinion or secure a wide-spread consensus, often as a collaborative collective endeavour (Gale 2013). As embodied notions of political and creative consensus, printed visual arguments from the Italian Futurists and UK-based Vorticist movements were introduced to help the students explore an experimental mode of communication through practice. For the Futurists, typographic experimentation allowed language itself to be a tool for attacking, disrupting or subverting convention, appropriating the most effective means of communicating an urgent message to the masses, forming a sphere of popular public opinion. As designed artefacts, the manifestos employ a dynamic integration of form and content to engage the public in ideas.

The original Word As Weapon manifesto project was absorbed into the graphic design degree course at second year level in 2005 in response to student requests for sustainability to feature more prominently in the academic programme as an integrated component. At the time, the ecological and social impact of design was framed as a specialist research subject in the third year, due to staff bias but also a historical ambivalence in the student cohort to incorporating the political and ecological impact of the discipline in their portfolio work. Word As Weapon sought to draw the attention of practice-led graphic design students to the role and value of graphic authorship as a significant asset in visual communication. Over a two-week period, a cohort of approximately 80 students worked independently or in pairs to craft an original manifesto and embody their ideas in visual and material form. By exploiting a collective impulse amongst the student cohort to explore sustainability and contribute to social and ecological discourse I interlaced critical thinking on contemporary culture with significant artefacts from graphic design's heritage. This critical challenge through design extends the semiotic analysis of consumer culture developed by theorists such as Roland Barthes in *Mythologies*, which sought to reveal how visual culture and consumer demand is created and not natural or fixed. On the one hand, Barthes sought *"an ideological critique bearing on the language of so-called mass-culture; on the other, a first attempt to analyse semiologically the mechanics of that language"* (Barthes 1993, 9).

In a material argument, the familiar visual mechanisms and devices of commercial communication are reframed causing a double-take, inviting a closer look at and consideration of the message. For instance, student Mickey Yoo crafted a manifesto cut into ice that gradually melted, a material synecdoche embodying a global message of climate change while also capturing the ephemeral nature of public interest in ecological issues. Helen Perry redesigned and printed a traditional A4 foolscap writing pad so that it had much narrower lines thereby encouraging smaller handwriting and as a result, a less (wasteful) use of paper. As she says, *"bored with serious messages of sustainability, I wanted to communicate how a few small changes can help the bigger picture"* (Gale 2013, 8). Ben Roebuck employed a more dynamic direct intervention with a printed graphic design artefact which demanded the reader 'wake the fuck up!' substantiated by concise and appropriate research data. Ben Urbanowicz focused his attentions on the eco-political responsibility of design staff in the social context of the university by creating a badge for all tutors with the simple invitation: 'ask me about sustainability.' By embedding notions of design activism and political reflection into the graphic design degree curriculum at Kingston School of Art (London) graphic authorship (singular) and collective identifications of shared principles gained a firm foundation as core concepts of the discipline.

Whether the design manifesto leads to effective change in professional practice, ethos or philosophy has been contested since Ken Garland's 'First Things First' manifesto (1964) galvanised and then polarised opinion between design as service and design as conscience. Celebrated as a concise call for more meaning in professional practice at the time 'First Things First' has subsequently been criticised as reductive by placing social responsibility in opposition to the commercial sphere of graphic design. *"The critical distinction drawn by the manifesto was between design as communication (giving people necessary information) and design as persuasion (trying to get them to buy things)"* (Poynor 1999, 2). Yet Garland himself rejected any notion of abolishing the contemporary socio-economic and political system as unfeasible: such binary oppositions fail to acknowledge the complex interweaving of design within commerce *and* culture, consumerism and social change. In a development and expansion of the manifesto project Wall of Words represents a more open-ended synthesis of graphic authorship and artefact, focusing on design discourse itself as a dialogic activity captured in visual form.

Visual Rhetoric in Collective Design Activism: Wall of Words

Devised as an explorative component of the second year graphic design degree programme, but curated and produced collectively and collaboratively by the students, the 'Wall of Words' exhibition in January 2017, is introduced in this section as a dialogic mode of visual rhetoric. In a collective process the students involved in this event and exhibition were challenged to increase awareness of design's socio-political agency by responding to the question of how people relate to design discourse itself as a cultural product full of meaning (Melucci, 1996).

The exhibition comprised a selection of poster designs shown in a space adjacent to the original site of the symposium in a central social university location, created in collaborative partnerships between students participating in two electives. The Alternative Art School (AAS) is a student-led autonomous collective concerned with issues relating to contemporary design education and Reign concerns the typography and contemporary media: participation in the show was optional and extra-curricular. The copy used by students was drawn from edited samples of the recorded debates during the symposium.[1] Members of the AAS facilitated and co-presented on the day, while other students captured the atmosphere of debate in the live production of typographic GIFS, presented in the symposium venue during the day. Words and phrases from debates and conversational exchanges during the event were chosen as concise statements (fig 4) or more poetic expressive moments and developed in an intensive studio-based workshop for the Wall of Words show and printed using accessible college resources, exploiting both print and digital media in a social network.

The series of printed posters displaying fragments of debate from the AAS Symposium (1st November 2016), formed ambiguous invitations to the local student population and visiting public to engage in deeper discussions around their content and purpose. The visual language of protest in which form embodies meaning/ideology is co-created by students as mediators of political alternatives in a community of practice. The collaborative group was not fixed but allowed partnerships to shift and reform, and expanded in number as the show's opening neared. Working with a number of social and temporal conditions at that time of year – dark, cold weather, tired students finishing dissertations – the Japanese A2 riso printer provided a rapid and affordable resource for the students. Three colours – flourescent pink, yellow and blue – were chosen to draw attention to the show in a convergence of seeing and reading (fig 5). Experimental layout is employed in this context as a creative strategy to draw attention to the act of reading, leading to a more reciprocal mode of interpretation than conventional graphic design permits. The posters inspired dialogic debate around the issues tackled over the course of the symposium among divergent participants at the exhibition. Students were also delighted when their peers, friends and members of the general public, bought the individual images or enquired about purchasing the whole set. In a collaborative, co-operative and collective process the students created a unified visual argument for their macro and micro concerns around contemporary design education and practice. An unexpected outcome of the exhibition was increased involvement in the socio-political power systems within the university: for instance, the number of active student reps increased from a conventional three, to fifteen, by the end of the year. In addition, as more voices joined the social discursive space, more posters were produced and added to the unframed prints in the show: as a collective exercise, the exhibition and the works therein emerged as accumulative creative acts of design.

---

1   The Alternative Art School (AAS) Symposium, described in more detail in '#AlternativeArtschool // an Interstitial Space for Creative Dissent' (Gale 2017), was based around a number of provocations.

Figure 4: Images form the 'Wall of Words' exhibition, photo by Paul Jenkins.

Figure 5: Images from the Wall of Words exhibition, photo by Paul Jenkins.

The processes and outcomes of a dialogic design approach have been given visual and material form in the Word as Weapon and Wall of Words to provide diverse audiences or participants intellectual access to new ideas and social structures. Muf frame the co-production of socially-engaged art as a dialogic process: *"dialogic projects can change dominant representations of a given community and create a more complex understanding and empathy for the community with a broader public"* (Dodd 2012, 62). The same persuasive pictorial strategies employed in visual communication to increase consumer engagement and gain commercial advantage are deployed here to provoke discourse beyond the echo chamber of design in two pedagogic contexts. For the students, the agency and independence gained from participating in the symposium and exhibition inspired a broader critical perspective of (graphic) design's social, ecological, economic, cultural and political roles.[2]

Summary and conclusions

Designers operate in a multi-layered cultural landscape, a matrix of inter-relationships between media, people and place, within which the designer must always be on alert for unpredictable scenarios, new technologies, economic and political shifts. In pragmatic terms, connectivity, co-operation and hybridity have extended conventional relationships between the designer and audience to incorporate the critical implications of design beyond solely meeting consumer demand. In collaboration or co-operation designers and architects (can) actively contribute to shaping meaning through collaborative communication and, through that, social relations. As the examples from Matrix, Muf and Assemble demonstrate the collective processes of design represent flexible and fluid modes of design practice, in which the boundaries of this social model can be porous and versatile. In an organic sharing of resources – conceptual, creative, pragmatic, experiential – co-operative or collective design groups have resisted the singular author or 'celebrity' status that many designers and architects have sought for personal gain. The multiple demands made on young creatives underpins the necessity of testing alternative models for design practice.

In the context of young design graduates, under extreme pressure to pay back debt while attempting to sustain and build on the innovative ideas and methods developed while in educational institutions, the collective social and creative model offers an alternative. The collective value of design is identifiable through the artefacts and messages that coalesce to form a critical counterpoint to the fused wires of commerce and culture. In a more socially engaged model of collective and collaborative practice that simultaneously enables financial security within a larger group of diverse participants, the collective social inter-relationships facilitate more meaningful reflection on the discipline and practice of graphic design.

---

2   As a collective the Alternative Art School team went on to create two more events – in London and in Berlin – in which dialogic design helped give structure to an otherwise open-ended research project.

Spatial connectedness and ideological purpose inspire more critically-active design processes which coalesce the micro communities at university and the more global networks of the discipline.

Word As Weapon and Wall of Words have illustrated collective and collaborative design as a mode of activism through practice. The projects and shows were devised as educational experiments in forging a knowledge-commons for anyone interested in collective self-organisation, non-hierarchical structures and radical pedagogy but developed through co-creation and co-operation with the students into clearly framed pedagogic alternatives. Through collective action, internal and external discursive creative systems are connected for socio-economic benefit within a larger community, with diverse teams activating the multivalent touch points required for connected audiences. Design activism forms an alternative by challenging narrow definitions of identity and society and activating change by working in common *with* diverse design teams and/or the public. This dialogic method is extended in educational contexts by framing students as partners in a collective relationship underpinned by trust. In answering what a socio-political design means in practice perhaps we can establish some new collective co-operative methodologies or a broader territory of concern affecting the (graphic) designer as a cultural producer and socio-economic agent?

References

Assemble (2017): About. http://assemblestudio.co.uk/?page_id=48 (accessed: 16.08.17).

Barthes, R. (1993): *Mythologies* (trans. Lavers, A.). London: Vintage. Originally published in 1957 Paris: Editions du Seuil.

Bourriaud, N. (2009): *Altermodern: Tate Triennial.* London: Tate Publishing.

Bourton, L. (2016): Envisions Exhibition. http://www.itsnicethat.com/articles/envisions-exhibition (accessed: 24.08.2016).

Cumulus (2017): Call for Papers. http://www.cumulusassociation.org/call-for-papers-cumulus-paris-2018-together-to-get-there/ (accessed: 12.10.17).

Dodd, M. (2012): Practicing Generosity: The Hospitality of Collective Space. In: Edquist, H. and Vaughan, L. (eds.) (2012): *The Design Collective: An Approach to Practice.* Newcastle-upon-Tyne: Cambridge Scholars Publishing. pp. 54-67.

Dunne, A. and Raby, F. (2001): *Design Noir: The Secret Life of Electronic Objects* (Basel: Birkhauser).

Dwyer, J. / Thorne, A. (2007): Evaluating Matrix: Notes from Inside the Collective. In: D. Petrescu (ed.): *Altering Practices: Feminist Politics and Poetics of Space*, Routledge: London.

Edquist, H. and Vaughan, L. (eds.) (2012): *The Design Collective: An Approach to Practice.* Newcastle-upon-Tyne: Cambridge Scholars Publishing.

Experimental Jetset (2009): Experimental Jetset & Nille Svensson (Sweden Graphics). *Iapsis Forum on Design and Critical Practice __ The Reader.* Berlin: Sternberg Press. pp. 90-91.

Fisher, M. (2009): *Capitalist Realism: Is There No Alternative?* Hants: O Books.

Gale, C. (2013): Word As Weapon: Manifesto As A Catalyst For Design Activism. https://www. academia.edu/17930051/Word_As_Weapon_Manifesto_as_a_Catalyst_for_Design_Activism (accessed: 15.08.18).

Gale, C. (2017): #AlternativeArtschool // an Interstitial Space for Creative Dissent. In: *Art, Design & Communication in Higher Education, ADCHE Special Issue: Territories of Graphic Design Education*, Volume 16, Number 1, 1 April 2017, pp. 99-115(17).

Hess, C. / Ostrom, E. (eds.) (2007): *Understanding Knowledge as Commons: From Theory to Practice*. Massachusetts: MIT Press.

Julier, G. (2006): From Visual Culture to Design Culture, *Design Issues*, 22(1): 64-76.

Julier, G. (2011): Introduction. http://www.historiadeldisseny.org/congres/Design_History_Society_Annual_Conference.pdf (accessed: 15.03.17).

Ki-moon, B. (2012): International Year of Cooperatives 2012. https://social.un.org/coopsyear/ (accessed: 15.02.17).

Mason, P. (2016): *PostCapitalism: A Guide to Our Future*. London: Penguin.

Melucci, A. (1996): The Process of Collective Identity. *Challenging Codes: Collective Action in the Information Age*. Cambridge: Cambridge University Press.

Moline, K. (2012): The Legacy of Historical Design Collectives in Contemporary Experimental Design: A Case Study of *Global Tools* and *Digestion* by Matali Crasset. in: Edquist, H. & Vaughan, L. (eds.) (2012): *The Design Collective: An Approach to Practice*. Newcastle-upon-Tyne: Cambridge Scholars Publishing.

Moore, R. (2015): Assemble: the unfashionable art of making a difference. https://www.theguardian.com/artanddesign/2015/nov/29/assemble-architecture-collective-london-turner-prize (accessed: 11.03.16).

Poynor, R. (1999): First Things First Revisited. http://www.emigre.com/Editorial.php?sect=1&id=13 (accessed: 04.05.12).

Poynor, R. (2012): Power By Design. http://www.printmag.com/article/power-by-design/ (accessed: 11.03.16).

Sennett, R. (2012): *Together: The Rituals, Pleasures and Politics of Co-operation*. London: Penguin Books.

United Nations (2017): International Year of Cooperatives 2012. https://social.un.org/coopsyear/ (accessed: 15.02.17).

Vaughan, L. (2012): Design Collectives: More Than the Sum of Their Parts. in Edquist, H. & Vaughan, L. (eds.) (2012): *The Design Collective: An Approach to Practice*. Newcastle-upon-Tyne: Cambridge Scholars Publishing.

Wenger, E. (2010): Communities of Practice and Social Learning Systems: the Career of a Concept: in *Social Learning Systems and Communities of Practice* (ed. Blackmore, C.). The Open University: Milton Keynes.

Williams, Z. (2017): Sexual harassment 101: what everyone needs to know. https://www.theguardian.com/world/2017/oct/16/facts-sexual-harassment-workplace-harvey-weinstein (16 October 2017).

IV. PRINCIPLES AND PRACTICES

IN TIMES OF IRONY AUTHORITY BECOMES OVERWHELMING
A RHETORIC OF SUBVERSION

Pierre Smolarski

Irony and Authority

When the question of a connection of design and activism is asked, the question of a Rhetoric of Subversion emerges as well: subversion because the subverted, the contortion, the overthrowing seems to be an essential motive of any activism; rhetoric because the possibility to influence others with an action, maybe even to convince, but in either case to provide affiliation and identification for potentially like-minded, needs to be a fundamental part of any successful activism. Therefore a Rhetoric of Subversion shall be developed in the following, which is supposed to determine the persuasive potential of activist acts. This Rhetoric of Subversion will initially start with the confrontation of two concepts that stand in various conflicts but nevertheless influence each other in many ways: Irony and Authority. A better understanding of these two terms can contribute to view several essential aspects of our time in a new light and to confront them – especially in the terms of activism – differently.

Irony is an enigmatic term that currently experiences quite a boom. Frequently the motto of our ironic era is: 'This is so terrible, it's already good again' and usually refers to the performances in the entertainment industry, including everything from the TV program to the DIY YouTube video. The constant commentary of comments of the cultural rubbish that is presented to us, enjoy popularity, are positively viral. Their Likes are justified with the own misconception of irony, but basically just show the incapability to produce anything of importance. In 2012 Christy Wampole puts the ironic era in her article in the New York Times in a nutshell, using the archetype Hipster: *"If irony is the ethos of our age – and it is – then the hipster is our archetype of ironic living. The hipster haunts every city street and university town. Manifesting a nostalgia for times he never lived himself, this contemporary urban harlequin appropriates outmoded fashions (the mustache, the tiny shorts), mechanisms (fixed-gear bicycles, portable record players) and hobbies (home brewing, playing trombone). He harvests awkwardness and self-consciousness. Before he makes any choice, he has proceeded through several stages of self-scrutiny. The hipster is a scholar of social forms, a student of cool. He studies relentlessly, foraging for what has yet to be found by the mainstream. He is a walking citation; his clothes refer to much more than themselves. He tries to negotiate the age-old*

problem of individuality, not with concepts, but with material things." (Wampole 2012)
For the ironist in this case applies: *"He doesn't own anything he possesses."* (ibid.)

Irony as a term in this case seems to experience a kind of Renaissance, which makes a criticism of it inevitable, as it is not always clear what one wants to express with it. In its daily appropriation irony usually means a sort of absence. When you meant something "only ironically", it says nothing more than that you did not mean what you said. In the everyday life the ironic changes between an excuse that is supposed to avoid any kind of responsibility, a game of things one does not mean, a gesture of merely messing around and a dilemma that ultimately undermines the own authority auto-subversively. Immunizing oneself against any kind of criticism, like a spell the withdrawal to the irony of the said is supposed to make the said unsaid. Irony in this sense is not being serious.

This everyday use is rooted in a (mis)understanding of irony as a rhetorical figure. The figure of irony does not refer to the fact that one did not mean what was said, but that the exact opposite of it is meant and with that, the whole audience should know what one in fact wanted to say. Thus, the rhetorical figure of irony is in this sense basically a figure of enhancement that exaggerates the severity of the situation dramatically, instead of lacking it. This irony thoroughly depends on being seen as such, which is why there are certain indicators for its presence. The use of such a strong, partly declamatory, but still concentrated on exaggeration, figure is almost diametrically opposed to the auto-subversive undermining of the own authority. This counts particularly because the risk of irony not being seen as such is always given. At the same time the figure owes its impact on the fact that it is always on the verge of inappropriateness, aggravating, teasing and offending the counterpart. This offending is closely connected to the literary figure of Socrates. In the platonic dialogs his offend and attack aims at the assumed certainty of his counterpart, which he has to dissolve through his irony. Different to the previously mentioned kinds of irony, the everyday version and the rhetorical figure, the ironic of Socrates is more of a tactic, instead of a concrete statement. The irony of Socrates can be seen as art of performance, precisely: the disguise to something smaller, an understatement. Socrates ironic behavior is a trick, so the counterpart views themselves in a safe place. On the other a hand a fourth kind of irony that one could call romantic irony, can be distinguished as a general attitude towards certainty. The romantic ironist from Friedrich Schegel to Richard Rorty emphasizes the contingency of certainty.

Rorty determines the Ironists as *"someone who fulfills three conditions: (1) She has radical and continuing doubts about the final vocabulary she currently uses, because she has been impressed by other vocabularies, vocabularies taken as final by people or books she has encountered"* (Rorty 1989, 73).

Several aspects about this are remarkable. First of all, the romantic irony is not a quality of a sentence, not part of a rhetoric strategy. Additionally, the subordinate clause shows that the ironic attitude needs experience. Based on the experience of established vocabularies and speech that gave us orientation, but do not anymore, we get to the conviction of the contingency of all these vocabularies.

"(2) she realizes that argument phrased in her present vocabulary can neither underwrite

nor dissolve these doubts; (3) insofar as she philosophizes about her situation, she does not think that her vocabulary is closer to reality than others, that it is in touch with a power not herself." (ibid.)

According to Rorty the ironist knows – or better: presumes – that the use of vocabularies is not about whether it is closer or further away of a reality that is not touched by vocabularies, but rather that the reality itself only appears in one or the other way through vocabularies. Her choice – if she has one – is not one of the right and the wrong vocabulary, but solely one between the old and the new. *"Ironists who are inclined to philosophize see the choice between vocabularies as made neither within a neutral and universal metavocabulary nor by an attempt to fight one's way past appearances to the real, but simply by playing the new off against the old."* (ibid.)

It is certainly not as simple as that. The exaggeration to a question of old versus new blocks the view on the function of vocabularies as an instrument of power and a tool to rule that we are going to see with Jacques Derrida and Kenneth Burke later on. The old vocabulary is one of a class, it oppresses specific groups and supports some. The new vocabulary shall now support others, also at the cost that once more groups and interests need to be oppressed. It is virtually an essential element of the subversion to elevate the oppressed and bring the supported back to ground. This is the reason why the rhetoric of subversion primarily needs to be the subversion of rhetoric and will be elaborated as such.

We have now touched several kinds of irony, in the hope to stop the vulgar use of that word, and so that especially students of design don't excuse their written and said with alleged irony. After all irony seems to appear sometimes as an escape from responsibility, sometimes as a hyperbole, an expression or snappy punch line, sometimes as a strategy, a temptation or seduction, and also sometimes as a skeptical attitude and rejection of all certainty. What I am driving at now is that to every one of these kinds of irony, there is a corresponding kind of authority. Through that it gets apparent how related and connected these two concepts are. We know the reference to an authority as a rejection of any responsibility, not only with children, but with every segment of society: whether it is the student, who after a critical request about his unreflected, cultural-chauvinistic text in his self-created china magazine, claims the professor had asked for this Lorem-Ipsum-replacement, the government that uses EU instances as an excuse to get away – and in this way prefers to confess one's own, supposed powerlessness rather than one's own unwillingness –, or simply the bus driver who won't open the backdoor, because the instructions say that one should enter in the front. Authority is in all of these everyday examples a place of retreat of the responsibility the own action might bring with it, by putting the responsibility on other instances. Interestingly the retreat to an authority can be seen as ironic, because one is often not willing to accept this authority in other cases.

The irony as a hyperbolic figure emphasizes the rhetorical use that tends to seem empty and inappropriate when the own authority is missing. Thus, the rhetoric irony is not a rejection of authority per se, but rather of the authority of the other. It is like the trick or seduction of the Socratic irony, agonal and fierce. With the

Socratic irony and their reference to authority, we touch the stricter semantic field of authority, as both become apparent as leading and tempting (Führung und Verführung). Authority is primarily a term for social orientation. In any part of life, whether social, religious, scientific, ethical, political or economical, the authority leads or tempts us through unknown territory. Authority is in all of those cases ultimately the power to set an example. And this in two ways: on the one hand authority gives the example of itself, goes forward. On the other hand it allows for examples to create prototypes (Rosch 1978), to set individual cases paradigmatically (paradeigma = gr. example). Based on the attitude of romantic irony the authority gets distinguishable as what it is: an ascription. Authority, that shows the ironic doubt of certainty, is not an attribute of an institution or subject, but is based on processes of appreciation. Rhetorically this understanding is fundamental, because it shows that I can not rely on authorities that I see as such in a persuasive process, but only on those that my audience respects. As a left-winged politician in front of a conservative-market-radical audience, one would not quote Marx, Engels or Lenin, but rather the investor and capitalist George Soros, the thatcherist Charles H. Moore or the star of the conservative FAZ[1]-feuilleton Frank Schirrmacher, who all expressed criticism of capitalism in the context of the financial crisis 2008. Even if a rhetorical use of authority is not always based on an ironic attitude, and with that not always emphasizes the principal contingency of authority, so allows exactly this ironical attitude a way to deal with authority, like Alain de Lille summarizes in the 12th century, when he says: "authority has a wax nose, that is, it can be bent in different directions."[2] Particularly this handling has subversive potential.

Rhetoric of Subversion

Subversion is no exposed term in any rhetorical system.[3] Neither the classical rhetoric nor the *New Rhetoric* formulates a theory of subversion, that is to unfold *subversio* with own goals, strategies and means. A possible reason for that lacking of a rhetorical theory of subversion could be seen in the fact that the subversive act as a corrosive, disintegrative act radically overthrowing social order is in a certain sense always across the rhetoric, understood as an art of planful design of communicative means to establish new or to preserve present orders. As Joachim Knape emphasizes, the disintegrating doubt (Knape 2015) about the given situation is indeed a premise of every rhetorical invention to establish new ways of seeing something, but the persuasive process is finally built not upon doubt but on positive identifications. In short words: Although every rhetorical invention aiming on persuasion works with moments of disintegration and the evocation of doubt – to break the hegemony of the present –, building alone on disintegration will not reach the point of

---

1   The *Frankfurter Allgemeine Zeitung (FAZ)* is a liberal-conservative German newspaper.
2   Alain de Lille qt. after Eco 2007.
3   I have worked out this aspect of rhetoric elsewhere. See Smolarski 2017.

persuasion. To see subversion not only as means but as aim of a rhetorical act, is to understand the subversive as in close relation to irritation, provocation and in this sense to the anti-persuasive (Hagemann 2012) act of destruction and deconstruction (Gondek 1998, 571; Derrida 1986, 46; Derrida 1988, 47) of the prevailing opinions. The rhetoric of subversion, which will be unfolded in this essay, is in a sense the consequent rhetoric of a romantical ironists. The other forms of irony are just parts, sometime means or strategies of that ironic rhetoric.

The subversive is always the inversive, perversive (vertere (lat.) means to turn something, to twist it) and in that way, it is always the incorrect: oppositional characteristics are overthrown, moral values are revaluated, hierarchies are twisted and terms are turned into its opposite. For two reasons those reversals fall into the realm of rhetoric: First, those revaluations affect the linguistic structures, which have, as will be shown afterwards, a heavy impact on social frames of acceptance and are regulating our possibilities of acting. Those impacts can be understood by referring to the *New Rhetoric*, especially the motive-circle unfolded by Kenneth Burke. Second, subversion is meta-rhetorically bounded to the rhetorical process of persuasion itself, insofar as the subversive disintegrations touch the cornerstones of classical rhetorical means of persuasion – like Ethos, Pathos and Logos. A rhetoric of subversion is concerned with the paradox to analyze rhetorical strategies used to act against the persuasive process itself. In this sense a rhetoric of subversion reaches the border of an anti-rhetoric, precisely, of the anti-persuasion. In the following, the paper will help to draw this borderline by analyzing five meta-rhetorical disintegrations. Previously subversion has to be founded on a theory of deconstruction (Derrida) and a rhetorical theory of motive (Burke), which is a term that shapes our relations to our surroundings. Especially the connection to motives is important for any further possible relations to activism, since motives – as will be shown – are situational frames of action.

Deconstruction and Motive-Circle – Derrida and Burke

The premise for any kind of subversion is the existence of an oppositional structure in our use to label phenomena around us, that is an oppositional structure in our language, which is the initial point of the thinking of deconstruction. Derrida calls this kind of thinking *Différance*. Thus, our language and in the following our thinking is full of terminological, hierarchical oppositions, which are to be deconstructed. In a "double gesture"[4] the deconstruction achieves an overturning of classical antagonisms and a displacement of the whole system. The means for such an overturning and displacement are given by a continuous change of

---

4   *"Deconstruction cannot limit itself or proceed immediately to neutralisation: it must, by means of a double gesture, a double science, a double writing, practise an overturning of the classical opposition, and a general displacement of the system. It is on that condition alone that deconstruction will provide the means of intervening in the field of oppositions it criticizes"* (Derrida 1982, 195).

perspective (Kimmerle 1992, 50). Like a guerillero Derrida changes again and again the perspective on our naming – that is: our judging – of things and processes. To understand deconstruction as a practice and not merely as a method "is used by Derrida from a perspective to be taken in each case, which can not be described as a stand-alone viewpoint."[5] Similar to the tactician de Certeau describes, who never holds a fixed position but moves in time mostly dependent from the Kairos, the deconstructor, who wants to undercut and overturn apparently fixed and unshiftable perspectives, may not absolutize a perspective by its own. That's even the critical point in every ironic position, which left the ironic in the moment it refers to a position. Finally, the overturn and disintegration of oppositional structures lead to a *coincidentia oppositorum*, a coincidence of th e opposition, which – unlike Cusanus (1971) – does not seek to nullify the apparentness of opposites in the truth of unity but to show the opposites in their societal conditionality and to open a path into the plurality of perspectives. Thus, it is part of the *intellectio* within a rhetoric of subversion to describe the possibilities of deconstruction by detecting hierarchical oppositions, that is to be conscious that every revealment is at the same time a concealment (Kimmerle 1992, 29). Not only in this respect deconstruction is very close to Burke's understanding of language. He wrote: *"Any given terminology is a reflection of reality, by its very nature as a terminology it must be a selection of reality; and to this extend it must function also as a deflection of reality."* (Burke 1966, 45)

Insofar as both authors – Derrida and Burke – are clear about the fact that there is no usage of terminology and consequently no intellectual point of view, which does not to the extent it may be used to reflect reality also select and therefore deflect reality, for both ways of thinking – deconstruction and New Rhetoric – there is no Archimedean point outside the rhetorical system to analyze the structures of language itself. Derrida points out this subversive aspect of deconstruction: *"Operating necessarily from the inside, borrowing all the strategic and economic resources of subversion from the old structure, borrowing them structurally, that is to say without being able to isolate their elements and atoms, the enterprise of deconstruction always in a certain way falls prey to its own work."* (Derrida 1976, 24)[6]

What leads Derrida to the need of an ironic, radical multi-perspectivity, directs Burke to what he calls a perspective by incongruity, which he describes as *"a method for gauging situations by verbal 'atom cracking'"* (Burke 1984a, 308). He further notes: *"That is, a word belongs by custom to a certain category – and by rational planning you wrench it loose and metaphorically apply it to a different category."* (ibod.) In this way situations are redefined and established views are broken. What Burke termed "trained incapacity" (Burke 1984b, 7–9) after Thorstein Veblen, that is an acquired or trained inability to freely choose meaning, becomes ever again by a consistent perspective by incongruity a free play of signs without center in the sense of Derrida (Pekar 1994). The rhetorical dimension of this subversive process becomes clear when one binds the subversion of hierarchical oppositions to the motive term in

---

5   My translation. See Kimmerle 1992, 24.
6   See also Blakesley 1999, 73.

Burke. Then it will become apparent that the revaluation of the terminological opposition is not simply a hermeneutical practice, but may entail a revolution in the social orientation. It is therefore worth introducing the Burkean motive term for this purpose.

For Burke, motives are explanatory and justifying patterns that describe situations in such a way that actions taken in them become understandable. The term motive is therefore analyzable only in its relation to the terms situation and action, and at the same time always refers to a specific symbolic form of expression of precisely that motive. Thus, the terms motive, situation, action and symbolic form are inseparable for Burke. In *A Grammar of Motives,* he wrote: *"The stage-set contains the action ambiguously (as regard the norms of action) – and in the course of the play's development this ambiguity is converted into a corresponding articulacy. The proportion would be: scene is to act as implicit is to explicit. One could not deduce the details of the action from the details of the setting, but one could deduce the quality of the action from the quality of the setting."* (Burke 1969a, 7)

Although no action can be deduced and explained en detail from a given situation containing (ibid., 3–20) the action – situation does not determine action –, the quality of an action may be derived from the quality of the situation. Insofar, as Burke wrote, these qualities concern 'the norms of action', that is they create the frame of rhetorical acceptance and adequacy, the quality of an action is the underlying motive. The situation quality corresponding to this quality of action can – as Burke seems to understand this correspondence relationship as a bijection – be described as a situational motive. Finally, this is the reason why Burke can say of motives that they are "shorthand terms for situations" (Burke 1984b, 29). In particular, this relationship of situation to motive to action (and vice versa) implies that situations must already be motivational. Otherwise, they would have no quality that could lead to the derivation of any qualification of actions. Situations are thus, unlike sheer or mere events, already provided with action-qualifying and thus action-leading meaning structures. Therefore, situations also belong to the 'realm of action', whereas mere events remain in the 'realm of sheer motion' and do not offer any evaluable or qualifiable meaning structures.

If motives are the core concepts for describing situations and at the same time setting out action frames in the form of acceptance frames, motives thus become the elementary building blocks of any rhetorical practice, especially if *movere* is the goal of the rhetorical efforts (like in most kinds of activism). Inasmuch as the persuasive process is about moving an audience to actions that it would not have done itself anyway, it is always about redefining situations - which means nothing else than recourse to motives: *"One tends to think of a duality here, to assume some kind of breach between a situation and a response [the motive]. Yet the two are identical. When we wish to influence a man's response, for instance, we emphasize factors which he had understressed or neglected, and minimize factors which he had laid great weight upon. This amounts to nothing other than an attempt to redefine the situation itself."* (Burke 1984b, 220)[7]

---

7   See also Blankenship/Murphy/Rosenwasser 1993, 78.

The deconstruction of terminologies can be described with Burke as the deconstruction of motives. Accordingly, it is the task of a subversive deconstruction to make terms in the first place clear as motives, that is, to show that these terms not only describe but also generate situations, and within those situations evaluate certain actions as appropriate and disqualify others as inappropriate. Through the reversal and disintegration of oppositions and hierarchies, a perspective alienation effect can occur which helps to accomplish this task, and which always appears to the degree that it is perceived as disturbing and subversive, as a *perspective by incongruity* (a distorted, disturbed, inappropriate perspective). *"The names we give to motives shape our relations with our fellows. Since they provide interpretations, they prepare us for some function and against others, for or against the person representing these functions. Moreover, they suggest how we shall be for or against. [...] Call a man a villain, and you have the choice of either attacking or cringing. Call him a mistaken and you invite yourself to attempt setting him right."* (Burke 1984a, 4)

Anything that can be attributed to subversive tactics in terms of political and sometimes even emancipatory and enlightening potential is ultimately well grounded in understanding subversion as a reversal of motives, overturning one motive-circle into another, thereby unmasking both at the price, by unmasking itself to follow again a motive that awaits its deconstruction.

Subversion of Rhetoric

Subversion, understood as the recognition (intellectio) of the hierarchical motives and actions of their reversal, uses rhetorical tactics, which are used in particular even if the subversion refers to the rhetorical process itself. Insofar as for Burke language itself is a motive – the medium of domination to enforce certain hierarchies par excellence – a subversion of the rhetorical seems to be the primary goal of any rhetoric of subversion. By this means subversive tactics also show the limits of rhetoric.

In addition, five meta-rhetorical movements are to be distinguished:
a) subversion of the seriousness/earnestness
b) subversion of the rhetorical calculus
c) subversion of the ethos
d) subversion of the pathos
e) subversion of the logos

The main aspects of these forms of subversion are now to be explicated and understood as topoi of the subversive activism.

a) Subversion of Seriousness

Seriousness is a precondition of every rhetorical endeavor. The rhetor (vir bonus) as well as the declaimed subject must be rated serious. Otherwise neither the rhetors statements seem creditable nor would it be possible to change the audiences thinking, feeling or actions. In addition, the manner of treating the subject has to be serious, too.

The first part is connected with the rhetors ethos, the second stresses the pathos, because the assessment whether the topic of the speech is serious or not correlates with the audience's attitudes, opinions (doxa) and mood. Both cases will be discussed in part c) Subversion of the ethos and d) Subversion of the pathos. The third part has aspects of a process technology because seriousness is a keystone of every social community and social order. It regulates different phenomena such as the possibility to advance an academic view, the orders of a court case or the foundation of political parties.[8] All these examples have in common, that the formation of an speech-act depends on its seriousness (Austin 1972, 38–45 and 58–63). Odo Marquard points out: *"Funny and inciting to laugh is what makes the void visible in what is officially valid and the valid in what is officially null and void." (Marquard. Qt. After Hügli 1001, 15)*[9]. Thus procedures can be subverted by explaining constitutive aspects of the procedure for void or by claiming totally unimportant parts of the procedure for relevant. In this way either satire, comedy and parody prosper by reversal. Especially the classical comedy can often develop its critical function strongly by placing the venues of current political events in a trivializing setting. This turns validities into vanities and vice versa. In his definition of the comedy, Aristotle describes this as follows: *"The comedy is an imitation of the ridiculous as a special kind of the ugly and vile: it is a deficiency and something shameful, but that neither hurts nor brings to ruin."* (Arist. Poet., 1449a31-33) Cicero continues this provision to the conclusion that the comic is a certain kind of ugliness, but which is not rendered ugly, so that it is a form of disappointed expectation and that the result is in no relation to expectations (Hügli 2001). However, the subversive is also reflected in everyday practices, for example if children play a game in which they copy the behavior patterns of their families. What children represent seriously in this game are often, in terms of the social image of the family and from the perspective of adults spoken, inactions of everyday life, transformed by their play from their casual status into a substantial. However, this game only gets a subversive character if it is interpreted by adults. Here, too, the subversive power of Burke's perspective by incongruity is shown. But 'actual subversion', however, should only be discussed if it does not remain on the stage alone, where it may in fact not hurt or corrupt in the sense of Aristotle, but rather in places where it is not expected, – in short – if it is not the situation that the comic action already suggests, but the comical reversal is somehow produced by the subversive motive at all.

---

8   For Germany, see: §2.1 'Deutsches Parteiengesetz'.
9   My Translation.

b) Subversion of the rhetorical Calculus

"You persuade a man only insofar as you can talk his language by speech, tonality, order, image, attitude, idea, identifying your ways with his." (Burke 1969b, 55) Burke points out that the mutual identification of rhetor and audience forms the fundament of persuasion. In the terms of the New Rhetoric, 'identification' offers the possibility to understand 'persuasion'. Rhetoric is in this respect an art of overcoming given divisions by using identifications.[10] Especially effective are rhetorical strategies to create identification if they can't be identified by the audience as purposes of an *attentum parare, captatio benevolentia* or *perspicuitas* but sound somehow 'naturally'. Therefore, *dissimulatio artis*[11], the concealment of the artificial, is the main part of rhetorical strategies. Thus, it is a central rebuttal strategy to dissimulate the *dissimulatio* itself, to show that what seemed to be so natural for the opposing party and seemed to be so good to the audience's ideas, was simply populism. But this is nothing but the subversion, the decomposition of the opposing rhetorical calculus. In this case, however, the subversion is not the aim but only an instrument. However, a rhetoric of subversion must also illuminate the borderline case, in which subversion is the purpose and destroys its own aid: the persuasion. To see subversion as a purpose implicates to see it as anti-persuasive. In principle, two tactics can be distinguished. On the one hand, the own *dissimulatio* can be continually dissimulated, which puts the audience in such uncertainty, that it finally does not know what to believe and how to identify – the consistently deconstructive reading seems to follow this direction. It is the highly annoying-subversive art of consequent ironic speech. In this case, although offers of *identification* are made, they are always recognizable as *offers* of identification. This is the way Kierkegaard describes the anti-persuasive rhetoric, which for him the Christian speech should be: *"According to Kierkegaard, antipersuasive rhetoric must not advertise, in particular, it does not recommend Christianity to the benevolence of the listener, but rather makes him take offence at it. The Christian is offensive, the Christian speech a provocation for the nature of man. Also, a thorny path must not be weighed against the probability of salvation, but rather it must be described as the completely improbable that it is. 'Christian eloquence would differ from Greek eloquence in that it has to do with improbability alone, in showing that it is improbable, so that one can believe it.'"* (Hagemann 2012, 47)[12]

On the other side is it possible to avoid any offer of identification consequently. In this case, the rhetorical action, where it is not simply incomprehensible, will provoke a great impetus and thereby attract a great deal of attention, although it will experience little consent and benevolence. Insults of the audience, direct attacks on the same, which are not justified, or even making a laughingstock out of the audience are typical tactics of this type. In a radical form, this type of subversion no longer plays only with the limits of rhetoric, but transcends them and can be

---

10   For more details see Richards 2008, 161–175, or Kramer 2012.
11   See Népote-Desmarres/Tröger 1994. See also Till 2009.
12   My translation.

regarded as rhetorically failed. In a moderate form, however, this type is embedded in a rhetorical process which, above all, wants to use the advantage – the high attention – without giving up any endeavor of persuasion. As such, this type serves as a basis for aggressive advertising, which wants to place a brand or product on the market, also at the risk to kick people in the teeth. In this case, subversion is again not a purpose, it is a means in the persuasive process, but is simulated as a purpose. In short, the subversion is a common means of refuting and attacking opposing positions – in this way Aristotle's 'sophistical refutations' or Schopenhauer's eristic rhetoric could be read. If subversion is simulated as a purpose, we leave every ethical concept of an orator as a *vir bonus* and enter the – quite rhetorical – field that extends from showmanship to guerrilla marketing. As a real purpose, subversion remains in the field of rhetoric only if it occurs as ironic and deconstructive.

c) Subversion of the Ethos

Ethos is one of the three means of persuasion of classical rhetoric and describes the reasons for conviction that arise from the character of the speaker. It is not the actual congruence of the imagination of an audience with a speaker's values and his or her actual way of life that is primary, but rather the self-representation of the speaker, following on from the ideas and prejudices that already exist about him or her. In this way, for example, announcements of speakers (conferences) already serve to build ethos by emphasizing their expertise; small concessions of one's own weaknesses strengthen ethos by emphasizing one's own virtue; and when an American presidential candidate says "I was a farm boy myself" (Burke 1969b, xiv) in front of an audience of farmers, it provides an identification basis for those farmers which should enhance their goodwill. Expertise, virtue and benevolence represent the dimensions of ethos for Greek rhetoric and beyond.[13] A subversion of ethos will therefore find three places of attack: an undermining of expertise, virtue or benevolence, but also the possibility of suspending the entire category of ethos. Possible tactics used are any kind of ethos-parasitism, ranging from parodistic or satirical imitations to exaggerated monkeys and, above all, to ridicule the speaker.[14] This will be all the easier the higher the ethos of the speaker is proclaimed in the course of his self-portrayal and the greater the rupture will be. In fact, the ethos of the opponent can also be used parasitically to produce forgeries, false reports, false quotations and fakes that are either used to legitimize something and draw it from the parasitic use of a foreign ethos, or infiltrate the ethos of the opponent himself. This will be all the easier and more successful if ethos is not only understood as a factor for a speaker, but also related to what is meant by corporate image. With their corporate identity, large brands in particular are establishing signs that stand for the

---

13   See Plato: Gorgias. Kallikles functions in this dialogue as a touchstone of argumentation, because he is characterised by knowledge, goodwill and openness. See also Arist. Rhet. 1378a15f.

14   As Gorgias notes, you have to destroy your opponent's seriousness with laughter and his laughter with eager seriousness. Arist. Rhet. 1419b2ff.

corporate values of the company and are easy to use and alienate for subversive purposes.[15] One possible result of successful tactics of a subversion of ethos is the suspension of the entire category by revealing it in its strategies of ethos generation, as with other forms of subversion.

In contrast to subversive tactics of suspending the ethos category, a non-subversive case must finally be mentioned: Insofar as ethics is a means of persuasion that cancels out the distinction of genesis (Genese) and validity (Geltung) and makes the value of a thought, in the sense of its credibility, dependent on its genesis, and especially on the person or institution that represents it, it is a common strategy, especially in the case of a dubious ethos, to endorse the distinction of genesis and validity. However, this practice cannot be called subversive, because it does not undermine the category by a reversal, but dodges to a logos argumentation in order to be able to cover the ethos deficit persuasively.

d) Subversion of the pathos

Pathos is the means of persuasion, which works mainly with the emotions of the audience. More emotional topics in particular, and topics on which there are strong social conceptions, norms and conventions, can hardly be discussed without emotional linking (in the sense of identification) to them. A failure of the pathos thus has several faces: On the one hand, total neglect of the pathos can lead to the orator being denied empathy, goodwill or even expert knowledge (damage to ethos), on the other hand, pathos always generates more or less strong emotions which, if used correctly, can increase the attention and willingness of the audience to be convinced, but can also fall back negatively on the orator. A precise knowledge of what the audience thinks is worthy and unworthy is therefore the prerequisite for a successful pathos argumentation and equally successful subversion of the pathos. In the area of pathos, the subject of the persuasive speech is above all the positive reference to the desirable, respected, in short, normal and the negative reference to the outlawed, despised, in short, the perverted in the broadest sense of the word.[16] Consequently, a subversion of the

---

15   Referring to David Ogilvy - "a brand is the costumers' idea of a product" (229) -, Zec develops an understanding of the brand as an idea that interacts with other ideas. For Zec, the brand designates the non-static idea that the consumer has of both the products and the company. He states: *"Even if it always seems as though a particular characteristic of the brand is its unequivocal identifiability, this appearance is deceptive in that it obscures the essence of the brand. This is because the trademark must always be characterized by both ambiguity and self-similarity in order to remain a trademark"* (my translation, 231) Quotes from Zec 2001, 227-250.

16   Normal' is understood here as a combat term in opposition to the term 'perversion'. As such, it is based less on a clear definition than on current recognised values. Similar to the term 'natural', the proclamation of the 'normal' is used, depending on the context, to justify any, even contradictory theses. 'Perversion' summarizes in a general sense, as the wrong, what is done contrary to accepted norms, a whole range of possible counter-concepts to the 'normal', among other things: the antisocial, the crazy, *"unwillingness to work, disturbance of the life and family happiness of other people, lust for crime, sexual violations of norms"* (my translation, Pfäfflin 1989, 379).

pathos consists above all in recognizing and reversing normality and perversion as hierarchical oppositions. Normal is perverse, perverted is normal. This is all the more so if perversion is not only a sexual violation of norms, but perversion (in perversum (lat.) - in the wrong, twisted way) is generally a violation of norms. Subversion is therefore always perversion – even if not every perversion has to be subversive. Insofar as such a reversal does not offer a broad basis for identification, but rather pushes the division, the reference to the subversion of the rhetorical calculus becomes apparent. Possible tactics in the service of a subversion of the pathos are given by the use of alienating or breaking effects. The targeted use of vulgar language can be just as useful as provocative obscenities or the ridiculing of common values. A special form of subversion of the pathos is cynicism. "Cynical is the refusal to concede something tragic to human suffering and action." (Zinsmaier 2009, 1601) In this definition of cynicism, it becomes clear that cynical language is based on a negation of values (like irony) and thus of the entire pathos. In this way Oscar Wilde can also say that: "Cynicism is merely the art of seeing things as they are instead of as they ought to be." (Oscar Wilde qt. after Zinsmaier 2009, 1602) Insofar as there will hardly be any socially relevant subject matter that is completely free of pathos and completely independent of any values at all, cynicism always represents an *perspective by incongruity*, which not only allows an unusual, sometimes shocking and disconcerting view of the subject matter, but is even able to cancel it as a socially relevant subject matter of the investigation. A subversion of the pathos through cynicism thus also undermines broad societal assumptions of relevance.

e) Subversion of the logos

As a fifth form of subversion, the subversion of the logos can be considered. It is not a refutation or an attack on the argumentation structure of the opponent, a demonstration that the argumentation of the opponent is a pseudo-argumentation and therefore logically not sustainable, because this refutation leaves the structure of the logos intact. To call it subversive, on the other hand, would undermine the possibility of the logos at all, for example by reversing sense and nonsense. In this sense, the avant-garde in particular, and especially Dadaism, turned out to be subversive in that the latter radically cuts off the connection between word (verba) and meaning (res). In what is arguably the most obvious opposition within the res-verba problem, from an absolute determination, which Ivor A. Richards describes as "a proper meaning superstition" (Richards 1936, 11), and an absolute indetermination, according to which words simply mean nothing, the rhetoric, as the doctrine, whose objects can always mean something else (see Arist. Rhet. 1357a12.), always moves between the poles. Dadaistic sound poems, collages, performances and other forms of performance, on the other hand, irritate the limits of the variety of meanings until the possibility of attribution of meaning disappears anyway. When Kurt Schwitters says that the artist creates through "choice, distribution and demolding"[17], he clearly follows the rhetorical production phases of inventio, dispositio and elocutio. On the other hand, however, the elocutio, as demolding, in Schwitter's words means "sucking out the self-poison"[18] of the materials used, in short: a complete (ideally) emptying of the senses. On the one hand, it can be said that an action that actually transforms every sense into nonsense – be it a speech, a happening or something else – simply falls out of the realm of rhetoric, but this very transformation performance remains bound to rhetorical tactics. As much as it is a rhetorical achievement to steer attributions of meaning by an audience in such a way that the orator can say that he has been understood, so much so it is also a rhetorical achievement to consistently let attributions of meaning run into the void. The procedures chosen for both purposes will most likely be the same, with the opposite sign. In this respect, the subversion of the logos is based on a radical violation of the rhetorical virtues of perspicuitas, latinitas and ornatus.

All these forms of subversion clearly show one aspect which leads us back to the relation of irony and authority. Subversion needs affirmation, every subversive treatment of media needs a common sense, a basic concept which is accepted. Irony needs serious authority. Where this seriousness is lacking, where obstacles are removed and everything to say is equally possible and or irrelevant, there can be no activism. Obstacles which have to be overcome and the feeling of power because of this overcoming form is the source of all subversive and also all political action. The ironic form of oppression is the lie of powerlessness, which is laughing at the onrushing activist and thinks he is merely tilting at windmills, which has always been allowed and has always been ridiculous.

References

Aristoteles (2002): Rhetorik. In: Hellmuth Flashar (Ed.): *Werke in deutscher Übersetzung*. Translated by Christof Rapp. Vol. 4/1. Berlin.

Aristoteles (2008): Poetik. In: Hellmuth Flashar (Ed.): *Werke in deutscher Übersetzung*. Translated by Arbogast Schmitt. Vol. 5. Berlin.

Austin, John L. (1972): *Zur Theorie der Sprechakte*. Stuttgart.

Blakesly, Davis (1999): Kenneth Burke's Pragmatism – Old and New. In: Bernhard L. Brock (Ed.): *Kenneth Burke and the 21st Century*. Albany. pp. 71-95.

Blankenship, Jane / Murphy, Edward Murphy / Rosenwasser, Marie (1993): Pivotal Terms in the Early Works of Kenneth Burke. In: Barry Brummett (Ed.): *Landmark Essays on Kenneth Burke*. Davis. pp. 71-90.

Burke, Kenneth (1966): *Language as Symbolic Action. Essays on Life, Literature and Method*. Berkeley.

Burke, Kenneth (1969a): *A Grammar of Motives*. Berkeley.

Burke, Kenneth (1969b): *A Rhetoric of Motives*. Berkeley.

---

17 Schwitters cit. after Wiesing 1991, 21.
18 Schwitters cit. after Wiesing 1991, 102.

Burke, Kenneth (1984a): *Attitudes toward History.* Berkeley.

Burke, Kenneth (1984b): *Permanence and Change. An Anatomy of Purpose.* Berkeley.

Cusanus (1971): *Mutmaßungen: lateinisch-deutsch.* Translated by Josef Koch. Hamburg.

Derrida, Jacques (1982): *Margins of Philosophy,* trans. Bass, Chicago: University of Chicago Press.

Derrida, Jacques (1986): *Positionen. Gespräche mit Henri Ronse, Julia Kristeva, Guy Scarpetta.* Wien.

Derrida, Jacques (1988): *Randgänge der Philosophie.* Wien.

Derrida, Jacques (1976): *Of Grammatology.* Baltimore.

Eco, Umberto (2007): *Über Gott und die Welt.* München.

Hagemann, Tim (2012): Antipersuasive Rhetorik. In: Ueding, Gerd (Ed.): *Historisches Wörterbuch der Rhetorik.* Vol. 10. Berlin/Boston. pp. 45-51.

Gondek, Hans-Dieter (1998): Subversion. In: Joachim Ritter; Karlfried Gründer (Ed..): *Historisches Wörterbuch der Philosophie.* Vol. 10. Basel. pp. 567-572.

Hügli, Anton (2001): Lachen, das Lächerliche. In: Ueding, Gerd (Ed.): *Historisches Wörterbuch der Rhetorik.* Vol. 5. Tübingen. pp. 1-17.

Kimmerle, Heinz (1992): *Derrida zur Einführung.* Hamburg.

Kramer, Olaf (2012): Identifikation. In: Ueding, Gerd (Ed.): *Historisches Wörterbuch der Rhetorik.* Vol. 10. Berlin/Boston, pp. 372-379.

Népote-Desmarres, Fanny / Tröger, Thilo (1994): Dissimulatio. In: Ueding, Gerd (Ed.): *Historisches Wörterbuch der Rhetorik.* Vol. 2. Tübingen. pp. 886-888.

Pekar, Thomas (1994): Dekonstruktion. In: Ueding, Gerd (Ed.): *Historisches Wörterbuch der Rhetorik.* Vol. 2. Tübingen. pp. 512-521.

Pfäfflin, Friedemann (1989): Perversion. In. Joachim Ritter; Karlfried Gründer (Ed.): *Historisches Wörterbuch der Philosophie.* Vol. 7. Basel. pp. 379-382.

Platon (1957): Gorgias. In: Walter F. Otto; Ernesto Grassi (Ed.): *Sämtliche Werke.* Vol. 1. Hamburg. pp. 447-527.

Richards, Ivor A. (1936): *The Philosophy of Rhetoric.* Oxford.

Richards, Jennifer (2008): *Rhetoric.* New York.

Rorty, Richard (1989): *Contingency, Irony and Solidarity.* Cambridge University Press.

Rosch, Eleanor (1978): Principles of Categorization. In: *Cognition and categorization.* Ed. by Eleanor Rosch und Barbara B. Lloyd. Hillsdale. pp. 27-48.

Schopenhauer, Arthur (2009): *Die Kunst, Recht zu behalten.* Hamburg.

Smolarski, Pierre (2017): *Rhetorik des Designs. Gestaltung zwischen Subversion und Affirmation.* Transcript, Bielefeld.

Till, Dietmar (2009): Verbergen der Kunst. In: Gerd Ueding (Ed.): *Historisches Wörterbuch der Rhetorik.* Vol. 9. Tübingen. pp. 1034-1041.

Wampole, Christy (2012): How to live without Irony. (The Stone. The New York Times. November 17, 2012). https://opinionator.blogs.nytimes.com/2012/11/17/how-to-live-without-irony/

Wiesing, Lambert (1991): *Stil statt Wahrheit. Kurt Schwitters und Ludwig Wittgenstein über ästhetische Lebensformen.* München.

Zec, Peter (2001): Die Rolle des Design bei der Entwicklung von Marken. In: Manfred Bruhn (Ed.): *Die Marke. Symbolkraft eines Zeichensystems.* Bern. pp. 227-250.

Zinsmaier, Thomas (2009): Zynismus, Kynismus. In: Gerd Ueding (Ed.): *Historisches Wörterbuch der Rhetorik.* Vol. 9. Tübingen. pp. 1594-1606.

BEAUTIFUL STRANGENESS REVISITED
GENERATIVE, DISRUPTIVE, FABULATIVE, DESIGN-LED ACTIVISM

Alastair Fuad-Luke

The etymological root of care is grief. Care underpinned a call I made in 2009 for 'new visions of beauty' to address issues of sustainability, which I called 'beautiful strangeness', manifest in a brief set of principles (Fuad-Luke 2009). Grief was framed as the paradigmatic consequences of the axiological and existential impacts of economic, technical and political structures of European and North American ('Western') globalization, today further amplified by China, India and other emergent economies. Stone-Richards recently referred to these effects as, *"the violence of late modernity captured in the wasteful logic of para-state vampirism"* (Stone-Richards 2011). Strong words indeed, but we should acknowledge that we live in a period of neoliberal transnational capitalism where the marginalised in society are, shockingly, in the majority and environmental degradation goes unabated. So, I revisit my original conceptualization of beautiful strangeness to flesh out its mode of being, acting and making worlds in order to revitalize a sense of urgency to address our human|non-human contingent realities. I hope to give it more visibility and potential agency. Furthermore, I hope to posit renewed teleological possibilities for those who wish to extend the emergent practices of design-led activism as counter-narratives, dialogues and actions.

The key tenets of the micro-manifesto of beautiful strangeness I laid out invoked a beauty that:
- is not quite familiar, tinged with newness, ambiguity and intrigue.
- services all in society, healing society's divides.
- is adaptable to changing circumstances.
- does not de-future.[1]
- encourages new ideals, values and concepts of humankind's 'growth' beyond the blinkered thinking of neoliberal economic growth as 'progress'.

---

1   Here I referred to Tony Fry's concept of design as an activity that precludes certain futures, i.e. de-futures, by removing options for future generations. For example, by designing products or services that make resources unavailable in the future. The concept of de-futuring implies that the designing does not satisfy, or even denies, our fundamental human needs and destroys ecological capacity for future generations (Fry 2008). Manfred Max-Neef referred to these ways of doing things that do not meet our needs as pseudo-satisfiers or destroyers (Max-Neef 1991).

– acts in the 'now' while being aware of its ability to prefigure and give directionality (Willis 2006).

– democratises decision making through design to better reflect society as a whole.

This framing of beautiful strangeness was itself framed within a framework for design activism referencing Design for Sustainability pitted against neoliberal transnationalism (of governments, corporations and transnational organizations). Such neoliberal transnationalism was, earlier, identified and described by Felix Guattari as Integrated World Capitalism (IWC) – IWC *"is delocalized and deterritorialized to such an extent that it is impossible to locate the source of its power"* (Guattari 2014). Guattari noted that we are being *"mentally manipulated through the production of a collective, mass-media subjectivity"* (ibid.) and, so, to counter this there was a need for [new] mental ecology. Guattari wrote this in 1989, prior to the mass accessibility to desktop computers, mobile phones and the Internet. We could argue today that the *transmedia* subjectivity promoting IWC has intensified immensely colonizing the minds and daily realities of vast swathes of the human population, seducing governments and societies while further imperiling *us* in *our* biosphere. This worldmaking (Goodman 1978, 6)[2] is persistently brought into being, and reinforced, by what Petra Hroch calls 'images of thought' that generate an undifferentiated, capitalized, designed, materialized, hegemonic world-view (Hroch 2015). I have characterized this materialised world of IWC as *pharmaka-design*, that is things that are designed and act paradoxically as medicine *and* poison, meeting real and false needs through being 'pseudosatisfiers' or 'destroyers' that destroy other human and non-human freedoms (Fuad-Luke 2013). In their omnipresence, these designed things fulfil some needs, that is they can be 'satisfiers', but also act as palliatives, sedatives, toxins and placebos hiding their ugliness. They do not reveal the ethics of true-cost economics (Foundation Earth 2017), their coming into being is not through democratic processes, they hide social injustice and ecological disaster, and they continue to de-future. As these affects and effects intensify, there is an urgency to deepen our understanding of the philosophical, design and social *poïesis* (Ancient Greek) of beautiful strangeness. Poïesis, here, is defined as *an action that transforms and continues the world.*

Strangeness as differentiation from, and deterritorialisation of, IWC

All design plays a part in aestheticisation of experience (Folkman 2013) and, the act of designing is, somewhere, underpinned by a paradigmatic position supported by products, projects, programs and practices that can only be opened up with reference to Aristotle's concept of poïesis (Redström 2017, 36-41). The IWC socio-technical

---

2   Goodman noted that *"Worldmaking as we already know it always starts from worlds already on hand; the making is remaking"* (ibid.). In this sense I think remaking is also re-relationing, that is re-configuring relations.

regime de-futures through its inability, or unwillingness, to internalize the real costs of its goods to society and the environment within the market price of those goods. IWC rejects true-cost economics whose aim is that sustainable goods would be less costly than unsustainable goods where externalized costs are *added* to the market price making them more expensive. I argue, below, that a new approach is needed where there is an integration of design with philosophical and social considerations to re-envision a poïetic aesthetics to counter IWC. As philosophers Deleuze and Guattari note, and Petra Hroch emphasizes, activist design practices to *"re-conceptualise existing 'problems' and re-organise existing territories in order to contribute to the design of more equitable and yet* difference-sustaining connections *among humans and their more-than human environments"* (my non-italics) (Hroch 2015, 229). To enact this requires what Hroch calls a *deterritorialising* of the domains of thought, and, I would argue, achieves this partly through direct participation and action. This, I suggest, requires a placing of strangeness to disturb the hegemonic domains of thought that constitute IWC. Again, in Deleuze and Guattari's terms this strangeness means 'newness' in terms of the production of ongoing differentiation as an 'intensive resistance' (ibid., 221-222). This means moving well beyond the newness peddled by IWC that faithfully follows Raymond Lowey's formula of Most Acceptable Yet Advanced, MAYA, or the introduction of the new as a programme of planned obsolescence to protect market share. So, the 'strangeness' appropriate here is that the aesthetics are not driven just by market values, but by multi-valent concerns for human|non-human *co-futures*. The strangeness *should* disturb your thoughts and actions.

Intrinsic, extrinsic and 'futuric' beauty

Beauty, in 'beautiful strangeness', has, for me, specific characteristics. There is the intrinsic, tangible, material beauty that is constituted in properties of the artifact that deliver an extrinsic beauty constituting properties of the *affect* of the artifact, its processes and experiences, i.e. how we feel, are emotional, think and respond. Lastly, but most importantly there is what I will call 'futuric' beauty, that is the *effect* of the artifact on possible human|non-human co-futures. What habits does it reinforce or change? Does it prevent certain futures, does it permit or encourage others? This third, temporal, characteristic of beauty is essential to challenge the aesthetic regime of IWC. Furthermore, it embraces and yet goes beyond dimensions of Thomas Markussen's notion of the 'disruptive aesthetics' of design activism which tend to be oriented in the present (Markussen 2011). Temporal aesthetic concerns have been expressed by those exploring a new environmental aesthetics (Maskit 2011; Orr 2002), and through eco-efficiency by applying eco-design and sustainable product service systems (Fuad-Luke 2002; Manzini/Jégou 2003; McDonough/Braungart 2003). However, the latter approaches are, arguably, easily absorbed into the market and, hence, normalized through IWC practices. The intrinsic and extrinsic within beautiful strangeness must address the 'futuric' in order not to de-future and be degenerative. Instead, this beauty must be generative and re-generative.

Towards an integrated poïesis of beautiful strangeness

A philosophical poïesis

If philosophy is the creation of concepts (Deleuze/Guattari 1994) how can it act and transform the world? It acts by interrogating and shifting perceptual thought and space. In doing so, it changes what happens now and next. Thus phrased, it sounds as if there are many synergies with design(-ing) and conceptual art. Numerous philosophical stones give foundation to beautiful strangeness. I will select a few that appeal to me, you, reader, may have your own.

The Three Ecologies was written by Felix Guattari in 1989. It came after a decade of neo-liberalism promoted by President Ronald Reagan in the USA and Prime Minister Margaret Thatcher in the UK. They presided over the de-regulation of markets by the state and initiated instantaneous computerized financial trading, colloquially known as the 'big bang', that were key antecedents contributing to the global financial crash of 2007/2008. Guattari's interpretation of 'ecology' deeply questions the subjectivity of capitalist power relations through an intertwining of mental, social and environmental ecologies (Guattari, ibid.). The ecology of the mind targets the modes of production and subjectivity; the ecology of the social focuses on the rebuilding of human relations at every level of the socius; and the ecology of environment centres on an environment as a continual process of reinvention, well beyond the constraints of the human:nature binary. Nicholas Bourriaud referred to Guattari's ecologies as a *potential* aesthetics and as an ethical-cum-political articulation between the environment, the social and subjectivity (Bourriaud 2002, 86, 101). We then need to address how the aesthetic emerges through these subjectivities. For this Bourriaud's concept of 'relational aesthetics' (Bourriaud 2002) and Jacques Ranciere's concept of an 'aesthetic regime' and its control of the 'distribution of the sensible' (Rancière 2013, 86) are useful. They see aesthetics as a socio-political process rather than simply the intrinsic and extrinsic properties of an artifact or experience. Relational (aesthetics) is an *"aesthetic theory consisting in judging artworks on the basis of the inter-human relations which they represent, produce and prompt"* (Bourriaud 2002, 112). Here we can extend artworks to 'designworks'. Bourriaud sees aesthetics as deeply relational, and therefore always marked by social processes. Ranciere's position is summarized as *"aesthetics as the distribution of the sensible that determines a mode of articulation between forms of action, production, perception and thought"* (Ranciere 2013, 86). Markussen picks up on Ranciere's understanding of dissensus to place design activism as aesthetic disruption through a way of doing things in a designerly way that produces a horizon of affects (Markussen 2011, 105-106), but hesitates in going further to discuss how the relationality of these modes of articulation might effect a socio-political, and therefore aesthetic, regime.

IWC, with its omnipresent reach through transmedia, has the ability to dominate our images of thought through its hegemonic distribution of its version of the sensible. So, how do we disturb the IWC aesthetic regime, how do we create new relational aesthetics, new distributions of the sensible? In short, we have to unbalance the regime by making what Jean Francois Lyotard calls *paralogic moves* (Woodward, unknown).[3] Lyotard sees innovation as being controlled by the system, so we have to make a move, the impact of which we are not absolutely sure other than that it goes *beyond* the rules of the system.

Beautiful strangeness also insists that the discourse of aesthetics moves beyond the passive gaze of the spectator as conferred by the creator or curator, to an active participation of the *spect-actor*, the co-creator.[4] Moreover, the futurity implicit in the aesthetics i.e. beyond the immediate aesthetic experience of the here and now, is central to the concept of beautiful strangeness. Beautiful strangeness must strive for active, inter-generational and inter-human|non-human aesthetical experiences and possibilities. Furthermore, it must help develop new mental, social and environmental ecologies, especially challenging the socius of IWC by developing new relations, through new channels and unexpected moves.

A design poïesis

Design-led activism acts within and on conceptualized, actualized and realized worlds while simultaneously being activist *on* the 'world' of design itself (Fuad-Luke 2009). Design-led activism re-conceptualises and re-materialises design as interventions, interruptions, irritations through unexpected acts, paralogic moves and processes. Design-led activism is re-constituted through human and non-human 'complementary relational designers' as 'relational design' (Fuad-Luke 2014)[5] and as an 'intra-domain mode of thought' (Hroch 2015). Design, in this sense, can be seen as an 'undiscipline' or 'practice-based knowledge-utilisation discipline' (Harfield 2008) or as 'design without discipline' (Bremner/Rodgers 2013), because design, when it is activist, is both fertile and promiscuous with other disciplines.

To qualify as beautiful strangeness the design act(-ion) cannot simply be to bring attention to or raise awareness of an issue or to posit things as questions about the future. A design that entails beautiful strangeness must exercise direct participation,

---

3   *"Paralogy is the movement beyond or against reason. Lyotard sees reason not as a universal and immutable human faculty or principle but as a specific and variable human production; 'paralogy' for him means the movement against an established way of reasoning. In relation to research, this means the production of new ideas by going against or outside of established norms."* (Woodward, unknown).

4   Augustus Boal created the word 'spect-actor' to indicate that we are all actors and spectators in life, and switch continuously between the two. See, http://beautifultrouble.org/theory/theater-of-the-oppressed/, accessed 01 November 2017. This concept is important when we consider collaborative, participatory, and open or co-design activities and how creative exchanges take place.

5   *"Complementary relational designers' are professional designers, other professionals designing, pro-am designers, amateur designers and citizen designers; 'Relational design' is an evolving set of design practices which found their theoretical and practical directionality on the whole of human and non-human interaction within their social context. This involves considering the human and non-human actors, actants and their socialy perceived and understood material assemblages as a unified living entity with mutual and respectful relationality. Impicit in relation design is the embedding of an ethically driven design enquiry."* (Fuad-Luke 2014).

wherever possible, that encourages or enables paralogic moves and generative constructions in the present that *disrupt* the [IWC] present, that generate diverse things to *displace* the currently projected future [IWC]. My insistence on people participating, by applying the principles of co-design and relational design, is to see the humans|non-humans active in the designing process, that is, creating *actions* together. It is not sufficient to simply aesthetically disrupt in a Markussian sense, the disruptions have to be personal, participatory, and beyond our anthropocentric gaze. This includes deciding what should be designed for whom and who could or will benefit, human and/or non-human. For me this is always at the root of my design-led activism. This is where, I believe, some of the beauty and the strangeness is generated; it is held deeply within the collective and individual actions. In this sense, Koskinen's proposal for an agonistic, convivial and conceptual aesthetics of social design, an aesthetics of action in 'new social design'[6] feels aligned, although I have noted elsewhere that the framing of design activism confers greater teleological freedoms to change our habitus than social design (Fuad-Luke 2015). Social design can be constrained by negotiated interests in representative democracy dominated by key stakeholders in existing power structures.

However, with all this stressing of participatory design processes, we should also not lose sight of maverick designers or design researchers intervening of their own volition to activate or catalyse participation or actions. Many of these maverick designers contribute to the debates around critical, speculative and adversarial design (DunneRaby 2013; Malpass 2017; DiSalvo 2012). However, to enact beautiful strangeness more effectively they need to move more into the field where other professionals and citizens can be actively involved beyond the confines of the lab and showroom (Koskinen et al. 2011). Markussen also notes that Di Salvo's adversarial design positions itself more as contesting power and authorities, but is less forthcoming as to *"how activist artifacts may also enter directly into the realm of real-life human interactions" (Markussen 2011, 105)*. I suggest that the maverick designers need to think more about their strategic and tactical approaches to interventions and how they can, and should, move between dissensus and consensus, between agreement, agonism and antagonism in direct participatory social settings (fig 6). In short, they need to establish better relations with the existing canon of work around design activism and social design.

---

6   'New Social Design' is a term coined by Ilpo Koskinen, where he explores aesthetics in the context of emerging social design practice (Koskinen 2016a/b).

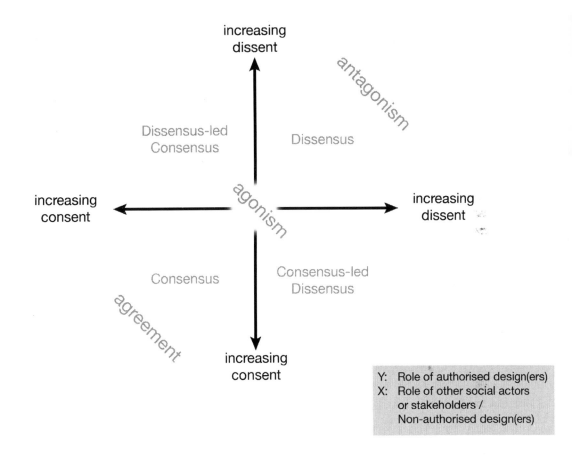

Figure 6: Strategies for authorised and non-authorised designers and others toward consensus or dissensus through agreement, agonism or antagonism.[7]

7   Based on a diagram originally presented in keynote talk at *U Design '12* conference at the University of Aveiro & University of Porto, Aveiro, 14 July 2012, as Fuad-Luke, A. 'Design(ing) for Transition and contingent eco-socio-political realities'. See also http://window874.com/2013/03/13/activist-strategies-agreement-agonism-antagonism-2/. Updated with 'authorised' and 'non-authorised' designers, July 2014.

A social poïesis

The transition to more sustainable ways of living and working is a societal journey. Cornelius Castoriadis thought that each historical period develops its existence – the imaginary of society – as specific ways of living, seeing and making (Castoriadis 1998). Jacques Lacan later noted that this structuring of human existence is real, symbolic and imaginary where the latter appears as fictional, unreal *and* real (Lacan 1956). Arjun Appadurai saw the social imaginary embedded within ethno-, media-, techno-, finance- and idea-scapes, all working as an active process of the *imagination as social practice* (my italics) (Appadurai 1996). Therefore, understanding the social imaginary, and how it can elicit new behaviours and modes of organizing, is critical to the task of designing sustainability transition. Social practices act as a bridge between *and* within immaterial/intangible and material/tangible spaces/ places. These practices challenge dominant or hegemonic social imaginaries through emergent everyday activities. This resonates with what Appadurai calls 'social-structures-in-the-making'. These emergent structures are linked to social aesthetics, identified by Arnold Berleant as a sub-category of everyday aesthetics, which he believes determines the moral character of persons, their actions and human interactions which promote the cultivation of virtues through everyday practice (Berleant 2012). As designers and design researchers, we can place new everyday aesthetical possibilities into people's lives through designing the artifacts and experiences encountered. We can also move people from a state of *anaesthesia*, induced by an overload of stuff, things, design – i.e. the humdrum materialization of modern life – by disrupting their imaginations through our design interventions. This aligns with Ranciere's sense of politics as a form of experience and an aesthetic act. Hence, *design* (the product in Redström's terms) and *designing* (the paradigm in Redström's terms) (Redström 2017, 36-41) become difficult to separate from the social and political practices they affect and effect.

Today, with the presence of ubiquitous computing and the Internet, imaginaries collide and reside in diverse places/spaces. Whomever enters these places/spaces can contest control of dominant or hegemonic aesthetic regimes, the distribution of the sensible, and, hence, the generation of 'images of thought' that can exercise pervasive control on the social imaginary. Beautiful strangeness seeks to disrupt the images of thought of IWC through displacement in the present and through re-directing the future toward regeneration, not degeneration. From a design perspective, we can disrupt through fictions and frictions that challenge the existing social imaginary (see below). Placing design in the public domain as an act of beautiful strangeness requires that it disrupts the aesthetic regime of IWC and the negative, unsustainable, social habits and practices it creates. More challenging is how we insert these designs to disrupt the distribution of the sensible of IWC effectively.

An integrated aesthetic poïesis?

If we wish to talk about an 'integrated aesthetic poïesis', where the philosophical, design and social poeïsis come together, then we need to take the disciplinary-held discourses on aesthetics beyond present confines. Aesthetics of the everyday focuses on the present, the immediate, either as action-orientated aesthetics aligned with social aesthetics, or, spectator-orientated aesthetics, the latter being the arena in which much discourse about art and aesthetics, predominantly judgment-orientated, was developed by Western philosophers (Saito 2015). Of course, these positions have some bearing on beautiful strangeness, but a better orientation is through relational aesthetics or dialogical aesthetics[8] where art/design and aesthetics enter everyday (social) practices to re-direct human activities. Yet, still this in not enough to combat IWC. An integrated aesthetic poïesis has to deal with 'what is' *and* 'what will the thing that 'is' do to us and non-humans in the future?' In Latourian terms we have to address both 'matters of fact' and 'matters of concern' (Latour 2008). In short, beautiful strangeness asks us to peer into the future while aesthetically experiencing and practicing in the present. It does this by combining action-oriented, social, relational and dialogic aesthetics through the experimental, paralogic aesthetics of the design(-ing). It is, in this sense, *'design-ing* as an (emergent) social practice'.[9]

Generative, disruptive, fabulative, beautiful strangeness

Beautiful strangeness contests the aestheticisation by and through IWC. As Folkmann recently noted, challenging the distribution of sensual material, challenging discourse and distributing knowledge differently is a way of challenging the ontology, extension and structure of aestheticisation (fig 7). I believe beautiful strangeness addresses all three of Folkmann's categories of extension and the degree of reflection/level of representation *while* also addressing the dimension of futurity.

To illustrate beautiful strangeness I have chosen design-led activism case studies from 'agri-culture' (Hooker 1993). Hooker coined agri-culture to bring attention to the relationship between a culture, its agriculture and the dynamic practices that maintain its viability. This is a topic that deserves serious attention from design-led activists, designers and design researchers given that IWC agriculture is a key contributor to global warming, social injustice and environmental degradation. The 2009 report by the International Assessment of Agricultural Knowledge, Science and Technology for Development (IAASTD), commonly known as the *World Agriculture Report,* described the failure of conventional Agriculture Knowledge, Science and Technology

---

8   'Relational aesthetics' and 'dialogical aesthetics' characterize activist art, socially engaged art, envrionmenatl art and other art practices embedded in social settings and participation in changing life through participating in changing the everyday aesthetics (Saito 2015).

9   I would like to thank my colleague, sociologist Dr. Alvise Mattozzi, at the Free University of Bozen-Bolzano, who is researching, 'design as a social practice'. Here, I emphasise activity; design-ing.

(AKST) to adequately address grave issues around: Unsustainable land and soil use by industrial agriculture; hunger in times of plenty contrasted with obesity through unhealthy industrial food; dubious ethical practices in meat production; issues of food sovereignty; land grabbing; and bio-fuels (McIntyre et al. 2009).

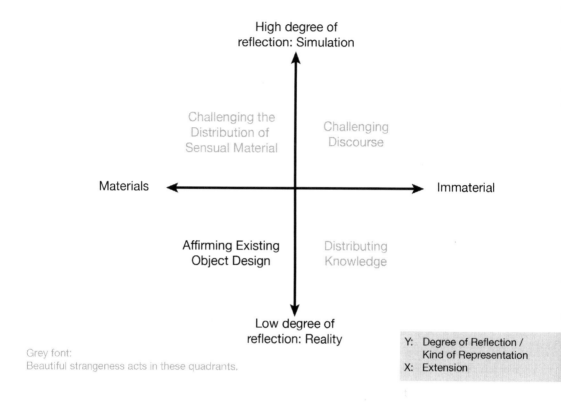

Figure 7: Framework for the approaches of design toward the field of aestheticization (redrawn after Folkmann, 2013) and how 'beautiful strangeness' acts, potentially, in three quadrants simultaneously.

This led to the Foundation on Future Farming to call for an urgent re-assessment of transition to sustainable agriculture by adopting a multifunctional and agroecological approach to farming (Beck et al. 2016).

My three agricultural case studies are: Agricultural Printing and Altered Landscapes by Bendikt Groß; the Colorado Top Bar and Barcelona Warre beehives from OS Beehives; and Outside Brewery by designer/artist Henriette Waal, part of the Edible Landscapes project. These case studies provide examples of sustainism[10]; as they meet questions of futurity through regenerating or renewing the future, rather than de-futuring, so they also align with beautiful strangeness by being *generative, disruptive* and *fabulative.*

Generative. The designing does something in the present to lean into a future that is not degenerative but is, rather, generative and re-generative, i.e. beautiful strangeness focuses on the potentiality for renewal in the future. It is a re-directive design practice than can affect and effect thoughts and actions to re-direct us away from IWC toward more sustainable alternatives.

Disruptive. The designing challenges the distribution of the sensible of IWC through paralogic moves that simultaneously alter perceptions while encouraging participation and actions. These moves enable participation as a collective *or* individual, action. In becoming open and participatory, the way in which beautiful strangeness challenges the dominant aesthetic regimes is unpredictable and indeterminate but, importantly, it is active, resistant and exploratory. We need a combination of open designers, complimentary relational designers, co-designers and maverick designers to elicit micro-paradigmatic shifts.

Fabulative. The designing hovers between fictions and frictions (Fuad-Luke 2016), with the potentiality to go to work on the imagination, the real and unreal (fig 8). They are frictions because they grasp or hold attention, they contest the normative, affirmative, invisible machinations of IWC, and they generate agonism. They are fictions because they are precedents and, not yet, established as visible cultural production in the dominant aesthetic regimes. Hence, they are not yet *fresh* images of thought, except to those who have participated in their creation. However, if they become better distributed then they can help enact new tensions in a dominant or hegemonic aesthetic regime.

10   'Sustainism' refers to a set of four interlocking principles developed by Michiel Schwarz and Diana Krabbendam where localism, sharing, connectedness and proportionality ensure activities that reinforce behaviour that increases social relationships for the common good while caring for our environment and local economies (Schwarz/Krabbendam 2013).

Figure 8: Edible Landscapes and Outside Brewery by designer/artist, Henriette Waal, 2009 onwards.[11]
Photo: Jorn van Eck.

11   Waal designed a portable brewery that travels to different locations where she brings together her
      expertise, local amateur brewers and citizens, ecologists and others. Exploring locally found resources,
      water, special herbs and, of course, local knowledge, and mixing this with malt, she creates what she calls
      'landscape beer', *Landschaps bier*. Her first project in the city of Tilburg in 2009 harvested locally available
      red clover (*Trifolium pretense*) as one of the main ingredients to produce Klavertje Bier. Such catalytic
      design facilitation re-combines resources in interesting hybrid ways, setting up possibilities for locally-
      based enterprises to emerge. Source: https://www.stroom.nl/paginas/pagina.php?pa_id=752085.

These selected case studies address relational/dialogical aesthetics through their generative, disruptive and fabulative matters of concern expressed by the aesthetics they generated through the issues they address *and* through their specific ways of designing and storytelling. As Folkmann emphasizes *"...the organizing principle of aestheticisation is fundamentally marked by groundlessness, instability and production of acts of assertion...each act of the aesthetic has to stake its claim..."* (Folkmann 2013, 60). The designers in my selected case studies have, I believe, staked a claim for an aestheticisation for *re-generative futures* that aligns with my original and expanded conceptualization of beautiful strangeness.

My original mini-manifesto for beautiful strangeness can, thus, be expanded by adding some additional principles. It is a beauty that:
- constitutes an integrated poïesis of philosophical, social and design thoughts and actions.
- contests the socio-technical, socio-political and, hence, the aesthetic, regimes of IWC.
- embraces paralogic moves to disturb the IWC regimes.
- encourages social practices catalysing new social-structures-in-the-making and by developing our social imaginations.
- applies strategies of consensus and dissensus through design to catalyse new social imaginaries.
- challenges the way of design(-ing) within IWC, so is, by default, activist on the discipline and practices of design(-ing).
- produces disruptive images of thought, frictions, fictions and fabulations, to displace the IWC aesthetic regime.
- encourages new symbiotic human|non-human relations.
- is (re-)generative in the present and the future.

I have also staked my claim here. I hope that the reader can now imagine and generate *their own* manifestations of beautiful strangeness that disrupt and displace the untruths of Integrated World Capitalism.

References

Appadurai, Arjun (1996): *Modernity at Large: Cultural Dimensions of Globalization.* Minnesota: University of Minnesota Press.

Beck, Angelika / Haerlin, B. / Richer, L. (Ed.) (2016): Agriculture at a Crossroads. IAASTD findings and recommendations for future farming. Berlin: Foundation on Future Farming (Zukunftsstiftung Landwirtschaft).

Berleant, Arnold (2012): Aesthetics Beyond the Arts: New and Recent Essays. Aldershot: Ashgate) cited in Yuniko Saito, 'Aesthetics of the Everyday', The Stanford Enclyclopedia of Philosophy, Winter 2015 edition. Available at https://plato.stanford.edu/entries/aesthetics-of-everyday/, accessed 01 November 2017.

Bourriaud, Nicholas (2002): *Relational Aesthetics*, trans. by. Simon Pleasance and Fronza Woods with the participation of Mathieu Copeland, (Les presses du reel, 2002,). First published in France, *Esthétique relationnelle*, 1998. pp. 86, 101.

Bremner, Craig / Rodgers, Paul (2013): Design Without Discipine, Design Issues, Volume XXIX, Number 3, Summer 2013, pp. 4–13.

Castoriadis, Cornelius (1998): *The Imaginary Institution of Society.* Cambridge, Massachusetts: MIT Press (First published in France in 1975).

Deleuze, Gilles / Guattari, Félix (1994): *What is Philosophy?,* trans. by H. Tomlinson and G Burchell, New York: Columbia Press, p. 24 cited in Hroch, 219.

DiSalvo, Carl (2012): *Adversarial Design.* Cambridge, Massachusetts: MIT Press.

Dunne, Anthony / Raby, Fiona (2013): *Speculative Everything. Design, fiction and social dreaming.* Cambridge, Massachusetts: MIT Press.

Folkmann, Mads Nygaard (2013): *The Aesthetics of Imagination in Design.* Cambridge, Massachusetts and London: MIT Press.

Foundation Earth (2017): 'True-cost economics', *Foundation Earth*, 2017. Available at http://www. fdnearth.org/essays/true-cost-economics-toward-a-model-to-ensure-fair-play-long-term-survival/, accessed 01 November 2017.

Fry, Tony (2008): *Design Futuring: Sustainability, Ethics and New Practice.* Oxford: Berg Publishers.

Fuad-Luke, Alastair (2002): *The Eco-Design Handbook.* London: Thames and Hudson.

Fuad-Luke, Alastair (2009): *Design Activism: Beautiful Strangeness for a Sustainable World.* London: Earthscan, pp. 188–189.

Fuad-Luke, Alastair (2013): Towards eudaimonic possibilitarian design(-ing)..., *Window874*, 9 February 2013. Available at https://window874.wordpress.com/2013/02/09/towards-eudaimonic-possibilitarian-design-ing/, accessed 01 November 2017.

Fuad-Luke, Alastair (2014) 'Design(-ing) for Radical Relationality: 'Relational design' for confronting dangerous, concurrent, contingent realities', in *Emerging Practices in Design. Professions, Values and Approaches*, ed. By. MA Jin and LOU Yongqi, Shanghai: Tongji University Press, pp. 42–73.

Fuad-Luke, Alastair (2015): 'Design Activism's Teleological Freedoms as a Means to Transform our Habitus, in *Agents of Alternatives: Re-designing Our Realities*, ed. By. Alastair Fuad-Luke, Anja-Lisa Hirscher and Katharina Moebus. Berlin: AoA, 2015.

Fuad-Luke, Alastair (2016): Fictions, frictions and functions: Design as capability, adaptability and transition, in *The Pearl Diver. Designers as Storytellers*, ed. By. Elisa Bertolotti and Others, (Milan: DESIS Philosophy Talks, 2016), pp. 90-95, available at https://archive.org/details/ThePearlDiver_DESIS, accessed 01 November 2017.

Goodman, Nelson (1978): *Ways of Worldmaking.* Indianapolis, Indiana: Hackett Publishing Company.

Guattari, Félix (2014): *The Three Ecologies.* London: Bloomsbury, trans. By Ian Pidar and Paul Sutton. (English translation first published in 2000 by The Athlone Press, First published in France 1989 by Editions Galilee).

Harfield, Steve (2008): 'On the Roots of Undisciplined', in *Undisciplined!* Design Research Society Conference, Sheffield Hallam University, Sheffield, UK, 16-19 July 2008.

Hooker, Cliff (1993): Value and System: Notes toward the definition of agri-culture. Available at http://www.researchgate.net/publication/265309571, accessed 16 July 2016.

Hroch, Petra (2015): Sustainable Design Activism: Affirmative Politics and Fruitful Futures, in *Deleuze and Design*, ed. by Bettie Marenko and Julian Brasset. Edinburgh: Edinburgh University Press, pp. 219–248.

Koskinen, Ilpo (2016a): The Aesthetics of Action in New Social Design. Design Research Society 50th

Anniversary Conference Brighton, UK, pp.1–12.

Koskinen, Ilpo (2016b): Agonistic, Convivial, and Conceptual Aesthetics in New Social Design. Design Issues, Volume XXXII, Number 3, Summer 2016, pp. 13-29.

Koskinen, Ilpo / Zimmerman, John / Binder, Thomas / Redstrom, Johan / Wensveen, Stephan (2011): *Design Research Through Practice. From the Lab, Field, and Showroom*. Amsterdam: Morgan Kaufmann.

Lacan, Jacques (1956): 'Symbol and Language' *The Language of the Self*, Baltimore: The Johns Hopkins University Press.

Latour, Bruno (2008): 'A cautious Prometheus?' In *Networks of Design*, Proceedings of 2008 Annual International Conference of the Design History Society, University College Falmouth, 3-6 December 2008, pp. 2–10.

Malpass, Matt (2017): *Critical Design in Context. History, theory and practices*. London: Bloomsbury Academic.

Manzini, Ezio / Jégou, François (2003): *Sustainable Everyday: Scenarios of Urban Life*. Milan: Edizioni Ambiente.

Markussen, Thomas (2011): 'The Disruptive Aesthetics of Design Activism: Enacting Design Between Art and Politics', *Making Design Matter!* Nordic Design Research Conference 29-31 May, 2011, Helsinki, pp. 102-110. Available at www.nordes.org, accessed 01 November 2017.

Maskit, Jonathan (2011): 'The Aesthetics of Elsewhere: An Environmentalist Everyday', *Aesthetic Pathways*, 1 (2), 2011: 92–97.

Max-Neef, Manfred, A. (1991): *Human Scale Development*. New York and London: Apex Press.

McDonough, William / Braungart, Michael (2003): *Cradle-to-Cradle*. New York: North Point Press.

McIntyre, Beverly D. et al. / IAASTD (Ed.) (2009): Agriculture at a Crossroads. Global Report. Berlin: Foundation on Future Farming (Zukunftsstiftung Lanwirtschaft).

Rancière, Jacques (2013): *The Politics of Aesthetics*. London: Bloomsbury Academic (First published in France under the title Le Partage du sensible: Esthétique et politique, La Fabrique-Éditions, 2000).

Redström, Johan (2017): *Making Design Theory*. Cambridge, Massachusetts and London: MIT Press.

Orr, David (2002): *The Nature of Design: Ecology, Culture, and Human Intention*. Oxford: Oxford University Press.

Saito, Yuniko (2015): 'Aesthetics of the Everyday', The Stanford Enclyclopedia of Philosophy, Winter 2015 edition. Available at https://plato.stanford.edu/entries/aesthetics-of-everyday/, accessed 01 November 2017.

Schwarz, Michiel / Krabbendam, Diana (2013): *Sustainism*. Amsterdam: BIS Publishers.

Stone-Richards, Michael (2017): 'Care Comes in the Wake of Retreat'. Eflux. Available at http://www.e-flux.com/architecture/future-public/151953/care-comes-in-the-wake-of-retreat/, accessed 01 November 2017.

Willis, Anne-Marie (2006): Ontological Designing, *Design Philosophy Issues*, Volume IV, Issue 2, 2006, 69–82.

Woodward, Ashley: 'Jean-François Lyotard (1924-1998)', in: *The Internet Encyclopedia of Philosophy*. Melbourne, Australia. Date unknown, ISSN 2161-0002. Available at http://www.iep.utm.edu/lyotard/#H9, accessed 01 November 2017.

DESIGN ACTIVISM IN THE CONTEXT OF TRANSPORT AND MOBILITY

Ann Thorpe

During the 20th century, our transportation network developed by optimizing roads, automobiles and economic growth. As the 21st century dawned, these narrow priorities for transport and mobility began giving way as technology and concerns about climate change, health, and congestion increased.

Technological change in the transport sector proceeds at a furious pace. We are rethinking vehicles in terms of fuel types, zero emissions, and self-driving. Increasingly we have 'big data' about many aspects of transport and mobility systems; wearables, sensors and the internet-of-things all signal further fundamental shifts. Meanwhile, digital networks enable the 'gig' and the 'peer to peer' economies, affecting the way we ship, travel, and commute (for example Deliveroo, Zipcar, Uber and remote working). Is any of this activism?

Activism describes the work of framing or revealing a problematic or challenging issue through disrupting routines, social practices, or systems of authority; this disruption characterizes activism as being unconventional or unorthodox – outside traditional channels of political change (Beissinger 2002, 15; Taylor/Van Dyke 2007). Social movement activists often turn to disruption as a form of influence because their other resources are limited (Olzak/Uhrig 2007; Traugott 1995). A classic example is activists putting their bodies on the line to create a 'manufactured vulnerability' that reveals exploitative power (Jordan 2002, 61–63). Activism also acts on behalf of a 'deprived, excluded, or wronged population' or 'issue' in the case of the environment (Tilly 1995, 37). For our purposes, activism addresses largely progressive social and environmental issues.

Design activism follows this description of social movement activism, over and above any profit-driven or aesthetic agendas that are most common in design. The types of tactics and concepts found in conventional activism apply to design activism as well (Thorpe 2014). Design activists use disruptive methods to try to bring about change in arenas where the issues are typically cash poor and value rich.

Considering these characteristics of design activism, we'd expect to find it in the areas of transport that we understand to be fundamentally connected to an array of serious societal challenges and feedback loops. For example, our sedentary travel and the inactive lifestyle it enables, have a huge public health cost. At the same time, the historically fossil fuel-based transport sector is typically responsible for around 25% of greenhouse gas emissions in developed economies and its rate of emissions is growing faster than other sectors (International Energy Agency 2015). As the world urbanizes, city transport systems are being overwhelmed by population increases. Active travel (walking and cycling) is a cheap yet rewarding contribution to solving all three of these challenges: improving health, reducing greenhouse gas reductions, and reducing demand on mass transit.

There are also profound social implications of transport networks. Arguably we discovered this the hard way, designing for cars instead of people. Motorways and major roads severed communities and many have not recovered (Anciaes et al. 2016). Public transport – its speed, character, stations, and paths – affects the quality of civic spaces in terms of safety, the environment, equity and prosperity.

Transport sector activists also work on behalf of various user groups such as women (safer travel), disabled people (better transport options), vulnerable road users (safety and comfort for cyclists, pedestrians, children, the elderly). Still other activists focus on livable streets, greening freight, and re-configuring access patterns and the physical materials on roads and other infrastructure.

Although the transport sector seems heavily planning-based, more than design-based, everything for transport is designed. There may be differences in the sequencing, for example the points at which designers are brought in to the process, and existing systems may pre-configure what designers can do. But transport is designed in terms of architecture, product design, landscape architecture and related design disciplines that have spatial and material manifestations. Examples include the design of stations, streetscapes, signaling systems, or vehicles.

There is of course a wide range of motorized vehicles – boats, trains, planes, cars, trucks, motorcycles and so on. At the time of writing, many cities and governments around the world are particularly concerned about the link between health and transportation, particularly how 'active' forms of travel such as cycling and walking can improve physical health, reduce air pollution, and reduce congestion.[1] In this sense 'feet' are arguably a 'vehicle.' Shoe design, walking aids and other pedestrian support may be relevant cases for design activism.

Design Activism in Social Movement Terms

Designers can learn a lot from thinking about activism in social movement terms. Social movement scholar Charles Tilly suggested that there are 'repertoires' of activist tactics that persist across time and across different causes. By studying many social movements, scholars proposed a stable set of tactics that protestors use, such as sit-ins, blockades, vigils and petitions. Stability in tactics is important for gaining wider participation. Activism is often constrained by what people know how to do. And yet tactics are ultimately flexible to suit different social causes. Consider the versatility of a

---

1   Mayor of London, Healthy Streets for London: Prioritising walking, cycling and public transport to create a healthy city. London: Transport for London. February 2017.

sit-in or 'occupy' tactic. It can become a 'teach-in' or even a 'die-in' for health activism (Tarrow 1995, 91). I propose that designers also have a repertoire of tactics constrained by what they know how to do (Thorpe 2012, 138). Instead of signing petitions, they hold design competitions. Instead of blockades, they create demonstration products and services. This repertoire is shown in broad terms in Table 1 (Thorpe 2012).

Tactic	Description
Demonstration artifact	Demonstration structure, system, product, space, place, plan or graphic: a better alternative to the status quo, typically seen as a positive, if imperfect effort, a model that others can use.
Service artifact	Service structure, system, product, space, place, plan or graphic: providing services where the market and governments have left gaps. Examples include clean teach, humanitarian aid to victims (war, disaster or poverty).
Protest Artifact	Protest structure, product, space, place, plan or graphic: often opposed, offensive or confrontational artifacts that make a cutting, critical statement prompting reflection on the morality of the status quo. May also be a specific tool of protest.
Communication	Make information visual or tactile (or both), create symbols or preserve or extend symbols.
Connection	Linkages such as doorways, gateways, borders, bridges or view corridors: attempts to make physical or visual links that often repair, restore, signify or enrich social and environmental conditions.
Rating System	Criteria, guidelines, rating schemes: includes formally structured rating systems or labeling systems, but also guidelines and criteria that typically set out metrics by which we can measure performance.
Competition	Competitions that call for proposals or that call for already complete work, award schemes.
Exhibitions	Exhibits, gallery and museum shows, site-specific installations.
Research and Critique	Design research, critiques, polemics, manifestos: the process of using research results or critical thinking as evidence or basis for change, often takes the form of written arguments.
Event	Conferences, lectures, seminars, workshops.
Conventional	Testimony, petitions, policy drafts, fundraising, books, publications, TV shows, films, demonstrations.
Social Exchange	Links among people, consultation/stakeholder input, self build, co-design: efforts to make social connections, and weave social fabric, hinging on specific relationships (as opposed to general ideas of "community").

Table 1: Tactics and Descriptions.

The usefulness of this framework is that it helps designers think strategically about change. Architects typically create buildings, but considering the broader tactical repertoire, they might think to ask, 'is a demonstration building the most effective tactic for bringing about change in this situation?' The repertoire of action directs design activists to think about actions they might take relative to other actions available in the repertoire. As the repertoire explicitly highlights a call for change, it also directs designers more explicitly to consider how their actions might fit into the broader social movement that is calling for that change.

Social movement activism has a reputation for being negative – trying to stop, block, or otherwise protest things. Traditional activist methods reinforce this notion through 'resistant' tactics – blockades, sit-ins, or boycotts. Design activists often practice a different form of activism, trying to bring about change by generating positive alternatives to the status quo. Its disruptions are generative rather than resistant (Hess 2007, 85).

Social movement activists diagnose a problem and come up with a solution that they use to motivate action. When they protest a new road being built by lying in front of heavy equipment, they have to feel confident that the road is wrong. By contrast, design activism is often more concerned with understanding, or diagnosing, the problem than it is with offering the 'right' solution. Many designers see their work as experimental and iterative, where each new project, whether their own or others, informs about what works and what doesn't. Rather than stop a road, design activists are more likely to explore the problem that 'a road' tries to solve.

However not all design activism is generative, and as the table indicates, designers do take up 'protest artifacts' where a confrontational, even offensive artifact makes a critical statement. An example described below is the white ghost bike, placed around cities at points where cyclists have been killed, a constant reminder of failures in the transport system.

Design Activism in Transport

In this section we look at examples from transport for the design activists tactics described above.

Demonstration Artifact

Roads have changed little since the late 1800's, but Dutch designer Daan Roosegaarde proposed 'Smart Highway,' supported by Dutch infrastructure company Heijmans Infrastructure (Wysocky 2014). The smart highway has a kit of parts. For example luminescent paint soaks up energy by day and gives off light by night, eliminating the need for as much street lighting. Temperature sensitive coatings indicate when the road is cold enough to form ice. These techniques work on bike paths as well as streets designed for cars.

Other design activists have worked on road surfaces, for example Wattway is a road 'paved' with solar panels, and was developed through five years of research with the French National Institute for Solar energy and company Colas.[2] PlasticRoad is a prefabricated hollow modular structure that is lighter than asphalt with a longer expected lifespan. The hollow area can temporarily store water, for example, to prevent flooding.[3]

An example of a demonstration streetscape is London's 'Mini Holland' scheme: in the London Borough of Waltham Forest. The project tested out ways to reconfigure streets to reduce rat-running, enhance public space, and improve cycling and pedestrian experience. During a pilot test there were eight temporary road closures designed from surplus barriers, trees in planters, and street furniture. After a community engagement to finalise the design, the scheme has dramatically lowered traffic levels and increased places for people to walk, cycle and enjoy the place.[4]

A demonstration vehicle is the Copenhagen Wheel. MIT university researchers developed the red hub, built directly into the rear bicycle wheel, to simplify electric-powered bikes. The wheel 'learns how you pedal' and the motor automatically kicks in when you need it.[5] An easy electric bike aims to get more people cycling, extend the season for cycling, and lengthen the distances cycled. Increasing the uptake of cycling has benefits for human health, road congestion, and the environment. Design of the wheel played a large role in the framing of the issue – it's visible and symbolic – and in disrupting the norms of electric assisted bikes which typically have motors built on to the frame.

Service Artifact

London-based design and invention studio, Vitamins, created the first folding wheel. Originally intended for high-end bikes, the wheel turned out to be life changing for wheelchair uses. The designer learned, *"There are so many problems associated with storing and transporting wheelchairs, and the biggest problem is wheel size"*. The new wheel enables wheelchair users to travel with their wheel chairs more easily stowed in vehicles ranging from cars to planes.[6]

In conjunction with the Royal College of Art's Helen Hamlyn Centre, Turkish

2   Wattway, online http://www.wattwaybycolas.com/en/ accessed 28 October 2017.

3   PlasticRoad (online: Index Design to Improve Life) https://designtoimprovelife.dk/plasticroad/ accessed 20 Octobr 2017.

4   Ross Lydall, "Mini Holland" scheme in Walthamstow hailed as major success as traffic falls by half,' London Evening Standard 8 November 2016, online https://www.standard.co.uk/news/london/mini-holland-scheme-in-walthamstow-hailed-as-major-success-as-traffic-falls-by-half-a3389936.html) mini Holland accessed 27 October 2017.

5   Copenhagen Wheel, The Copenhagen Wheel official product release. (online: Copenhagen Wheel, Dec 3, 2013) https://www.youtube.com/watch?v=S10GMfG2NMY accessed 27 October 2017.

6   Reinventing the Wheel (Online: Index Design to Improve Life, 10 April 2013) https://designtoimprovelife. dk/wheel-vitamins-westaway/ accessed 27 October 2017.

company Karsan has developed a next generation taxi that is wheelchair-compatible and features other elements such as wide dual doors, automated wheel chair ramp, and illumination both for visually impaired and as a signal to cyclist and pedestrians that doors are opening.[7]

Although many struggles in transport are about reallocating infrastructure, especially giving more road space to non-motorised vehicles, there is a parallel movement to bring mobility to areas where we might not expect it. An example is architect Michael Herrman's Nomadic prayer space, a portable, self-assembled structure that fits in the back of a compact car, yet enables communities to "temporarily 'construct' their own culturally specific spaces" (Herrman 2008, 279). Other examples include mobile urban farms, mobile park spaces, mobile performance spaces, and 'popup' venues such as libraries. These examples often aim to widen access to services in underserved communities, and re-configure the narrative of place.

Protest artifact

Ghost bikes are memorials for cyclists killed or hit on the road. The all-white ghost bike is locked to a signpost near the crash site, with a small sign. The ghost bike organization comments that the bikes, *"serve as reminders of the tragedy that took place on an otherwise anonymous street corner, and as quiet statements in support of cyclists' right to safe travel".* They originated in Missouri in 2003 but have since grown in use globally.[8]

Another protest artifact was developed for the Mexico City subway. An installation replaced regular seats with a naked torso/penis, to highlight the problem of sexual violence towards women. The seat's sign read *"It is uncomfortable to sit here, but that is nothing compared to the sexual violence that women suffer on daily journeys".*[9]

Communication/Visualization

The act of making something visible is natural for design, and one common expression takes the form of a map – particularly suitable for transport. An example is Crashmap, which enables users to see the location and severity of road crashes in their areas. The aim was to create a way for the public to easily see the most relevant road safety data for them.[10]

Another example is the first unofficial transport map for Amman, Jordan. The

---

7   Max, Blue Badge Style Blog, (Online: Blue Badge Style, 7 February 2014) https://bluebadgestyle. com/2014/02/knowledge-new-generation-black-cabs-accessible-eco-friendly-taxis/ accessed 20 October 2017.

8   Ghost Bikes (Online: Ghostbikes.org) http://ghostbikes.org accessed 27 October 2017.

9   Matt Saunders, The Campaign highlighting sexual harassment on public transport (Online: Design is Political, 6 April 2017) http://designispolitical.com/activism/the-campaign-highlighting-sexual-harassment-on-public-transport/ accessed 20 October 2017.

10   http://www.crashmap.co.uk/Search

designer, Ahmad Humeid, was driven to create the map after decades of investment in private vehicles and their roads, but no tools for making public transport accessible and clear. He commented, *"I am dismayed that our city authorities have not been able to produce a map for us in the past decades. I get angry when I see Amman's streets clogged with ever worsening traffic jams. I am sad to see the indignity of those who do not own cars, struggling to use a weak transportation system".*[11]

Connection

Design activism is often involved in stitching together, or connecting, places and activities that have been diminished by being separated or partially disused. These projects can take the form of reclaiming train tracks for bike and pedestrian paths, such as rails to trails programs or New York City's highline. In Paris, Mayor Anne Hidalgo has implemented some progressive re-connection policies, for example closing a central highway that ran along the Seine and replacing it with a pedestrian park – reconnecting people with the river.[12]

In another approach to connection, pedestrianized bridges enable more accessible cycling and walking. One example is the Christchurch cycle and pedestrian bridge in Reading, which makes the town and the rail station more accessible for non-motorised visitors.[13]

Rating system

Designers who want to signal that their work has met higher standards, for example in terms of environmental performance or fair trade, often have no way to indicate this without some sort of rating system. While ratings have been more common for products such as food or packaging, there are well known ratings for green buildings, such as the US Green Building Council's LEED rating system. Recently London has introduced a set of indicators for Healthy Streets, developed by Lucy Saunders, as part of the Mayors initiative for active travel and improved air quality in the city.[14]

The Institute for Sustainable Infrastructure has introduced the ENVISION Rating

11   Ahmad Humeid, Designing Amman's Unofficial Transport Map: Transformative design meets urban activism (Amman: Syntax, 9-3-2016 http://syntaxdesign.com/blog/designing-ammans-unofficial-transport-map-transformative-design-meets-urban-activism/ accessed 27 October 2017.

12   Metropolis contributors, The World's Best Design Cities 2017: Metropolis editors choose 15 cities around the globe that set the bar highest for progressive design and good living (2017). http://www.metropolismag.com/cities/the-worlds-best-design-cities-2017/ accessed 25 October 2017.

13   Chartered Institute for Highways and Transportation, CIHT/Costain Sustainable Transport Award: Commended, Christchurch Bridge, Peter Brett Associates LLP, Reading Borough Council, Design Engine, Balfour Beatty, Hollandia Infra and Schreder, (London: CIHT, 2017) http://www.ciht.org.uk/en/events/ciht-awards/ciht-awards-2017/ciht-awards-2017-winners/ciht--costain-sustainable-transport-award.cfm accessed 20 October 2017.

14   Mayor of London, Healthy Streets for London: Prioritising walking, cycling and public transport to create a healghty city (London: Transport for London, 2017) p.12.

system for sustainable infrastructure projects. The system has 60 sustainability criteria that are arranged in five categories including Quality of Life, Leadership, Resource Allocation, Natural World, and Climate and Risk.[15]

Competition

'Ideas' competitions are common across many types of design activism, from emergency shelter to environmental cleanup. An example in the transport arena is the Cambridge to Oxford Connection Ideas Competition sponsored by the National Infrastructure Commission. The competition sought visionary design ideas for the Cambridge – Milton Keynes – Oxford corridor. They were particularly interested in integrating place making with infrastructure.[16]

In the arena of transport there is another common type of competition based around alternative vehicles – challenges, races and journeys. An example is the World Solar Challenge, a 1,860-mile (3,000k) solar car race across Australia's outback.[17]

Competitions are ways of introducing a big range of demonstration and service artefacts, often conceptually, all at once.

Conventional

In terms of conventional activism, designers sometimes take approaches from 'classic' social movements. For example, urban 'hacktivist' designers have been popping up anonymously in some American cities to 'direct traffic' – typically creating bicycle lanes that the cities have been slow to implement. In conventional activist terms we might characterize this as a form of 'civil disobedience.' The design twist is that the 'disobedient' element is not the designers and their physical presence, for example at a sit-in, but the materials and symbols marking out the cycle lanes.

San Francisco's group is known as the San Francisco Municipal Transformation Agency, with an acronym SFMTrA very similar to the city's official transit agency SFMTA. The activists are responding to several deadly hit-and-run accidents and have performed interventions in many hazardous areas.[18]

---

15   Institute for Sustainable Infrastructure, Envision's critical role in infrastructure sustainability (online: Institute for Sustainable Infrastructure, no date).

16   National Infrastructure Commission, The Cambridge to Oxford Connection: Ideas Competition (London; Malcolm Reading Consultants, 2017).

17   Greg Beach, The Netherlands' sun-powered Nuna9 race car wins the World Solar Challenge, (New York: Inhabitat,   10-13-2017)   https://inhabitat.com/dutch-team-nuon-wins-world-solar-car-challenge-again/ accessed 27 October 2017.

18   John Metcalfe, 'Building DIY Bike Lanes as a Form of Activism' (Online: City Lab, December 23 2016) https://www.citylab.com/transportation/2016/12/san-franciscos-anonymous-diy-bike-lane-builders-qa/510989/ accessed 24 October 2017.

Figure 9: Guerilla cycling: San Francisco activists create their own bike lanes with traffic cones. Photo courtesy of San Francisco Municipal Transformation Agency (SFMTrA).

Social Exchange

Design activism also works to disrupt social relations, often by connecting people to each other through service or design processes, for example 'co-design.' In a digital, social media environment, we see more designers involved in creating online tools to better connect people around transport. An example is Getaround, an online peer-to-peer car sharing service that allows drivers to rent cars from private car owners and owners to put up their own car for rent as well. As the Getaround website explains, there are a billion cars in the world and most of them sit idle for most of the day.[19]

Reflections

Clearly there is overlap among the tactics and the way they work. A ghost bike, while serving as a 'protest artifact' also visualizes a crash; hacked bike lanes 'demonstrate' an alternative signaling system. As with wider, conventional social movements, forward progress is complex and overlapping.

These examples also illustrate the interdisciplinary nature of design and its multiplicity of stakeholders. Activism expressed through design usually sits alongside other 'expressions' in the design, such as function, appearance or budget. For example, the Copenhagen wheel is not just a way to 'raise awareness' about how we extend cycling, it has to function for key audiences, someone has to be able to fabricate it and it has to be financially and physically accessible. These factors impinge on activist expression in material and spatial form, whether on a road, a vehicle or a signaling system. Similar multiplicity exists in more conventional social movement protest. For example, Jasper has noted that in addition to their concern for the cause, activists also engage with causes for reasons of friendship obligations, improvement of skills, enjoyment or entertainment and personal taste (Jasper 1997, 237).

How does activism 'work'?

The tactics outlined above rarely work by themselves. To move beyond simply 'raising awareness' activism has to build power to make change. In simple terms, power struggles are usually enacted through several means (often combined), particularly organized money, organized people, and from a design perspective, organized representations, materials and spaces (Gecan 2004, 36). This is another reason why it is important for design activists to think of their work in social movements terms.

---

19   Rent Your Neighbour's Car and Reduce the World's CO_2 (Online: Index Design to Improve Life, August 18, 2013) https://designtoimprovelife.dk/getaround/ accessed 22 October 2017; Getaround (online: https://www.getaround.com) accessed 22 October 2017.

The key capacity designers have for building power is physically and visually disruptive framing. With generative activism, designers are often proposing real alternatives to the status quo, they are putting 'offers' on the table that people can bargain for ('we want that in our neighborhood') or use as a persuasive tool. These disruptions relate to codes of behavior and protocols, narratives and physical configuration. Hacktivists re-configuring cycle lanes create positive experiences for cyclists while embarrassing city officials, increasing pressure for change. The bargaining power of people who want improved bike lanes is enhanced in a way that is experientially different than petitioners showing charts and graphs of number of cyclist deaths from road accidents.

Many of the above examples also affect the distribution of and access to resources. This perhaps marks design activism out from conventional activism as well. Rather than simply bodies-on-the-line as a resource, design activism brings a shifting of physical configurations, alternative access and other resource implications. In many of the examples above, the focus is on changing the resource allocation among road users, in addition to shifting the physical configurations of roads (smart roads) and vehicles (Copenhagen wheel). These change our notions of how roads and vehicles can be part of positive change.

Who can be an activist?

In the examples above, the activists include a city government and a company. It's fair to ask, can these entities really be activists? Must activism always be from the bottom up, or from the outside in? Historically social movements aimed to correct the wrongs of dominant powers, typically governments. Classic social movements fought for the right of women to vote, or for black people to gain civil rights. In our global, connected world there is a growing sense that change doesn't come either solely from the top or solely from the bottom of society. Robin Murray, Julie Caulier-Grice and Geoff Mulgan of the Young Foundation suggest: *"Most social change is neither purely top-down nor bottom-up. It involves alliances between the top and the bottom, or between what we call the "bees" (the creative individuals with ideas and energy) and the "trees" (the big institutions with the power and money to make things happen to scale)"* (Murray et al. 2010, 8).

More people are also recognizing that buildings, material objects, landscapes, technologies or spaces play a distinct role in power relations (See, for example, Miller/Martin 2003; Pinch 2008; Soja 2010, 91). This idea comes from the notion that material objects and spaces both constitute and are constituted by social relations. Markus suggests that there exists no a-social space or place, just as there is no a-spatial or a-material social relation. Social relations always take place somewhere (Markus 1993, 13–14). Since power emerges in social relations, materiality and spatiality have a role in extending, reproducing or even shifting the balance of power.

Michael Gecan echoes this idea of tension between being on the 'inside' and the 'outside' of established systems of power. He notes that for many individuals there is a challenge in *"maintaining a conservative's belief in the value and necessity of stable institutions, along with a radical's understanding of the need for persistent agitation and reorganization. We are called to love, engage and uphold our most cherished institutions, while watching them, questioning them, and pressing them to change, all at the same time"* (Gecan 2004, xix).

Designers already work in a client-service model and take into account a range of users – they already work collaboratively. In many cases design activism is just as collaborative. A number of the examples above involved companies working with 'social good' organisations such as universities or cities. The bottom line is that these activities have the characteristics of activism, where there is a framing of a problem related to a disadvantaged or excluded group or issue, there is a public call to change, and the approach disrupts routines, social practices, or systems of authority.

Conclusion

Design activism in the transport sector fits generally with patterns of design activism in areas such as architecture or products, but there is a sense that the balance of activism in this sector tips toward planning rather than design.

That may be partly because so much of the transport system is publicly owned and often sprawling. There is less leeway for individual experimentation and for progressive clients to push forward radical action, in the way a progressive building owner might. For example, one progressive building owner, Harlem's Schomburg Center for Research in Black Culture, implemented 'material justice' by specifying a brick building (Hosey 2005, 128). Research showed that masonry union members included a relatively high percentage of minorities from Harlem.

That kind of action is harder to imagine in a city street network or a project such as Britain's High Speed Rail 2, which have to be at once both more specific and more generic. They are more specific in terms of being controlled through publicly accountable specifications, contracts and regulations. But they are also generic in terms of adapting to all contexts and all users along the route.

In many of our transport networks we are also 'locked in' to existing infrastructure assets and legacy methods. Although designers never truly 'start from scratch' – there are always social practices and technological systems that they must respond to – there is surely a continuum along which designers have more or less freedom or capacity to frame issues. The continuum may run from the specialist private facility (such as Harlem's Schomburg Center) on the one hand to a system like London's underground on the other. Recently Mark Curran, of Transport for London, spoke about how difficult it was to convert several of the London Underground lines to 24-hour service.[20] Everything from the ticketing machines, to train maintenance, to

---

20   Mark Curran, Night Tube: Research Past, Present & Future, presented at *Night Moves: Understanding and shaping Transport and Mobility at Night*, University College London, 17 October 2017.

the on-train passenger announcements required re-working in a system that was never designed for 24-hour use.

Transport, beyond the flashy vehicles, is a complex system that can be difficult to capture in one showy drawing, show-stopping model, or signature photograph. Although architecture in particular is frequently criticized for its 'starchitect' personality cults around 'spectacular architecture,' the fact is that design activism trades partly on this very ability to create strong visual and physical framing of issues (Foster 2008). Where the transport system makes this is hard to create, there may be a more challenging role for design activists.

The examples covered here show that despite some of the limitations, there is still plenty of scope for design activism in the transport sector. Considering design activist tactics may help uncover more opportunities and ultimately link designers with movements that can leverage design's unique activist contributions.

Rapid transformation in the transport sector, combined with its ownership, scale, and other constrictions, probably means that the role of activists, innovators, profiteers and end users will continue to be mixed and complex. Social movements rarely proceed neatly in one, straight-forward direction. Yet we push for and expect change in the transport sector and design activism has a useful role.

References

Anciaes, P R. / Boniface, S. / Dhanani, A. / Mindell, J S. / Groce, N. (2016): Urban transport and community severance: linking research and policy to link people and places. *Journal of Transport and Health 3(3)*, 268–277.

Beissinger, Mark (2002): *Nationalist Mobilization and the Collapse of the Soviet State*. Cambridge: Cambridge University Press.

Foster, Hal (2008): *Skin as Spectacle, in Architecture: Between Spectacle and Use*, edited by A. Vidler. Williamstown: Sterling and Francine Clark Art Institute.

Gecan, Michael (2004): *Going Public: An Organizer's Guide to Citizen Action*. New York: Anchor Books.

Herrman, Michael (2008): *Hypercontextuality: The Architecture of Displacement and Placelessness*. Rome: Consiglio Nazionanale Delle Ricerche.

Hess, David J. (2007): *Alternative pathways in science and industry: Activism, innovation, and the environment in an era of globalization*. Cambridge, MA: MIT Press.

Hosey, Lance (2005): The Ethics of Brick, in: Metropolis (June 2005), p. 128 ff.

International Energy Agency (2015): Energy and Climate Change: World Energy Outlook Special Report. Paris: International Energy Agency.

Jasper, James M (1997): *The art of moral protest: Culture, biography and creativity in social movements*. Chicago, IL: The University of Chicago Press.

Jordan, Tim (2002): *Activism! Direct Action, Hacktivism and the Future of Society*. London: Reaktion Books.

Markus, Thomas (1993): *Buildings and Power*. London: Routledge.

Miller, Byron / Martin, Deborah G. (2003): Space and Contentious Politics, in: Mobilization: An International Journal, Vol. 8, no. 2 (2003), pp. 143–56.

Murray, Robin / Caulier-Grice, Julie / Mulgan, Geoff (2010): *The Open Book of Social Innovation*. London: The Young Foundation and NESTA.

Olzak, Susan / Uhrig, S. C. Noah (2007): The ecology of tactical overlap. *American Sociological Review*, 66 (2001). Taylor & Van Dyke, pp. 694–717.

Pinch, Trevor (2008): Technology and Institutions: Living in a Material World, in: Theory and Society, Vol. 37 (2008), pp. 461–83.

Soja, Edward W. (2010): *Seeking Spatial Justice*. Minneapolis: University of Minnesota Press.

Tarrow, Sidney (1995): Cycles of Collective Action: Between Moments of Madness and the Repertoire of Contention, in: *Repertoires and Cycles of Collective Action*, ed. Mark Traugott Durham, NC: Duke University Press.

Taylor, Verta / Van Dyke, Nella (2007): "Get Up, Stand Up": Tactical Repertoires of Social Movements, in *The Blackwell Companion to Social Movements*, ed. David A. Snow, Sarah A. Soule and Hanspeter Kriesi. Oxford: Blackwell.

Thorpe, Ann (2012): *Architecture and Design versus Consumerism*. London: Earthscan.

Thorpe, Ann (2014): Applying Protest Event Analysis to Architecture and Design. *Social Movement Studies*, 13:2 (2014), 275–295.

Tilly, Charles (1995): Contentious Repertoires in Great Britain, 1758-1843, in *Repertoires & Cycles of Collective Action*, Ed. M. Traugott. Durham: Duke University Press.

Traugott, Mark (Ed.) (1995): *Repertoires and Cycles of Collective Action*. Durham, NC: Duke University Press.

Wysocky, Ken (2014): In the Netherlands, luminous lines guide drivers. London: BBC, 2 December 2014) http://www.bbc.com/autos/story/20141202-in-the-netherlands-a-luminous-highway, accessed 27 October 2017.

V. REFLECTIONS AND PROJECTIONS

THE ART OF RESISTANCE
ON CONTEMPORARY RESPONSIBILITY OF ART AND DESIGN

Marcel René Marburger

In the 1980s Norman Junge, a Cologne based artist, offered his services to the *Bundeswehr*, the German military. In a letter to the head of the Ministry of Defense, Manfred Wörner, he referred to „a long tradition in the history of military" that had not been cultivated any more: *"In the past it was a matter of course that painters artistically documented battle scenes"*. This representation, that „resulted from a lively experience", had been completely replaced by photography. Since „our *Bundeswehr*", as Junge wrote, would not fight battles anymore but now had the mission "to prevent armed conflicts", he had a „deep desire" to attend a military exercise as a painting observer.

Surprisingly even for him, Junge was invited to a military exercise of the NATO the following year, taking place from the 18th to the 25th of September 1985 in Southern Germany. Armed with typical artistic tools – brush, oil paint and easel – Junge was painting rolling tanks and soldiers crawling through the underwood. Doing so, as it is not just obvious in the historical retrospect, the artist was undermining the genre of battle painting as well as he was ironically mirroring the alleged seriousness of the participants of the NATO military exercise. According to his own words, Junge was sapping the demonstrated pathos as well as the evident absurdity of such an event: In a situation in which military actions are just being simulated, soldierly virtues like braveness or honor are outdated. In a simulation, heroism is inappropriate and therefore doesn't need an artistic documentation.

Interestingly enough, Junge combines two very different art historical phenomena in his performance: the genre of battle painting and the ironical and as such humorous gesture – which was an often chosen weapon in history being the only one available for artists. While battle painting through all times had been a serious medium of communication (and as such a constitutive one, since it consolidated power relations instead of questioning them), the graphical medium of the caricature was used to criticize authorities, by holding a distorting mirror up to them. One of the best known representatives of this genre was the French artist Honoré Daumier, who in 1832 was even sentenced to a six month term in prison for a caricature of King Louis Phillippe.

Already a generation before Daumier, French painter Jacques-Louis David became famous for immortalizing the assassinated revolutionary leader Jean-Paul Marat in the moment of his death. Being an artistic chronicler of the French revolution and a member of the revolutionary national convention, David is said to be the first revolutionary artist in history. But just as he was presenting himself as an advocate for revolutionary ideals in the late 18th century, David also worked for Napoleon Bonaparte, who with his efforts to gain power eroded democratic ideas of *liberté, fraternité* and égalité just as successful as he brought fear to European monarchies. In this sense David is a tragic character: While he is said to be the first revolutionary artist he becomes at the same time the first revolutionary artist who betrayed his ideals. Resulting from this, the following rule can be formulated: Believable resistance requires political independence; an embracement of those who are in power is to be avoided at all costs.

For contemporary understanding and definition of artistic resistance though, neither Jacques-Louis David nor Honoré Daumier proved formative, but Berlin based Dadaists like George Grosz and John Heartfield did. Being members of the Communist Party since 1918, they weren't political neutral either, but since the KPD wasn't in power in Germany and had little influence on the political processes in the Weimar Republic, their artistic activism cannot be called constitutional in regard to a perpetuation of power. In opposite to this, the artworks and happenings of Berlin Dadaists were directed against the war supporting bourgeoisie as well as against the rise of National Socialism.

In this regard especially the photomontages of John Heartfield are worth mentioning, which were mostly published in the weekly magazine *Arbeiter Illustrierte Zeitung* that was circulating all over Germany in up to half a million copies at the time. In his photomontages the critical and ironical messages result from the juxtaposition of text and picture – so like Daumier and Junge Heartfield also used irony as his main tool.

The idea that art not only *can* be political but *must* be political came from this period and this might be owed to the particular situation of the Weimar Republic. In addition, Heartfield with his photomontages created – parallel with Hannah Höch – a new artistic medium, a fact not only relevant for art historians. Eventually, the communicative success of Heartfield's pictures is owed to this innovative technique – photographic and therefore seemingly more realistic pictures were more impressive and more up to date as for example drawings – and therefore their communicational impact was stronger. Nevertheless, the success of Heartfield's artistic resistance was little: Whereas the Nazis took power in January 1933, Heartfield and his Dadaistic collaborator George Grosz where forced into emigration. The millionfold murder they couldn't prevent.

In a similar way, the inefficiency of the *Situationistic Internationale* can be stated – the Situationists are considered as the second important artistic-political initiative of western European modernity. Differing from Honoré Daumier or the Dadaists, the Situationists around Guy Debord though did not criticize particular people who were in power in the 1960s but the system itself, or more accurately they opposed structures of power that can't be assigned to specific individuals but that are systemic – meaning that they in some sense concern all of us.

is lacking: While more and more information is shared at perceivable surfaces, often enough leading to useless gossip levelling and weakening each participant's output, essential operations are taking place under the surface – e.g. in the shape of surveillance technologies that are based on algorithms.

Therefore, an effective intervention can't remain on the surface but needs to progress into deeper levels. Creative resistance must generate innovative technological ideas not just communicative ones: Art and design should be subversive and inventive. In the tradition of the modern term *avant-garde,* artists and designers should discover unknown territories and doing so they should camouflage themselves and disguise their intentions. To exemplify this, I will give three artistic examples from recent years: In 2001, Austrian artist Herwig Weiser, in collaboration with Hannes Baumann and some other friends, removed the Olympic rings from the *Bergiselschanze* – the famous ski jumping hill in Innsbruck. Even though the group has filmed the nightly activity, the actual artwork is not the experimental film that resulted from it but rather the unlawful appropriation of the symbolically charged rings itself. In 1994, Weiser spontaneously stole a Pinocchio mask that was part of the exhibition *Pinocchio Pipenose Household Dilemma* by Paul McCarthy that was shown in the Cologne art gallery Esther Schipper. In a car ride, shortly after, Weiser and his collaborator Gabriel Lester were wearing the mask while they were trying to activate a permanent installed speed trap by driving faster then allowed. Unfortunately, as they reported, the speed trap was out of order and so their attempt did not result into a photographic picture. But even if there had been a photographic proof about their ‚performance' the actual artwork would still be the appropriation and humorous misuse of the mask and not the picture that would have proved their activities. Since in both examples an appropriation of iconic charged media took place, both artworks could easily be connected to the genre appropriation art and it might be interesting to discuss this further. But my intention is to demonstrate that the given example of an artistic practice is living very little of the communication and much more of the action – the act that rather wants to be concealed then to be communicated. In the given examples, it can be stated that the relation between act and communication is shifting towards the act.

Even more, this can be postulated for the *Image Fulgurator* – an invention by Berlin based artist Julius von Bismarck. The device he developed in 2007 is a transformed camera, that is not taking but projecting pictures. Von Bismarck's apparatus does so literally and automatically at the same time when another camera is photographing. The simultaneity in speed of light is generated through a light meter that is measuring the increase of the light intensity caused by the flashlight of the camera that is activated next to the *Image Fulgurator.* Now the special trick is, that the image which was projected by the *Image Fulgurator* is appearing on the picture the other apparatus is taking. As well as for the others it can be stated for this piece that it is not the photographic result that is important. It is not very relevant which pictures von Bismarck is implying other photographers. Essential for his artwork is that von Bismarck has invaded the apparatus on a structural level and therefore has influence on how pictures are created generally and not so much which particular picture is being generated.

Relevant from my point of view is the surprising and transgressive aspect of the works presented, since these aspects constitute art equally as a given aesthetic quality. Now this is an issue which is despite the oeuvre of Marcel Duchamp or conceptual art from the 1960s still hard to convey in a reality that is dominated so much by visual representations. Even for political art it is demanded constantly that besides other qualities it nevertheless must be convincing aesthetically. This might be true in the sense that otherwise it could be difficult to exhibit or sell such pieces of art. But outside these, well established, interests there certainly are ways to state artistic qualities on levels that are not visible, and being like that, show little or no aesthetic quality at all. Maybe such artworks should be appreciated even more if they are not keen on a convincing visual appearance: If the idea is about going beyond the surface, naturally resistant art and design cannot take a rest on an aesthetical level. With regard to the military vanguard, the *avantgarde*, artistic resistance should be interested in remaining invisible.

For several reasons this is especially true for the last artwork I like to finish my line of argumentation with – for reasons of camouflage I don't want to name its inventor: The piece of art is a construction which can generate electrical tension out of lightning strikes. Potentially as a side effect, this tension would destroy every computer which is located nearby in a range up to several hundred meters. Used as a subversive weapon, even large server facilities could be closed down with a rather simple equipment. Independent of how reasonable it would be to – for example – shoot down certain sections of the internet, this example demonstrates that based only on creative potential it can be possible to ensure an extensive impact even with simple instruments. It just requires first of all to leave the hermetic and self-referential art world and secondly to find outstanding and unexpected solutions: If it comes to efficient resistance, creativity is needed – and isn't this a quality that artists and designers are famous for? Especially at a time when computer programs – which are prescribed instructions – influence and structure our ways of thinking, acting and designing. The *derivé*, the deviation of the French Situationists from existing structures and regulations might work as a mental template. Just as Survival Research Laboratories could be pointing the way, as they face complex technological challenges by collaborating into constellations which include all kinds of different skills and knowledge. Following this, artists and designers should start to collaborate more often and systematically to connect their talents and creative skills in a complementary way. If the implementation potential and technical capabilities of designers are combined with the passion many artists have for experimentation and the unknown, a real powerful resistant unit could emerge.

DESIGN AND ACTIVISM IN THE AMERICAS

Fernando Luiz Lara

When Tom Bieling invited me to write this essay it brought me the question of the existence (or not) of a unique kind of design activism in the Americas. In order to elaborate later on the kinds of activism currently being practiced by designers in this continent of ours, please allow me to define the urban history that created the contemporary challenges. For they are the very roots calling for Design Activism.

America the Unequal

The latest OECD report on inequality shows that the three most unequal countries of the so-called „developed" countries are in the Americas: United States, Chile and Mexico in that order. Add Brazil, Colombia, Venezuela, and Peru to the list and we have the following picture: the Americas are much more unequal than the rest of the world, including most of Africa and the Middle East. This alone would induce the need for strong design activism in our continent for in the context of high inequality and weak social safety net it is up for the third sector to lead the fight for a better built environment. What we see in the Americas today is a strong drive for design activism in the sense that architects, students and community leaders are coming together to improve their neighborhoods with any means at their disposal. In this essay I will briefly review the roots of high inequality and fragile welfare state in the Americas in order to discuss the impact of different modes and practices that we shall label *design activism*.

To explain this scenario requires a dive in the colonial enterprise that dominated us for over three centuries. For instance, after 200 years of independence the Americas has a gross domestic product almost identical to Europe: 24.5 trillion this side of the Atlantic, 24.4 trillion over there (2013 data). Our population is 20% higher, 930 million people, compared with 730 million Europeans. In a hypothetical egalitarian world Europeans would be 20% richer than we in the Americas. However, our levels of poverty and sheer inequality are rampant when compared to Europe. It seems important to acknowledge that our cities function as an important facet in our outrageous inequality. In Europe cities have always been synonymous with inclusion: "Stadtluft macht frei" (city air makes you free) says the old dictum. In the Americas, since the colonial enterprise, cities have always been an exclusion machine (Mignolo 2011).

The Americas are not only unequal, they are also oblivious. Our cities were designed to exclude and to forget. To exclude any non-white, non-wealthy citizen and to forget their histories. The land here is stained by two enormous tragedies: the Amerindian holocaust and slavery. The Amerindian holocaust is the name given to the massive loss of life during the 16th century. From an estimate of 10 million inhabitants in 1500, the Amerindians were decimated to less than 2 million one hundred years after. Only one in every 10 persons born during the 16th century survived the arrival of measles, chicken pox and influenza, accompanied by guns and metal swords. In the course of the following 150 years an estimated 8 million (such a coincidence!) Africans were enslaved and sent to work the land, making sure it remained productive and extremely profitable. Anything we discuss in the Americas to this day is framed by those twin tragedies. Our space was made and remade by those tragedies. Our architecture is the result of those tragedies. Our activism is a response (pale most of the times) to those tragedies.

We know very little about how the Americas were before the arrival of the Europeans in 1492 but we know enough (and we learn more and more each day) to understand that it was no utopia, no paradise on earth (Cardinal-Pett 2015). The two most advanced pre-Columbian societies, the Inca empire in the Andes and the Aztec empire in the central valley of Mexico were exceedingly stratified, with an army of peasants serving a small military and clerical elite. It indeed did not change with the arrival of European Christians. Much to the contrary, the Spanish *conquistadores* replaced the very top of those stratified societies and put everybody else to work for them. In an effort to organize the colonial settlements, the king of Spain in 1572, Felipe II, decreed the famous Law of the Indies. Among the 148 articles that organized the Spanish bureaucracy in the Americas there were several that dictated how cities should be designed and built. One amongst those are of ultimate importance to us. While several articles talk about converting the natives and treating them well, article 137 explicitly says that: *"while the town is being completed, the settlers should try, inasmuch as this is possible, to avoid communication and traffic with the Indians, or going to their towns, or amusing themselves or spilling themselves on the ground [sensual pleasures?]; nor [should the settlers] allow the Indians to enter within the confines of the town until it is built and its defenses ready and houses built so that when the Indians see them they will be struck with admiration and will understand that the Spaniards are there to settle permanently and not temporarily. They [the Spaniards] should be so feared that they [the Indians] will not dare offend them, but they will respect them and desire their friendship"* (Lejeune 2005).

Such was the beginning of town planning in the Americas: a city to exclude and to induce respect by fear is very different from a city to make people free. Since the early 16th century such was the rule: a city as a machine to exclude. The move from colonial rule to independence did little to change that in the 19th century, except for small rural communities in the northern United States where there was a significant level of inclusion by homogeneity, meaning everybody not conforming to WASP[1] characteristics was therefore expelled or shunned into oblivion. For the large metropolitan areas exploding with urban growth, the rule was an urbanization of exclusion that concentrated wealth and power in the hands of a few, from New York to Buenos Aires, From San Francisco to Lima.

To reflect on our urban heritage in the Americas is to reflect on a spatial history of violence and exclusion. The first Europeans to travel (and rape) this land like Hernan Cortez wrote about complex and wealthy cities much beyond the well-researched Cuzco and Tenochtitlan (See Stannard 1992; Cañizares-Esguerra 2006). Cities in the heart of the Amazon, cities in the Mississippi valley, cities by the island of Santa Catarina in southern Brazil. The ones who came one century later to take possession of the land saw nothing and called the old explorers liars. Four hundred more years would pass before the remains of those great cities start to be unearthed. The early explorers' awe was justified and their word vindicated, but the holocaust they provoked is made even more shocking. Eighty percent of the population died in the first century after the encounter, many by gunpowder, but many more by viruses and bacteria.

America the Activist

With a rooted history of exclusion and erasure, the Americas also have developed in the last 50 years a tradition of participation and activism that, despite its successes, have been mostly invisible in the design scholarship. This essay will depart from the troubled history of 23 de Enero in Caracas (1956-58) to analyze PREVI in Peru (1966-70); Rural Studio in Alabama (1990s); Favela-Bairro in Rio de Janeiro (1994-97) and the contemporary *colectivos* that are taking matters in their own hands and pushing architecture away from its elitists quarters and straight to the streets.

In January of 2016 the Pritzker Prize was announced to Chilean architect Alejandro Araveña. His practice Elemental is a leading firm on societal engagement, their housing schemes an award-winning proposal that unites incremental design with social awareness. Later that same year Araveña would curate the Venice Bienalle with the theme of "reporting from the front". Perhaps, as I will argue in this article, the tide is changing and we will see more and more architecture celebrating their social roles and engaging the "front" instead of banking on elitism and exclusivism. But only hours after Araveña's prize the internet was full of traditional architects denouncing his choice as "political correctness" and decrying that "feel good" intentions have trumped good old architectural judgment. Back in 1972 Giancarlo de Carlo had already demonstrated that architecture was losing its engagement with reality but it would take several decades for his words to be heard. As I hope to show in this essay, architectural excellence is only heightened, never shortened by social

---

1   WASP is the acronym for White, Anglo-Saxon, Protestant.

engagement. It is about time that we stop selling exclusivity under the banner of art. Exclusivity, individualism, exceptionalism are disguised instruments of exclusion, and it is about time that architecture gets more inclusive in all aspects: race, gender, class, region, taste, you name it.

The issue of design activism in the Americas allows me to bring together a series of practices and experiences that together make for a robust body of knowledge that, as I just stated, have not been much explored yet. The reasons why the architecture of social engagement have not yet reached the level of dissemination that it deserves are many. First and foremost, because architecture has distanced itself from the idea of social transformation, or as I shall discuss, mainstream architecture has dislocated utopian ideals to the margins of the discipline. While modern architecture was developed with strong emphasis on social transformation one century ago, the critique of the 1960s set the discipline in an introvert and centripetal path that remained in place for decades (de Carlo 1972). It would take forty years for social issues to come back to the agenda of architecture schools in the North Atlantic. The Reagan-Thatcher dismantling of the welfare state set architecture in a search for exclusivity at any cost, without ever considering its dark side: exclusion. After the global financial meltdown of 2008, architecture, as defined by the North Atlantic circuit of media, lectures and exhibitions, started to value social engagement again. It was about time.

Second in my reasons on why social engagement has not occupied the central position it deserves is the fact that it implies, by definition, less control on the part of the architect. British educator Jonathan Hill has elucidated two decades ago the processes by which "the architect" resists the occupation of the profession by any "other", be it clients, users or the construction industry that together make it possible (Hill 1998). Since the publication of "Occupying Architecture" the profession has indeed witnessed the decline of the lone genius creator and the rise of collaborative collectives, but it has still not embraced society at large in the definition of what comprises good architecture.

It hasn't been always like that, much to the contrary. From antiquity to the end of the 19th century architects have served those in power, designing cathedrals and castles. The dawn of the 20th century witnessed a transformation in architecture clients and programs. At last architects were designing schools, hospitals, train stations, worker's clubs, sports facilities, public infrastructure of every kind. There was also more interest in urban transformations, mostly confined to slum removal and opening of arteries, the American cities following Haussmann's compass (See Almandoz 2002; Fishman 1989). New York's Slum Clearance Committee in the 1930s and Detroit Black Bottom demolition in 1943 are some of the famous cases but the infamous precursor was Rio de Janeiro with the reforms of mayor Pereira Passos in 1906, expelling thousands of poor families from crowded downtown to make room for boulevards and new development.

One good point for us to discuss is to what extent we can call activism the practice of modernist avant-garde. The protagonists surely proposed housing solutions for the masses. In the USA Frank Lloyd Wright designed his Usonian houses; in

Europe Mies van der Rohe designed several multi-family buildings; in Mexico Juan O'Gorman built four public schools for the price of one earlier design; in Brazil Oscar Niemeyer dreamed of a communist government that would provide houses for all. They did not engage much with the clients nor did they think of architecture as a collective endeavor. They were, in a way, architects in the old sense of the term: genius creators that had solutions for everything. That said, they deserve credit for calling the responsibility to themselves in hopes of transforming society. It is just that they did not think – or at least recognize – society should have a say in such transformations.

23 de Enero

Later on, when governments finally accepted that housing was a major issue to be urgently addressed, the solutions were all top-down such as the now famous Prutt-Igoe in Saint Louis; Cabrini Green in Chicago; Forte Apache in Buenos Aires or the most interesting of all, the 23 de Enero in Caracas. The 23 de Enero housing complex is the perfect example of the fate of such large projects hailed as the solution for housing problems in the mid 20th century. Designed by Carlos Raul Villanueva, the most celebrated Venezuelan architect, in 1956 it was first named 2 de diciembre for the day that general Perez Jimenez came to power in 1952. When he commissioned Villanueva to design the complex in 1956, the idea was to celebrate his government with a successful relocation, building high rises where slums previously existed. Fifty large blocks of fifteen floors each should provide nine thousand apartments for the Venezuelan working class (Carranza/Lara 2015, 155).

However, before the buildings were completed, another coup ousted Perez Jimenez and the unfinished apartments were occupied by the rioting crowd. People occupied also the open spaces between the buildings and the barrio returned blanketing all the ground area. The complex was renamed for the date that celebrates the end of the Perez Jimenez era: January 2nd, 1958. Moreover, it was at 23 de Enero that young army colonel Hugo Chaves Frias got in touch with the realities of exclusion and developed his political theories during the time that he was in charge of the Quartel de la Montaña, located on the hill adjacent to the complex. When Chavez was ousted for 48 hours in 2002, it was the people of 23 de Enero that blocked downtown Caracas, paralyzing the city and frustrating the coup supported by the Bush administration in the USA.

Design activism matters, huh?

PREVI

Experiments with more awareness of social engagement were happening all over the world in the 1960s but the protagonist (also not widely known) would be again in Latin America. In 1967 the United Nations consultant Peter Lang convinced the government of Peru that they should hold a competition with the best architects in the world to design incremental housing (Kahatt 2015). With an architect – Fernando Belaunde – in the presidency, the Peruvian government called the PREVI (Proyecto Experimental de Vivienda) competition with 13 invited architects from all over the world and 13 selected from Peru.[2] The competition brief called for the design of 1500 low rise housing units clustered around smaller neighborhoods, connected to schools, community and commercial facilities. The competition also asked the architects to consider the need for future expansion embedded in the structural and spatial concepts, the incremental mandate being as much social engagement as they could handle at the time.

The idea was so good that one might wonder why it hasn't been done more often. Invite the best architects of the world to design for the poor, connect them with another selected group of local designers, arrange for the United Nations to provide technical support and develop a finance mechanism that ensures the economical sustainability of the process. Nevertheless, PREVI had already disappeared from the architectural radar by the time the houses were inhabited in 1978.

To understand the value of PREVI we need to consider that it was proposed only a few years after Jane Jacobs (1963) and Venturi's (1966) books, a time in which most cities were still insisting in towers in the park as a solution for low-income housing. The master plan does resemble Brasilia's super-quadras but the low rise high-density cluster which incorporates growth and adaptation as an integral component of the concept was quite radical at the time. PREVI was also designed before John Turner published his studies defending self-built informality as a solution rather than a problem, something already incorporated at PREVI (Carranza/Lara 2015, 263). Besides, PREVI is not social housing as we know it in the developed north. The inhabitants own the units and the need for future self-help growth was part of the concept since the beginning. Indeed, it is very much possible that the modifications built by the families were partially to blame for PREVI's falling off the architectural radar.

One of the main disciples of PREVI is the Elemental scheme developed by Alejandro Araveña. The Venice Biennale curator and Pritzker Prize 2016 devised a tiny 300sq ft house that should work as a seed space for low income families in Chile. The brilliance of the design is that the houses were understood as spaces to be later expanded and modified by the inhabitants themselves. Elemental gets the best of the construction industry standardization (good plumbing, good structure, organized access) and the best of self-built logic (flexible spaces, incremental changes).

The 1960s was surely a time of enchantment with social engagement on the part of architects but unfortunately the great experiments of the Unidad Vecinales in Chile; Cajueiro Seco and Bras de Pina in Brazil would all be shelved by the military dictatorships

---

2   The 13 foreign architects were: James Stirling (UK), Knud Svenssons (Dennmark), Esquerra /Samper /Sáenz /Urdaneta (Colombia), Atelier 5 (Swizerland), Toivo Korhonen (Finland), Charles Correa (India), Kikutake / Maki /Kurokawa (Japan), Iñiguez de Onzoño /Vásquez de Castro (Spain), Hansen, Hatloy (Poland), Aldo van Eyck (Netherlands), Candilis /Josic /Woods (France), and Christopher Alexander (USA). The 13 Peruvian were: Miguel Alvariño; Ernesto Paredes; Miró-Quesada /Williams /Núñez; Gunter /Seminario; Morales /Montagne; Juan Reiser; Eduardo Orrego; Vier /Zanelli; Vella /Bentín /Quiñones /Takahashi; Mazzarri /Llanos; Cooper / García-Bryce /Graña /Nicolini; Chaparro /Ramírez; Smirnoff /Wiskowsky; Crousse /Páez /Pérez-León.

that swiped the continent as collateral damage of the cold war. Another two decades would pass before a major project with strong social engagement was built.

Favela Bairro

In 1994 a competition for ideas on how to intervene in mid-size informal settlements, was called in Rio de Janeiro. Thirty-two local firms submitted proposals and fifteen were selected (one for each of fifteen areas prioritized). The first phase of Favela-Bairro (1994-1998) had an integrated approach, in which accessibility and connectivity would be addressed by building roads and public space infrastructure which would also improve drainage and sewage connections, relocating as few families as possible from risky areas and building new housing for those inside each community (Duarte/ Magalhães 2009). The Favela-Bairro project became the model for larger interventions all over Brazil during the presidency of Lula da Silva (2003-2010). Many of those interventions were based on a participatory process of making budget decisions that was the trademark of Lula's party, the PT, in the 1990s. In the participatory budget process the inhabitants were encouraged to organize in assemblies and vote of the priorities for the city public works budget (Lara 2010). The process, when continued over decades (spanning many different administrations) had the power to bring the population to the forefront of discussions around infrastructure. It also inspired other actors such as Bacho Gibran, a biologist that led a remarkable landscape initiative in Belo Horizonte. Hired by a construction company to re-vegetate the park area after the roads and sewage main were built, Gibran decided to work with the community of an ambitious but very successful project. Instead of just purchasing plants and seeds from the nurseries Gibran built a greenhouse and trained local youth on the processes of caring and splitting mature plants into seedlings. The team went door to door on the houses that were scheduled for demolition and/or relocation and retrieved hundreds of plants before the families moved out. One year later, Gibran's team invited the families to choose where in the park their plants should be located. This fostered a connection between the neighbors and the new park, the result being that the community feels much more responsible for the area. With densities above 300 inhabitants per hectare there is no question that green open space is a much-needed improvement but without the engagement component people feel alienated from the park and less inclined to care for it (Lara 2010).

Cantinho do Céu

Elsewhere in Brazil informal settlements were transformed and conditions improved for millions. But as a rule of thumb I am confident that the more participation opportunities the better the results. One of the best examples is the work of Marcos Boldarini at Cantinho do Céu, a very vulnerable community at the southern periphery of São Paulo. Working around the margins of a lake once used as garbage dump the Cantinho do Céu project stitches together social awareness and elegant details to water filtration, an important example of how architecture could make a difference regarding the contemporary challenge of balancing social and environmental sustainabilities. Local participation was not the tradition in São Paulo's government when Boldarini got the commission, but his sensibility and his commitment to spend time there and listen to the community made all the difference.

Marcos Boldarini started his career working for the Erundina administration at the city of São Paulo (1989-1993) and brought a strong community engagement as a basis for his design practice. Moreover, Boldarini and his team (led by Lucas Nobre at the office) has been able to achieve the highest quality of detail and construction, a rare feature in Brazilian contemporary social-housing. His dedication to the communities can be seen in the first book published about his work (Boldarini 2018). Where other architects talk about gestures and artistic intentions, Boldarini interviewed community leaders to test how they perceive the architecture produced by the office.

In his own words: *"Yes, Cantinho do Céu, like other recent projects, is a consequence of the learning and experimentation carried out in the public projects, understanding these first projects as a cumulative process of experiences and production of knowledge. Before we get to Cantinho do Céu in 2008, it is worth mentioning, as part of this training process, a set of important projects developed since 2004 for the Project of Technical Assistance to the Sanitation Program for Populations in Low Income Areas - Prosanear implemented by the federal government in partnership with municipalities. Those interventions for Prosanear presented popular participation as one of the structuring and obligatory components of the methodology for the development of the works. And in addition to this obligation to work with participatory processes - something that we are developing until today - it mandated a local office in the communities. We rented spaces within the areas of intervention and worked there, participating in the daily life of these communities, a very rich experience"* (ibid., 32).

Today, few years later only, Boldarini is being recognized as the best architect in the country for projects of high complexity in informal areas, and his investment in social engagement paying dividends for several communities that are lucky enough to have him guiding their projects.

Medellin

Medellin, Colombia's second largest city, was aiming even higher that its Brazilian neighbors in the early 2000s, and reaping its deserved rewards. The city known in the 1980s for its infamous drug cartel became a poster child for Colombia's urban renaissance. Galvanized around Sergio Fajardo, a professor at Universidad Nacional with a PhD in math that was elected mayor of Medellin in 2003, the local institutions combine a strong belief in architecture as catalyzer for change with creative initiatives such as community leaders signing documents pledging to maintain a new park after inauguration.

A city with strong institutions: the EDU - Empresa de Desarollo Urbano, and the

EPM - Empresas Publicas Municipais are able to finance and manage great projects all over the city, poorest peripheries included. Some are most iconic buildings such as Parque Biblioteca de España, a library and community center built in the hilly informal sector of Santo Domingo. Organized around three monolithic dark volumes enveloping the spaces, the library complex sits like "rocks" on the site, recreating the mountain profile according to architect Giancarlo Mazzanti. Unfortunately, this iconic work presented construction problems since inauguration and is now closed to the public, awaiting the courts decide who should pay for repairs. Other less visible parts of the projects are perhaps more important such as the "park" side of the complex, a series of ramps that makes the library and the community more accessible.

Several other projects in Medellin deserve praise and were extensively published since: the intervention at Praca de Cisneros by Juan Manuel Pelaez; the Leon de Greiff library by Mazzanti; or the Hontanares School by Felipe Mesa and Alejandro Bernal (Plan B Arquitectos). My favorite is the Orquideorama (also by Mesa and Bernal), a shade and support for a collection of orchids in Medellin's botanical gardens, designed as a sequence of hexagonal shaped roof structures that are grouped together.

Rural Studio

While Brazil and Colombia have used the public sector as catalyzer of those projects, other countries and/or initiatives are less based in governmental budgets and large construction companies, more taking the matters in their own hands. The model for them all is the Rural Studio led by Samuel Mockbee at Auburn University in Alabama from 1993 until his death in 2001. At the core of the Rural Studio is the idea that the design studio should serve as real galvanizers for design and implementation of small projects in the poorest areas of the region. Students led by Mockbee designed, detailed, budgeted, fundraised, and built small structures in the rural backlands of Alabama. Since 1993 the Rural Studio, now led by Xavier Vendrell, has built 170 structures and engaged over 800 students – or citizen architects as they call it.

The process is now spreading like fire throughout the Americas. In Texas a long time collaborator of Mockbee, Coleman Cooker, has been doing the same with beautiful results and enthusiastic support of the participating students, designing structures that support the State Parks in the Gulf of Mexico. Also in Austin, TX Jack Sanders, another Mockbee collaborator, has founded Design Build Adventure, a workshop based on the idea that building is the basis for transforming the world. Sanders promotes camps for students and anybody interested, teaching them the basics of construction, craftsmanship, installation and furniture manufacturing. Several other university-based initiatives have sprouted all over the Americas following the lead of the Rural Studio.

In Queretaro, Mexico, Juan Alfonso Garduño came back from Harvard's GSD to found the Taller Activo under the auspices of the Monterrey Tech. At Taller Activo students interview the local communities, hold a design competition, detail the winning proposal (chosen with community input), fund raise and build the projects in the 16 weeks time of a college semester. Their project for Sombrerete for instance is a minimalist intervention: a light roof supported by two walls over a base of concrete pavers. Economy of materials and elegance of design used to transform the lives of a working-class community. In Paraguay students of Javier Corvalen have founded Acqua Alta, a collective that works on projects for the underserved communities of Assuncion. In São Paulo a group called Oficina Goma has sprouted from Escola da Cidade and is now changing the face of several communities with their light-weight light-based interventions.

Al Borde

In Ecuador a design collaborative founded by David Barragan and Pascual Gangotena – Al Borde - designed and built the Nueva Esperanza school in a remote fishing village. With a budget of around 200 USD, Al Borde relied on local timber and thatched roof to materialize a sophisticated diamond-shaped form. Built of course with the help of local fisherman, the Nueva Esperanza school launched them on a path of leadership on participatory design and construction. Now, a few years and several projects later, Al Borde is organizing workshops all over the world and proving that participatory design is indeed a big hit with students everywhere.

Grupo Talca

Less famous but probably more effective is the work of the Talca school in Chile. Located in the central valley and catering to the sons and daughters of farm workers, loggers and miners, the Talca school, led by Juan Roman, has one of the most radical pedagogies being experimented those days in the world. Inspired by the Valparaiso school experimentations of the 1960s and 70s, the Talca school requires that all students complete their graduation project in order to claim their diploma. And when I say complete their project I don't mean finish all the drawings. The school requires every graduate to build their project. Students are trained, since the beginning of the studio sequence, to work in groups, cater to the needs of the community, and only design what they can actually build. In addition, they have extensive exposure to issues of fund raising, craftsmanship and resource availability. The result is a school absolutely rooted in the community.

Optimist Conclusions

Despite the gloomy introduction discussing why is needed in such unequal parts of the world, I am actually very optimistic about the fact that the tide is indeed changing and more architects are paying attention to small scale interventions with high transformative potential. My data set is probably very biased but at least 50% of my students are interested in this kind of work, not at all interested in corporate jobs or fancy design firm (although the hard realities of life will probably make them reconsider). In addition, everywhere I go to talk about contemporary architecture in Latin America, those are the project that people are interested in, not the outrageously expensive museum by Calatrava in Rio or the new airport by Norman Foster in Mexico City. There is a strong realization that this is an important and feasible career choice, and Alejandro Araveña's Pritzker Prize of 2016 have certainly helped. We might be experiencing the very end of starchitects' era. We certainly are experiencing the dawn of a much more humble, connected and socially aware practice of architecture. The problem for me is that in library shelves, textbooks and syllabus reading lists we still have hundreds of titles celebrating the elitist genius of the past traditions and not enough exposure, not to mention good criticism and evaluation, of the impact made by a new more of socially engaged architecture.

It is my hope that this essay can work as a simple but effective map for navigating those new approaches. Here you have a few references and a few concepts. Go out and chart your path based on it.

References

Almandoz, Arturo (ed.) (2002): *Planning Latin America's Capital Cities 1850-1950*. 1 edition. London: Routledge.

Boldarini, Marcos (2018): "Interview" in Boldarini Arquitetos Associados (Fernando Lara, editor), São Paulo / Austin: Nhamerica Platform.

Cañizares-Esguerra, Jorge (2006): *Puritan Conquistadors: Iberianizing the Atlantic, 1550-1700*. Stanford, Calif: Stanford University Press.

Cardinal-Pett, Clare (2015): *A History of Architecture and Urbanism in the Americas*. Routledge.

Carlo, Giancarlo De (1972): *An Architecture of Participation*. Royal Australian Institute of Architects.

Carranza, Luis E. / Lara, Fernando Luiz (2015): *Modern Architecture in Latin America: Art, Technology, and Utopia*. Austin: University of Texas Press.

Duarte, Cristiane / Magalhães, Fernanda (2009): Upgrading Squater Settlements into City Neighborhoods, the Favela-Bairro program in Rio de Janeiro, in *Beyond Brasilia, Contemporary Urbanism in Brazil*, Gainseville, University Press of Florida, pp. 266-290.

Fishman, Robert (1989): *Bourgeois Utopias: The Rise and Fall of Suburbia*. 3.1.1989 edition. New York: Basic Books.

Hill, Jonathan (1998): *Occupying Architecture: Between the Architect and the User*. London / New York: Routledge.

Jacobs, Jane (1963): *The Death and Life of Great American Cities*. New York: Random House.

Kahatt, Sharif S. (2015): *Utopías Construidas - Sharif Kahatt*. Fondo Editorial PUCP.

Lara, Fernando Luiz (2010): Beyond Curitiba: The Rise of a Participatory Model for Urban Intervention in Brazil. *Urban Design International* 15, no. 2 (May 2010): 119–28.

Lejeune, Jean-François et alli. (2005): *Cruelty & Utopia: Cities and Landscapes of Latin America*. New York: Princeton Architectural Press.

Mignolo, Walter D. (2011): *The Darker Side of Western Modernity: Global Futures*, Decolonial Options. Durham: Duke University Press Books.

Stannard, David E. (1992): *American Holocaust: Columbus and the Conquest of the New World*. New York / Oxford University Press.

Venturi, Robert / Museum of Modern Art (1966): *Complexity and Contradiction in Architecture*. New York: Museum of Modern Art.

CRITIQUE OF THE ACTIVIST-DESIGNER PHENOMENON BASED ON ARAB SPRING EXPERIENCES

Maziar Rezai

The main idea of this chapter is inspired by changes that have happened during the last eight years in Arab countries called Arab Spring. These changes and movements happened to pursue democracy in these countries; although the result of many of them was not democracy. Tunisia's political and social situation changed peacefully, Egypt has changed by a semi-revolution and some other MENA[1] area countries such as Libya, Iraq, and Syria have collapsed in a pit of violence. As for just six years, about 550.000 people have been killed and hundreds of thousands of people displaced in these three countries. In fact, the democratic movement of the Arab Spring, unfortunately, changed its route to the appearance of ISIL and tragedies that are objective evidence of crimes against humanity.

The starting point of the Arab Spring was affected by the controversial presidential election of Iran in 2009. When thousands of Iranians took to the streets of Tehran[2], to protest the election outcome (Karagiannopoulos 2012). I (as a designer and as witness), in the middle of all these happenings, could observe acts of design through people's expressions of change in the course of the revolution that brings many questions to mind: what is the role of design in this situation? In addition, what can be a meaningful act provided or supported by the designer in this atmosphere? This chapter attempts to review this action and this role.

Designers Action

Herbert Simon in *The Sciences of the Artificial* states: Design in itself is always about *"courses of action aimed at changing existing situations into preferred ones"* (Simon 1969). This proposition was a route to the conclusion that designers should see the world as something that can be changed by their acts; although to devise *courses of action* is different from taking action.

In 1971, Victor Papanek published his famous work, *Design for the Real World* that quickly became the bible of the responsible design movement, and Papanek himself

---

1   Middle East and North Africa.
2   Those days in June, I was in Tehran, following the events, closely.

became a leader to the dissatisfied or disaffected in design practices (Whiteley 1993). After this book, in the seventies, many designers wanted to save the world by their own actions – and considered themselves strongly responsible for the developments around them. Designers wanted to solve every problem from abortion to the Vietnam War and to abandon design for profit (Hiesinger/Marcus 1993). The old *form follows function* or fitness for purpose slogan was changed to fitness for need at the Design and Industries Association in 1975 (ibid). Designers also saw themselves opposing to large corporations, which were seen as capitalist exploiters – a rather double-faced approach considering that the designers were employed by the same companies (Valtonen 2006).

Against this background, Ann Thorpe has been exploring the Activism phenomenon, stating that Activism starts when groups within society call for change and society responds – either resisting or incorporating the values encapsulated by activism: *"I define activism as taking intentional action to instigate change on behalf of a neglected group"*. And with making a relation between designers and activists, she continues: *"Designers are working across a range of groups and issues, ranging from victims of war or disaster to minority groups"* (Thorpe 2008). In fact, the picture she presents, tells us that interest in public service design and design activism has been rising. Yet in conversations, it is also common to hear the suggestion that since most design seeks to improve the conditions of life, most of it must – in some senses – be activism.

This picture, in my view, opens up a new horizon to look at the concept of design. However, this new vision is completely affected by activism. Especially where Thorpe concludes that drawing on concepts of activism from social movement research and conventional activist practice, we can formulate a more useful, robust characterization of design as activism (w 2010). She believes this definition helps designers and social movement actors to gain a better understanding of the spatial and material possibilities of design's role in activism, but she forgot that design's role should not merely lead to the pursuit of activism structures or the loss of creativity (Rezai/Khazaei 2017). Activism is a dynamic process and a good exemplar for design; of course not to imitate, but to follow.

The relation of Design and Activism is not all of our discussion here. Another determinative critique in this regard is the role of the Designer and the boundary of being 'Activist-Designer' and being 'Activist'. To illustrate the dimensions of this critique, we shall examine the *Forms of Resistance* project, as a case study.

Tehran _ Gothenburg: Forms of Resistance

Forms of Resistance is an instance to express the perception of design action. The project was a collaboration of two female activist groups, one in Tehran (Iran) and one in Gothenburg (Sweden). The purpose of this project has been to record the process amongst activists under the supervision of two designers without the intervention of them in designing the process. The process that could change some ordinary workshops for women subjected to violence and find impressive results to show the problem of violence against women and making discussion in the society.

The first experiment took place in November 2010 in Tehran, based on experiences of violence or resistance against violence in everyday life. The activists set up three writing workshops in three cities of Iran, in which the activity of writing was understood as a performative tool to make a common sense of women's experiences. Around 100 short stories were written, most of them based on an object or an image from a place that reminds the sense of violence for women who attended the project. Some of these stories were selected by the activists and were exhibited in a café in a highly frequented street in Tehran, in which pedestrians would encounter them in the course of their everyday activities.

The second experiment was a collaboration that took place in February 2011, with an activist group concerned with violence against 'undocumented' women in Sweden. It took the form of documenting the experiences of these women, a process that the women themselves initiated in order to overcome the temporariness of their situations, their 'bare life'. At the end of the Gothenburg experiment, the outcome of the collaborative activity was a pocket book including photos taken by one of the women and materials she gathered from her everyday life, such as notes, diaries, etc.

The results of these two experiments were shown in an exhibition and a series of workshops at Konstfack University of Arts, Crafts and Design in Stockholm, Sweden, in May 2011.The exhibition and workshops were set up for people to browse through the materials.[3]After a brief introduction, the participants of the workshop sessions were invited to select and sequence some of the papers on the blank pages of a provided book. Five sessions were conducted, in which about 45 pages of the book were produced, co-authored by the participants including the provided materials.

The feature of this project, especially in the Tehran part, was putting two designers aside; designers who companioned women activists in this project. One key task for them: "not being designers" and "not using creative techniques to manage ideas" in the design process. Of course, this absence could make a space for activists to do what they have to do, but raise an important question: Does being 'Activist-Designer' mean not being 'Designer'? This question imposes the necessity of reviewing the Activist-Designer notion.

---

3   The images and texts appeared as an abstract translation of the original materials.

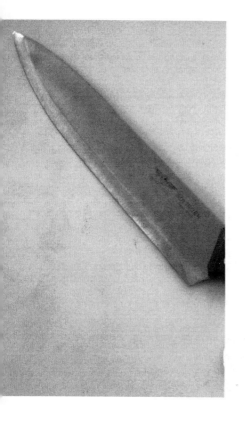

خشونت هم میان کدا از نامعینی پیداست که کلمه‌ای
است که هم از اسم آن ناراحت می‌شوند
من در اوایل از دواجم یک روز همسرم ماهیتابه‌ای
را که پر از غذا بود به سقف اتاق پرتاب
کرد که من از آن روز از این طرف بدم
می‌آمد
ولی بارم هرا بخاطر حرفی که زده بودم
با چاقوی بزرگی که در منزل داشتیم
مرا تهدید کرد که با آن طوری به من
می‌زنند من از آن چاقو
خاطره بدی بجا کردم

Figure 10: Experience of resistance: A note by a woman subjected to violence.
Photo by Mahmoud Keshavarz, 2010. www.experienceofresistance.com

Figure 11: Book by participants. Photo by Mahmoud Keshavarz. www.experienceofresistance.com

Arab Spring: Nondesigner's Designs in Revolutionary Squares

The Arab Spring (Arabic: الربيع العربي), also referred to as Arab Revolutions was a revolutionary wave of both violent and non-violent demonstrations, protests, riots, coups and civil wars in North Africa and the Middle East that began on 17 December 2010 in Tunisia with the Tunisian Revolution.

The Tunisian Revolution had a great impact on five other countries: Libya, Egypt, Yemen, Syria and Bahrain, where either the regime was toppled or major uprisings or social violence occurred, including civil wars or insurgencies in Syria and Iraq, for instance. In addition, sustained street demonstrations took place in other Arab countries.

In this way, the Egypt Revolution provides a good example for change by action of design. Here again, the change has been activated by "nondesigners" on the streets of Cairo; Change as reformation, redesigning, reassembling and remaking. On 25 January 2011, the Egyptian semi-revolution, locally known as the January 25 Revolution, began and took place across all of Egypt. It consisted of demonstrations, marches, occupation of plazas, riots, non-violent civil resistance, acts of civil disobedience and strikes. Millions of protesters from a range of socio-economic and religious backgrounds demanded the overthrow of the Egyptian President Hosni Mubarak. Violent clashes between security forces and protesters resulted in at least 846 people being killed and over 6,000 injured.[4] The protests took place in Cairo, Alexandria and other cities and one of the most important places of demonstrations in Cairo was Tahrir Square. The word Tahrir (Arabic: تحرير) means 'Freedom', and Tahrir Square as one of the city's main squares, appears to be the most important one in Cairo, in terms of public gatherings, national events or demonstrations happening there.

Eray Cayli explained the situation of the square in an analytic report for the Turkish newspaper *Radikal*: "*What really highlighted the spatial characteristics of the demonstrations in Tahrir was the fight between pro- and anti-Mubarak demonstrators for domination over the square. Once the latter won, they decided to settle in the square, in order to protect this hard-earned victory. So committed were they in this regard that they converted Tahrir into a small-scale neighbourhood*" (Cayli 2011).

Cayli describes the self-initiated redesigning of Tahrir accordance with demonstrator's needs as a new birth to a unique kind of political activism, which in turn led to their success (ibid.). For instance, the demonstrators took over a fast food restaurant and turned it into a hospital. This and a number of smaller healthcare centres set up in and around the square would provide handy, immediate and free of charge services that under 'normal' conditions would not have been available to all. The protesters who brought their children along to Tahrir redesigned a corner of the square as kindergarten. In another corner, a wall was furnished with newspapers so that people, who could not afford them, could

---

4   https://en.wikipedia.org/wiki/Egyptian_revolution_of_2011 [retrieved 12.05.2018].

keep themselves up to date. Right in the heart of the square, the roundabout was used to host overnight campers. A group of demonstrators showed environmental concern by setting up recycling points. Food stalls and flag vendors illustrated a functioning economy that had been formed in the square. Furthermore, a speakers' corner had been installed in Tahrir, as a platform for people to share and discuss thoughts with others. Probably the best example that illustrates the protesters' political power, which was directly linked to the creative use and spatial redesign, is this one: Protesters who spent the nights in tank wheels, in order to prevent the army's feared advance into the square (ibid.).

Actually, what happened in Tahrir Square on an urban/social level was exactly what had been analysed before in Design as a phenomenon called "Design by Use". In 2009, Uta Brandes explored this special kind of design, in which people with no formal design-training reuse things (using things for different purpose rather than what they are designed for), thus converting them to new uses, in short, "misuse" them in the very best sense of the word. Brandes and Michael Erlhoff describe this as *Non-intentional design* (NID), a term meant to illustrate the everyday redesign of designed objects by users that do not create a new design, but through using an object, create something new or replace the old. Such kind of Redesign through reuse can make things multifunctional and cleverly combines them to generate new functions. It is often reversible, resource-friendly, improvisational, innovative, and economical (Brandes/Stich/Wender 2009). This is what happened in Tahrir as well, which can be examined in Design Activism context: Protesters created a new story, a new experience and a new identity for an urban square. However, in this significant case too, there is no designer for designing these creative actions; design made by people in an extraordinary situation, that naturally implied a perfect design thinking process every day and transformed each single element of the square to a meaningful tool.

Another case: the Pearl Roundabout or Lulu Roundabout in Manama, Bahrain. A striking example not because of people's actions, but rather because of the government's reactions. The Pearl Roundabout used to be the central site during the 2011 protests, which began in February.

On March 18, 2011, government forces destroyed the roundabout as part of a crackdown on protesters. After demolishing the Pearl Monument, the government announced that the roundabout would be replaced with traffic lights, possibly to ease congestion in the financial district. The government also changed the name of the site to Al Farooq Junction, a reference to Umar ibn al-Khattab, a historical figure revered by Sunnis and considered by Shiites to be against their cause, as the main part of demonstrators was Shiites. The governmental plan to destruct and eliminate the Pearl Roundabout and change its name can easily be interpreted as a message to the demonstrators; A signal of control and sovereignty as a reaction to people's actions by eliminating, reuse and redesigning an urban element.

Design Activism: A Review

In these cases, practically, Design/Action has occurred but quite often, the operator was not a designer who is aware of his or her design action, but a nondesigner. In fact, the 'Design Activism' phenomenon, here, as well as the 'Design by Use' notion, although shows everyone can be a designer, helps for democratizing the Design and makes a new understanding of it but considering the designer absence can be a critical point, unless we review the concept of Design Activism.

We know this absence could make a space for activists or nondesigners to do what they have to do, but shows us a challenge in the Design Activism discourse and make an important issue: "What is the exact border between nondesigners and Activist Designers?" Therefore, I think there is a gap here that needs to be analysed: How we can separate the results of people who design by their ordinary actions and the designers who act by their designs.

As before this, we analysed these actions by people in the design activism area and we knew that they are not designers, activists or Activist-Designers. We, now, need a new term to do this division. Therefore, I would like to borrow this term from the 'Design by Use' concept and bring it to the Design Activism area. I would like to call it *Design by Act*. From my perspective, 'Design by Act' is the exact term to express the situation of those people who design by their acts, based on their social, political or cultural needs.

In other words, designer, here, is user itself; The people, who change their area, reform the products and design or redesign things or systems for sending a message to other people, government, or both. This message in diverse areas is different and can be a social, political or cultural message. What an Activist-Designer does is giving this message by its design and what these people do, is giving the message by their Act, while design serves their Acts in the purest mood.

Nevertheless, the key point here is that what guided us (Designers) to produce a new concept for our role in the society, Activist-Designer, was not desire to be an Activist; It's a need and passion to be critical and to be more effective in tackling social problems and not being the mere "servant problem solvers" or "service providers"(Keshavarz 2015). This made evident that Design goes something more than past and Designers called for more roles in the society. In my view, this need and passion is a kind of Intellectualism.

Intellectualism, in modern use and not in mere philosophical meaning, referred to the responsibility of elites of communities and reminded us of the *Dreyfus affair* and the reaction of Émile Zola and other French intellectuals in that historical case.[5] I do not want to open a new discourse, but I believe what the designer has to do as an Action in a Design Activism process, is not only being an activist. In fact, it is

---

5   The Dreyfus Affair was a political scandal that divided the Third French Republic from 1894 until its resolution in 1906. The affair is often seen as a modern and universal symbol of injustice, and it remains one of the most notable examples of a complex anti-Semitism. The major role played by the press and public opinion proved influential in the lasting social conflict.

Creative Enlightenment.[6] Otherwise, how can we determine the border of *Activist* and *Activist-Designer*? Thus, it may be possible to divide the Design Activism area into two contexts of Design by Act and Design Intellectualism.

In the Design Activism area, Intellectual-Designer is an Activist-Designer who first is a thinker, who observes, discovers, analyses and with a creative enlightenment reacts by design. However, like an ordinary designer, his or her reaction can be a confrontation with the society that can be a product, service or a political, social or cultural action/message as an intervention. We know what designers do, is creating value, but in this context, it is not an economic value only, but rather a value in a multi-dimensional form with an emphasis on social, political or cultural aspects.

This is the same perspective on Design, which can help to reframe design as the result of an active and conscious thinking process that creates a strong social, political and cultural message, action or some kind of other results that we may not be able to foresee. Therefore, it seems that the Intellectual-Designer concept follows the same route that Carl DiSalvo has described before in *Adversarial Design* with some differences (DiSalvo 2012).[7]

In this regards, Samer Akkach uses the Arabic word chosen for design: *Tasmim* (تصميم). *"[T]asmm (design)...[In] current usage, however, seems to be based on tasmim as 'determining,' 'making up one's mind' and 'resolve' to follow up a matter. Thus in linguistic terms 'design' is an act of determination, of sorting out possibilities, and of projecting a choice. It has little to do with problem-solving, the prevailing paradigm, as the designer (musammim/مصمم) seems to encounter choices, not problems, and to engage in judging merits, not solving problems. It is closer to [active] 'decision-maker'"* (Akkach 2003); who makes decisions to influence changes in specific directions.

From this perspective, Intellectual-Designer is a musammim or decision-maker who is effective in the community; at the same time, he is not outside the realm of design. Although his/her design is often action-oriented, but s/he has come to the action scene to take advantage of design, not because of being Activist. Maybe an Activist and a Designer, both opt for the common problem or they might be the same person, who requires thorough reflection of one's own role; severe role-conflicts may emerge. Therefore, a designer and activist, both, have chosen the case with awareness. However, there is a difference: an intellectual-designer would be far more creative and more responsive (in terms of feedback from the target group/audience/people).

---

6 I am using Creative Enlightenment as a term because, from my perspective, an Activist Designer usually works in an extreme, extraordinary or not ordinary atmosphere. This abnormal situation often is the encounter scene of social, political and or cultural problems. Therefore, at that moment, first, you are one person among ordinary people (nondesigners), second, a creative person at the maximum and third, a designer/Activist-Designer who is searching for a time to do something as a performative role. Here, 'creative enlightenment' can find a meaning in the square of being activist, being designer, thinking intellectual and raising awareness.

7 DiSalvo strives to question conventional approaches to political issues while interpreting politics is not our merely focus in this text.

Conclusion

The aim of this chapter was dividing the Design Activism area into two different contexts; Design by Act phenomenon and Design Intellectualism notion with a specified role, Intellectual-Designer. Intellectual-Designer, in a Design Activism area, is a necessity for the future of societies and aims at gaining a better understanding of how the designer can effectively work and interact with social and political problems; Problems that often need a kind of creative enlightenment for all parties envolved, in order to have a real and effective impact on the situation. Otherwise, the design work (the message) and/or the designer's role might disappear before reaching the audience.

In addition, this text tends to give an overview of the change in definition and the role of designers and their conscious interaction with society. The main questions of this research, including the role of the designer in a design activism area and at the border line of being Activist Designer and nondesigner. This has been approached by conducting multiple case studies analyzing the challenges for design activism in some significant cases over the last few years, looking at different contexts and conditions such as in Egypt, Iran, and Bahrain.

As Sara Ahmed proclaims *"what we 'do do' affects what we 'can do'. This is not to argue that 'doing' simply restricts capacities. In contrast, what we 'do do' opens up and expands some capacities, although an 'expansion' in certain directions might in turn restrict what we can do in others"* (Ahmed 2010). We, the designers, can do design. Acting with an intellectual mind is doing design on the new horizon, not only as an Activist but also as a Designer who has been introduced here as Intellectual-Designer. This horizon helps to reframe design as the result of an active and conscious thinking process that creates a strong message.

Acknowledgements: I am grateful to Prof. Dr. Michael Erlhoff, a person with whom I had the chance to discuss the ideas presented in this paper. In addition, I would like to express my sincere appreciations to Prof. Dr. Wolfgang Jonas, Dr. Mahmoud Keshavarz and Dr. Eray Cayli.

References

Ahmed, Sara (2010): Orientations matter, in Coole, D. and Frost, S. (eds.): *New materialisms: ontology, agency and politics.* Durham: Duke University Press.

Akkach, Samer (2003): Design and the Question of Eurocentricity, in: Design Philosophy Papers, vol. 1, no. 6, pp. 321–326.

Brandes, Uta / Stich, Sonja / Wender, Miriam (2009): *Design by Use: The Everyday Metamorphosis of Things.* Board of International Research in Design, Birkhäuser Architecture.

Cayli, Eray (2011): The Vernacular of Insurrection. Radikal Newspaper's monthly design supplement (published on 27 February 2011).

DiSalvo, Carl (2012): *Adversarial Design*, MIT Press.

Hiesinger, Kathryn B. and Marcus, George, (1993): *Landmarks of Twentieth-Century Design*, Abbeville Press.

Karagiannopoulos, Vasileios (2012): The Role of the Internet in Political Struggles: Some Conclusions from Iran and Egypt. New Political Science. 34 (2): 151–171.

Keshavarz, M. (2015): Design-Politics Nexus: Material Articulations and Modes of Acting, No 6 (2015): Nordes 2015: Design Ecologies, ISSN 1604-9705. Stockholm, www.nordes.org

Rezai, Maziar and Khazaei, Mitra (2017): The Challenge of being Activist-Designer. An attempt to understand the New Role of Designer in the Social change based on current experiences, The Design Journal, 20:sup1, S3516-S3535, DOI:10.1080/14606925.2017.1352855

Simon, Herbert A. (1969): *The sciences of the artificial*, Cambridge, MA: The MIT press.

Thorpe, Ann (2008): Design as Activism: A Conceptual Tool. In: *Changing the Change: Design Visions, Proposals: An international conference on the role and potential of design research in the transition towards sustainability* - Torino 10th – 12th July 2008. Available from: http://www.allemandi.com/university/ctc.pdf

Thorpe, Ann (2010): Defining Design as Activism, Available from: http://designactivism.net/wp-content/uploads/2011/05/Thorpe-definingdesignactivism.pdf

Valtonen, Anna (2006): Back and Forth with Ethics in Product Development: A history of ethical responsibility as a design driver in Europe: https://www.academia.edu/972634/Back_and_Forth_with_Ethics_in_Product_Development

Whiteley, Nigel (1993): *Design for Society*, 1993, Reaktion Books, Islington UK.

CAN DESIGN EVER BE ACTIVIST?
THE CHALLENGE OF ENGAGING NEOLIBERALISM DIFFERENTLY

Guy Julier

While its effects continue to unfold, the economic crisis of 2008 was a watershed moment for design activism. It was swept along by the activities of the Occupy Movement, including Occupy Design or the horizontalist actions in recession struck countries such as Spain and Greece. Meanwhile a number of academics attempted to provide re-framings for design practice and education (Fry 2008; Fuad-Luke 2009; Julier 2013; Thorpe 2012). These challenges to design sought alternative pathways that took it out of its historical service to industry.

In the meantime, neoliberal economics has stumbled on, perhaps in a zombie state (Harman 2010), but nonetheless it has continued to dominate and guide politics, society culture and everyday life, as if there was no alternative. The rise of populist politics, embodied, for example, by President Trump and or in the Brexit process in 2016, while claiming some form of alternative perspective, nonetheless embeds these even deeper into neoliberal logics of individualism, endless economic growth and competitivity – hallmarks of neoliberalism. Twitching and dribbling, though it may be, neoliberalism doesn't want to die off. And yet, commentators and institutions from the hard left through to the liberal right have warned of its unsustainability as a system. From its unhappiness-inducing individualism (Davies 2015) to its clear impact on global warming (Parr 2015) to the mere suggestion that wage inequality in fact stagnates growth (Swanson and Tankersley 2017), it surely should mean 'game over' for neoliberalism.

If we have zombie capitalism, then we also have zombie design. This is because design is the darling of neoliberalism. One need only track its inexorable rise since the 1980s against the rise of some of neoliberalism's key features to make the connection. The speeding-up of supply chains alongside flexible accumulation, the growth of intellectual property rights (IPR) in the competition of monopolies, the production of rational landscapes as part of the privatisation of spaces, the co-option of the commons into rent-producing assets, progressive outsourcing of public welfare services. All these express the material effects of neoliberalism's processes of deregulation, New Economy, financialization and austerity. And design does much, if not most, of the work of this alchemy.

The sheer weight of numbers suggests that there is no room left for manoeuvre. The countless reports that extoll the contributions that design in the creative industries makes to GDP suggest that There Is No Alternative: that the success of design and being successful as a designer is always going to be tied to a growth-based, capitalist economy of competitivity in which differentiating products, spaces and services is the core *raison d'être*.

Design and neoliberalism are good together not just because the latter provides plenty of work for the former, though. Design is also active in formatting particular dispositions, practices and structures of capitalism. It is not just a marriage built on economic arrangements, but a meaningful love affair.

But what can be done if we want that to re-boot that relationship? How might we re-cast that nexus of culture and economy where design becomes the active agent in new forms of everyday life that are more compelling in their environmentalism, concern for social justice and empathy for changing demographic circumstances? Can design ever be activist?

This chapter starts from a position that, first of all, we have to understand the tricky processes of neoliberalization and its continuing unfolding in order to then build design tactics toward a postcapitalist order. This is largely a pessimistic analysis, for as we begin to understand neoliberalism, so we see how it presents a moving subject that continually draws in its edges.

The story could have a happy ending, though. Through understanding these, some level of self-realisation might arise. And from this, perhaps a new, resilient and reflexive form of design could develop that moves beyond the porous, yet distinct parameters of neoliberalism.

The Co-Option of Design Activism

It seems that no matter how much design tries to break out of its abusive relationship with neoliberalism, it gets sucked back in. Or, rather, neoliberalism catches up with it to smother the life out any attempt at living on its own terms.

Neoliberalism is better understood as neoliberalisation. It involves continual processes of transformation: of individuals, of social relationships, of markets and of spaces. Design is an instrument of those transformations. At one level, it re-positions and re-organises matter to become neoliberal-friendly. But it also plays a strategic role in brokering change. It plays some of the role of softening consumers up for further change, making it appear 'reasonable'.

It is as subtle as it is pernicious. Those appealing, soft qualities are drawn in part from the experiments of counter cultural activities, if we are to follow Boltanski and Chappielo (2006). It is where the rhetoric of 'non-hierarchical, flat management', and 'the buzz' of creative work reside. It is where immaterial labour is presented as a lifestyle option, where the divisions between work and play are eroded.

The erosion of divisions is a key trope in processes of neoliberalisation. In this, it is parasitical, attaching to a variety of localised contexts as a transformatory process rather than an end. Thus its constant appropriation and reworking of activist initiatives is at work. Berglund (2013) explains how design activist initiatives – such as alternative food networks – get co-opted into city branding and creative city discourses, demonstrating 'edginess' and cultural capital to attract inward investment. Mould (2014) demonstrates how urban interventions of activists – such as guerrilla gardening or pop-up street benches – soon get framed as regeneration that in turn leads to gentrification. Valenzuela and Böhm (2017) argue that attempts to rebuild and reform economy towards more environmentally sustainable approaches – more specifically the promotion of circular economy – end up in the de-politicization of such efforts.

It seems to be an abusive relationship, then. In one way, designers continually fulfill the neoliberalism's appetite for the new, for something radical and edgy. That's how they get noticed. But they also get ignored in that the rewards make them think 'was that worth it?'. For example, in a survey of 576 people working in design in the UK in 2013, 85.6% said that 'clients expect more work for less money', around two thirds of respondents agreed that 'agencies are using more freelancers' (68.1%) and about two fifths (42.5%) agreed that 'agencies are using more unpaid interns' (Design Industry Voices 2013).

They then try and break out. Do something more transgressive. A bit of activism might shake things up, they think. But then neoliberal forces draw designers back in, offering some kind of security, albeit a temporary arrangement.

A bit of relationship counseling is needed here. What are designers doing to keep neoliberalism so self-satisfied? Designer's role in this is threefold: first in their relentlessly fashioning of objects that discipline subjects into neoliberalism's orbit; second, in engaging with the financialist logics of neoliberalism design conspires, quite literally, to forms of future value; third, its fashioning of intensities continually closes down possibilities for alternative possibilities. An understanding of these may lead to some points of exit from this current, unhappy relationship, though.

Neoliberal Objects

Designers do the cooking for neoliberalism. They don't do the clearing up afterwards, but they do serve up its meals, try out new recipes and make the next one something to be looked forward to. In this, they also fashion the objects that energize the rest of the family, keeping it disciplined and compliant with the father figure of neoliberalism. Briefly, what does this father figure stand for? Four things:
- the *deregulation* of markets and privileging of market forces, free of state intervention;
- the *privatisation* of state-owned enterprises and state services such as education, welfare and security;
- the foregrounding of *financial* interests over others such as societal, or environmental ones;
- an emphasis on *competitivity* and on *individual, entrepreneurial* practices and outlooks.

One might observe that these have been key features of capitalism in general. What makes these characteristics *neo*liberal as opposed to merely liberal? William Davies succinctly observes that *"the neo-liberal [sic] challenge was to invent instruments and mechanisms which made the philosophy secure"* (Davies 2012, 770). For the purposes of this chapter, one might take this very literally. Prior to the 1980s, full marketization and privatization was perhaps more of a political aspiration of the right and centre-right. The neoliberal order put in place not only laws and policies to ensure its dominance in the global north, but also specific material objects and systems that made it happen, from the macro-level of finance to the micro-level of individual thought and action.

Thus, if these features appear to be distant from everyday life, then it is as well to remember that social reproduction has to take place in order to undergird these. People have to be disciplined into undertaking the work that fulfils these aims. This is not just a case of turning up at the office on a Monday morning or going to the shopping mall on a Saturday. It is about a wholesale fashioning of the self to be compliant with neoliberalism's processes. Foucault (2008) expressed this disciplining process in terms of biopolitics – the wiring of power into the body.

Specific designed objects play their roles in this. Gadgets, particularly those that involve elements of quantification such as video games, personal organisers or sports apps, are mobilized in producing practices of calculation and anticipation (Ash 2015; Väliaho 2014). Just as neoliberalism requires us to constantly work out (our) value, so we are also engaged in the expectation of its near change and in preparing for that. Value *in potentia* is germane to both neoliberalism and design.

Thrift (2008) pays attention to what he calls the micro-biopolitics of contemporary life: small gestures and moments of cognition that we have adopted. These are: the prosthesis for cognitive assistance (think: Google maps on a smartphone); provisional spatial coordination (think: continual tracking of parcel delivery); continual access to information (think: newsfeeds at railway stations and in airports); an opening up of metrics (think: the multiple measurement systems in exercise apps); that places are less places of return (think: continual adjustments of supermarket aisles or updating of smartphone apps). All these examples are objects of design that point to the production of neoliberal subjects as competitive, rational, calculative, entrepreneurial, self-caring, choosing, networking actors (otherwise, homo economicus) (Verdouw 2016) or as insecure, confused and debilitated individuals (Chandler and Reid 2017).

Design isn't just producing objects. It's creating dispositions, ways of being, neural pathways and somatic memory. For the last 30 years these have almost exclusively been those that are concurrent with the capitalist living. What objects might we design that produce alternative dispositions? And which of these alternative dispositions might resist, fully or partially, co-option? Or if neoliberal objects live on, despite the failure of the neoliberal project, how do we kill these zombies off? Can something else be cooked up? Can the table be laid differently?

Financialized Objects

Not all objects are what they seem. They act as deep wells of investment and/or instruments of finance. As such as they participate in processes of financialization, an activity that has come to represent the leading edge of neoliberalism since 2000. In short, we may typify financialization by a greater emphasis on strategies to maintain value of shares, brands, real estate and capital flows. This means: the dominance of shareholder value within corporate governance; the pursuit of profit through financial rather than commodity production systems; the rise of financial trading.

Of the latter let us consider, for example, the Chinese bike rental firm Mobike. With 7 million bikes and around 100 million users, it requires a surety of 299 yuan ($45) from each user. This totals 30 billion yuan ($4.5b) that Mobike is then able to use as venture capital (Culpan 2017). Thus the objects – the bikes, that is – become ways by which money is gathered to be pushed into rentier financial flows. The existence of the bikes and, of course, their supporting infrastructure fulfill transport needs but also create a market. However, in turn, each participant in this new market, probably unwittingly, provides capital for Mobike to do other things. Similarly, and more generally, Sassen (2003) observes that a building is a security that allows finance to be gathered to then be invested elsewhere. Finance produces materialisations as materialisations lead to further financial recreation in a seemingly endless cycle.

As deep wells of finance, we may also consider the notion of spatial and technological fixes (Harvey 1989; 2001) and design's role in this process. Consider the $25 trillion held in pension funds in OECD countries (OECD 2015) or the €68 trillion of capital (derived through institutional investors and household bank accounts) that is dealt with by asset managers globally (EFAMA 2017). The point of such investments is to make profit. In order to make profit these investments have to go somewhere. Shopping malls, leisure attractions, hospitality offers, office developments and many other design-intense materialisations provide spatial fixes for this capital – somewhere for it to go. Another form of spatial fix is in the establishment, development and disciplining of new market opportunities, for example, in the global South. Technological fixes such as new forms of computer hardware or software, driverless cars or artificial intelligence provide other investment opportunities. The world is awash with money and, presently, we have to make places for it to go.

The logic here is in the continual search for sources of future value (Lash 2010) Design is wrapped into this process. It both fashions and points to these sources. Thus it is important not merely to view the economic role of design as a way of stimulating private consumption and the production of disposable products. This is where critiques of design have traditionally been placed, it seems (e.g. Crocker 2017). A key point of reference that takes us beyond this traditional view of design is Thomas Piketty's argument that through much of the twentieth century and increasingly into the twenty-first, return on finance has outstripped return on production in capitalist economies (Piketty 2014). Instead, therefore, we might view design within a wider field of financial circulation and value. At one level design provides nodes where finance is lodged, structuring these in such a ways to allow for returns on these investments. At another, it uses cultural value to increase the perceived attraction of such nodes. Thus, the use of place-branding to make a city attractive for inward investment, the establishment of an iconic building or piece of infrastructure such as a designerly bridge to support regeneration and thus property values or the re-design of a mobile phone ahead of a shareholders' annual general meeting (Aspara 2010; 2012) are some of the ways by which design takes on this secondary, financialist role.

Design Intensities

Within this financialist role we see design as the key factor in the creation of many different kinds of intensities for the logic of capital within neoliberalism. Here, design has not only acted as an instrument for fiat money but has shaped the pathways by which this process takes place.

In this, we note how design intensities act as points of value *in potentia*. They are where the possibility of future profit is based on the creation and protection of detailed and carefully planned and resolved forms of private property, be this intellectual or material. In effect, these are, as Lash (2010) notes, becomings. They are in constant states of development and roll-out: unfinished objects, as it were (Knorr Cetina 2001). Intensities become extensities as they are deployed into the marketplace. Brand signatures are applied to ranges of consumer goods. Franchise concepts are established in multiple high streets or as services through their licensee workers. While being individually designed and controlled, networks of shopping centres are held by property development companies, both as nodes in flows of capital but also as sources of market information, for instance. The table below expands on this idea through some examples.

design intensity example	some neoliberal effects
brand guidelines	• internal disciplining of employees into corporate culture; • brand valuation aiding shareholder value; • brand roll-out leveraging new markets.
creative quarters	• positions urban centres as innovation hubs to attract investment and more creative capital; • increases property values and acts as regeneration tool; • disciplines 'culture of innovation'.
franchise concepts	• licensing of intellectual property and material content to franchisees creates product and service monopolies; • investment can be put into concept development and marketing rather than full infrastructure (the latter borne by the franchisee instead).
global corporate design headquarters	• supports brand image and thus shareholder value; • leverages local resources (e.g. creative capital and milieux, tax breaks).
intellectual property rights	• maintains monopoly over design or invention; • licensing to third party producers.
movie franchises	• metadata licensed to third parties e.g. merchandise; • monopoly through IPR and metadata disciplines production network, including individual creative workers, to dominance of majors (little room for independent work, therefore).
prototypes	• materialisations based on high quality market information for testing profit potential.
shopping centres, hotels, leisure parks	• bounded, controlled spaces configured to create market demand and ensure steady return on investment, particularly interesting to institutional investors; • nodes for securitizing finance and moving it globally.
software programmes	• high value in prototyping and development; • marketplace becomes investment-free testbed; • licensing is source of profit with very low serial reproduction costs.
tax havens	• important nodes in tax avoidance and global circulation of capital, designed to be attractive to wealthy and as easy places for obfuscation and concealment.

Table 2: Design intensities (becomings) that lead to extensities (beings).

Design might be considered as something that is put into a pre-existing object, that is the fashioning of something to stimulate markets and consumption – sometimes referred to as 'value-added'. But here I want to push an idea that it is at the core of neoliberal systems of value creation through monopolies, the control of markets and disciplining. In this, orthodoxies are formed that either squeeze alternatives out or co-opt them in. As spatial or technological fixes, they provide points of focus for capital to be concentrated. Subsequently, their roll-out as extensities can be carefully measured and monitored in service of the investor class.

Fuck Neoliberalism

By shifting our point of reference of design from production to finance, we begin to see more acutely how it works within and at the service of neoliberalism, and how the rise of the two have gone hand-in-hand. Equally, by shifting design activism from ordinary points of everyday intervention and thinking more contextually about how neoliberalism functions through design, we might find some lines of attack. By asking, quite simply, 'what are we up against?', we can begin to understand the enemy. This then gives us a map through which may begin to see what, as activists who truly want to 'fuck neoliberalism' (Springer 2016). It might tell us how, despite all the best efforts of design interventions to disrupt, model alternatives and pre-figuratively explore other possibilities, we don't seem to be getting there fast enough. Design neoliberalism is in a constant and self-perpetuating circularity.

Neoliberal objects shape particular dispositions for operating under capitalism, where fiat money dominates and the securitization of individual lives requires acquiescence to certain modes of thought and action based on continual anticipation and calculation. Financialized objects provide an overarching, materialized logic and structure for the movement of capital, seeking sources of value. Design intensities are fashioned for the concentration of capital, the point of alchemy where, through their translation into extensities, profit is produced.

These processes are securitized through law, but also through their very refined qualities that make them difficult to assail. And this gives them their supposed resilience. At the same time, their continually unfolding, developmental and unfinished qualities keeps them moving and their borders flexible. It is this mixture of rigidity (power) and elasticity (dodging and weaving) that keeps the processes of neoliberalization just out of reach, just beyond being challenged and possibility defeated.

Machiavelli wrote in *The Prince*, "*People should either be caressed or crushed. If you do them minor damage they will get their revenge; but if you cripple them there is nothing they can do. If you need to injure someone, do it in such a way that you do not have to fear their vengeance*" (Machiavelli in Wootton 1996: 12). However, if we are to personify neoliberalism and design, such a bloody ending for either is probably not possible nor desirable. Instead, perhaps this abusive relationship can be healed through some gentle therapy. Through this, the benefits of change may surface. But it also requires

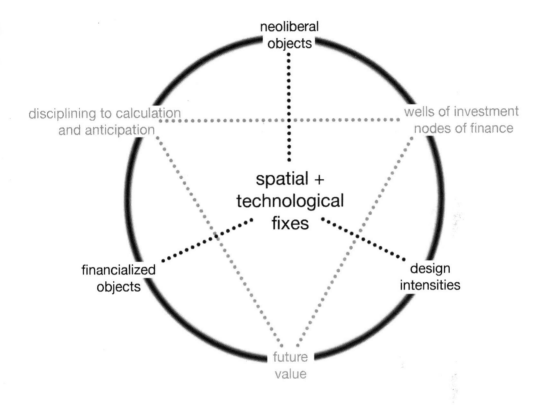

neoliberal
objects

disciplining to calculation
and anticipation

wells of investment
nodes of finance

spatial +
technological
fixes

financialized
objects

design
intensities

future
value

Figure 12: The interplay of neoliberalism and design in the context of financialization.

revealing and articulating how they both got into this mess.

Design activism may therefore be a process of discovery and description of the ways by which neoliberalism and design are acting on one another. How are they relational? How are the objects of design producing neoliberal subjects? And how might we undo this coding? Where are the key design points of financialization and how might we replace their logics while safeguarding security and welfare? How are design intensities disciplining particular commercial arrangements, leading to exploitation and suppressing creative action outside these? How do we work successfully outside these intensities and their extensities to create another world? These are some of the urgent questions we might be asking.

It seems, however, that it has only been when the financialist logic of neoliberalism falters, as it did in 2008, that chinks and fissures open up to explore them. Crisis sometimes offers opportunities. Neoliberal forces are very adept at exploiting these as we saw with the triumph of quantitative easing following 2008 or the advantages that natural disaster and war have offered (Klein 2007). Design activists might consider getting in their first, however, building their own reflexive processes where what has happened and what is happening is laid bare. Tactics for their own resilience and flexibility might be created and maintained. This is where neoliberalism might be engaged differently.

References

Ash, James (2015): *The interface envelope: Gaming, technology, power.* London: Bloomsbury.

Aspara, Jaakko (2010): How do institutional actors in the financial market assess companies product design? The quasi-rational evaluative schemes, in: *Knowledge, Technology and Policy. Vol. 22, No. 4*, 241–258.

Aspara, Jaakko (2012): The influence of product design evaluations on investors' willingness to invest, in: *Design Management Journal*, 6(1): 79–93.

Berglund, Eeva (2013): Design as activism in Helsinki: notes from the world design capital 2012, in: *Design and Culture*, 5(2), 195–214.

Boltanski, Luc and Chiapello, Eve (2006): *The New Spirit of Capitalism.* London: Verso.

Chandler, David / Reid, Julian (2016): *The neoliberal subject: Resilience, adaptation and vulnerability.* London: Pickering & Chatto.

Crocker, Robert (2017): *Somebody Else's Problem: Consumerism, Sustainability and Design.* Abingdon: Routledge.

Culpan, Tim (2017): The China Bike Rental Money Cycle, *Bloomberg Gadfly*, 04/10/17, https://www.bloomberg.com/gadfly/articles/2017-10-04/the-china-bike-rental-money-cycle

Davies, W. (2012) 'The emerging neocommunitarianism', *The Political Quarterly*, 83(4), 767–776.

Davies, William (2015): *The happiness industry: How the government and big business sold us well-being.* London: Verso.

EFAMA (2017) *Asset Management in Europe, 9th Edition, Facts and Figures.* http://www.efama.org/publications/statistics/asset%20management%20report/efama%20asset%20management%20report%202017.pdf

Foucault, Michel (2008): *The Birth of Biopolitics: Lectures at the Collège de France 1978–1979*. Ed. M. Sennelart. Tr. G. Burchell. Basingstoke: Palgrave.

Fry, Tony (2008): *Design futuring: sustainability, ethics, and new practice*. Oxford: Berg.

Fuad-Luke, Alastair (2009): *Design Activism*: Beautiful Strangeness for a Sustainable World. London: Earthscan.

Harman, Chris (2010): *Zombie capitalism: global crisis and the relevance of Marx*. London: Haymarket Books.

Harvey, David (1989): *The Urban Experience*. Oxford: Basil Blackwell.

Harvey, David (2001): Globalization and the "spatial fix", in: *Geographische Revue*, 2(3): 23–30.

Julier, Guy (2013): From Design Culture to Design Activism, in: *Design and Culture*, 5(2): 215–36.

Klein, Naomi (2007): *The Shock Doctrine: The Rise of Disaster Capitalism*. London: Penguin.

Knorr Cetina, Karin (2001): Objectual practice, in: T.R. Schatzki, K. Knorr-Cetina and E. Von Savigny (eds.), *The practice turn in contemporary theory*. London: Routledge. 184–196.

Lash, Scott (2010): *Intensive Culture: Social Theory, Religion and Contemporary Capitalism*. London: Sage.

Mould, Oli (2014): Tactical urbanism: The new vernacular of the creative city, in: *Geography Compass*, 8(8), 529-539.

OECD (2017): Annual Survey Of Large Pension Funds And Public Pension Reserve Funds: Report On Pension Funds' Long-Term Investments. http://www.oecd.org/daf/fin/private-pensions/2015-Large-Pension-Funds-Survey.pdf

Parr, Adrian (2014): *The wrath of capital: Neoliberalism and climate change politics*. New York: Columbia University Press.

Piketty, Thomas (2014): *Capital in the Twenty-First Century*. London: Belknap Press.

Sassen, Saskia (2003): Reading the City in a Global Digital Age: Between Topographic Representation and Spatialized Power, in: Linda Kraus and Patricia Petro (eds) *Global Cities: Cinema, Architecture and Urbanism in a Digital Age*, New Brunswick, NJ: Rutgers University Press, 15–30.

Springer, Simon (2016): Fuck neoliberalism. *ACME: An International Journal for Critical Geographies*, 15(2), 285–292.

Swanson, Ana and Tankersley, Jim (2017): 'I.M.F. Cautions Against Tax Cuts for Wealthy as Republicans Consider Them', *New York Times*, 11/10/17. https://www.nytimes.com/2017/10/11/us/politics/imf-tax-cuts.html

Thorpe, Ann (2012): *Architecture and Design versus Consumerism: How Design Activism Confronts Growth*. London: Earthscan.

Thrift, Nigel (2008): *Non-Representational Theory: Space, Politics, Affect*. London: Routledge.

Valenzuela, Francisco and Böhm, Steffen (2017): Against wasted politics: A critique of the circular economy. *Ephemera*, 17(1), 23–60.

Väliaho, Pasi (2014): *Biopolitical Screens: Image, Power, and the Neoliberal Brain*. Massachusetts: MIT Press.

Verdouw, Julia Joanne (2016): The subject who thinks economically? Comparative money subjectivities in neoliberal context, in: *Journal of Sociology*, 53(3) 523–540.

Wootton, David (Ed.) (1996): *Modern political thought: Readings from Machiavelli to Nietzsche*. Indianapolis: Hackett Publishing.

AUTHORS

Dr. phil. **Tom Bieling**, senior research fellow at the *Design Research Lab* of *Berlin University of the Arts*, has been visiting professor at the *University of Trento* and the *German University in Cairo*, and teaches Transformation Design at the *New Design University* St. Pölten. In his research he mainly focuses on the social and political dimensions of design, particularly on aspects of design for social innovation and inclusion. He is the Editor-in-chief at *DESIGNABILTIES – Design Research Journal*, Co-Editor of the book series Design Meanings (Mimesis), founding member of the *Design Research Network*, founder of the *Institute for Applied Fantasies (Institut für angewandte Fantasie)*, head of the *Ultràgallery*, Chief Editor at *Designforschung.org*, and Initiator of the *International Research Network on Design (and) Activism*.* He has held numerous guest lectures and run workshops at international universities (e.g. Mumbai, São Paulo, Rio de Janeiro, Milano, Portland, Nottingham, Budapest, Eindhoven or Rotterdam). His work has been presented at international exhibitions and museums in New York, London, Vienna, Manchester, Sheffield, Brno or St. Gallen. He was announced "Young Innovator of the Year" by the Falling Walls Consortium and has published over 100 research papers, book chapters and academic articles. Recent books: "Inklusion als Entwurf" (Birkhäuser/DeGruyter, 2019) and "Gender (&) Design" (Mimesis, 2020). www.tombieling.com

Gui Bonsiepe studied and graduated in the information design department at the HfG Ulm 1955-1959. Teaching and research activity at the HfG Ulm until 1968. Since 1968 design and consultancy services for multilateral and bilateral organizations for technical cooperation and in government institutions in Latin America (particularly in Chile, Argentina, Brazil). From 1987 to 1989 interface designer in a software house in California. 1993-2003 professor for interface design at the Köln International School of Design. Living and working in Argentina and Brazil. 2003-2005 Visiting Professor at the Design School Rio de Janeiro (ESDI). Numberous publications, including *Teoria e pratica del disegno industriale* (1975), *Interface – An Approach to Design* (1999), *Entwurfskultur und Gesellschaft* (2009), Do Material ao Digital (2015). www.guibonsiepe.com

Mikala Hyldig Dal is an artist, curator and writer based in Berlin. Her work evolves around the politics of art and language in transitory societies. A graduate of Media Art from the University of Arts Berlin, her work has been presented in Martin Gropius Bau Berlin, Townhouse Gallery Cairo and Nikolaj Kunsthal Copenhagen among other places; she has been involved in research and educational initiatives in Iran, Syria, Egypt and Germany. 2011-2014 she lived in Cairo where she taught at the AUC and GUC and published the book *Cairo: Images of Transition* with Transcript Verlag/Columbia University Press. Her text-works and essays have been published in Seismopolis, ...Ment, Itinerant and further journals. Mikala Hyldig Dal is currently an adjunct professor at Weissensee Art Academy in Berlin.

Stephen Duncombe is an activist and professor of Media and Culture at New York University. He is the author and editor of six books, including *Dream: Re-Imagining Progressive Politics in an Age of Fantasy* and the *Cultural Resistance Reader.* Stephen is the Co-Founder and Co-Director of the Center for Artistic Activism in New York City

Prof. em. Dr. **Michael Erlhoff** Founding dean of the school of design (today: KISD) at the Cologne University of Applied Sciences (CUAS). Dean of the CUAS department of cultural studies (2002 – 2006). Michael Erlhoff studied at the University of Hanover where he completed his PhD in German literature, art history and sociology. During his studies he also worked as assistant producer at the Staatstheater Hannover and as a teacher at a technical college. Michael Erlhoff worked for several years as research assistant and later as assistant professor at the University of Hanover. Together with Uta Brandes he published the magazine zweitschrift, he was editor-in-chief of the art magazine K; for more than ten years, he published an annual Kurt Schwitters Almanach and he was a member of the advisory committee for documenta 8 (1985-1987). From 1986 to 1990, he was director of the German Design Council in Frankfurt am Main. In 1991 he was appointed founding dean of the KISD Köln International School of Design in Cologne (KISD) where, until 2012, he was professor of design history and design theory. He also served as dean of the department of Cultural Studies at the Cologne University of Applied Sciences (2002-2006). In 1997 he was guest professor at the Hong Kong Polytechnic University. Michael Erlhoff was involved in the inception of the Raymond Loewy Foundation and was also the Foundation's president from 1992 to 2006. Together with Uta Brandes he organised the St. Moritz Design Summit (2000 – 2006). He is a member of the German Association for Design Theory and Research (DGTF), which he founded in 2003, and a member of AICA (association internationale des critiques d'art). He regularly gives guest lectures and runs workshops at international universities, e.g. in Tokyo, Nagoya, Fukuoka, Hangzhou, Shanghai, Beijing, Taipei, Hong Kong, New York and Sydney. Michael Erlhoff is a frequent member of national or international design juries. He also was coordinator of the Cologne Design Prize and the Cologne Design Prize international, which are among the awards with the highest prize money for talented young design graduates. He is author or editor of about forty books and of many other texts.

Anna Feigenbaum is a Principal Academic in Digital Storytelling. Before joining the department of Journalism, English and Communication, she was a Lecturer in Media and Politics at Bournemouth University from 2013-2015. Prior to this she taught at Richmond, the American University in London and held fellow positions at the Rutgers University Center for Historical Analysis, the London School of Economics and Political Science, and the Institute for Historical Research at University of London. She graduated from McGill University in 2008 with a PhD in Communication Studies. Her doctoral research on communication and creativity at women's peace camps was supported by the Social Sciences and Humanities Council of Canada and the Beaverbrook Fund at McGill. Beyond the university, she runs a variety of workshops on data storytelling for local businesses, NGOs and community groups. She also provides consultancy for campaigns, archives and museum exhibitions related to her research. This has included contributions toward the Signs of Change exhibition, Music & Liberation, and the Disobedient Objects show at the Victoria & Albert Museum in 2014.

Alastair Fuad-Luke works as a design facilitator, educator, writer and activist. His books include *Agents of Alternatives* (co-edited), *Design Activism* and *The Eco-Design Handbook* and *The EcoTravel Handbook*. He is a Professor of Design Research at the Faculty of Design and Art, at the Free University of Bozen-Bolzano in Italy. Previously he was Professor of Emerging Design Practices at the School of Arts, Design and Architecture, Aalto University, Finland, exploring approaches based upon co-design, openness and sharing, and at the Department of Communication and Art, University of Aveiro, Portugal. Present research explorations include: dissonant design; design f(r)ictions; design, agri-culture and Alternative Food Networks; complimentary relational designers; and the creation of new livelihoods within alternative economies.

Doctor **Cathy Gale** (MA: RCA) is a Senior Lecturer and level 5 year leader in BA (Hons) Graphic Design at Kingston School of Art London. She is also an Associate Lecturer at the London College of Communication (UAL) teaching across design theory and practice. She was awarded a Senior Fellowship of the Higher Education Academy (UK) for her radical design pedagogic projects, the Alternative Art School and Disco Dissent. Cathy is a graphic artist and educator researching *through* critical design practice. Her work is published with Cumulus Association and Intellect Books.

Gavin Grindon is a Lecturer in Art History and Curating and Director for Art History at the University of Essex. He recently curated The Museum of Cruel Designs and Guerilla Island at Banksy's Dismaland show. Cruel Designs was an exhibition of design for social control, from police tazers and anti-homeless spikes to booby-trapped border fences. Guerilla Island comprised several spaces for activist-art and workshops. Before this he co-curated the exhibition *Disobedient Objects* at the Victoria and Albert Museum, London, about objects of art and design produced by protest movements internationally since the late 1970s. It was the museum›s most visited exhibition since 1946. Gavin›s research focuses on twentieth century art, specifically activist-art and institutional critique. In 2010 he co-wrote the pamphlet *A User's Guide to Demanding the Impossible*, which has been translated into a number of languages, and he is currently completing a book on the history of activist-art. He has a particular interest not only in the particular histories of activist-art, but in new theoretical, methodological and curatorial approaches to social movement cultures which research and display with movements as well as on them. His PhD, completed at Manchester University under Prof. Terry Eagleton, comprised an intellectual history of political-aesthetic theories of revolution-as-festival, from dissident surrealist writers through to aspects of the 1990-2000s global justice movement.

Harald Gruendl (Dr. phil. habil.) works as a design practitioner, design theorist and curator. He founded the IDRV-Institute of Design Research Vienna (www.idrv.org) in 2008 and is partner at EOOS design (1995). As guest curator of the Museum of Applied Arts/Contemporary Arts in Vienna he was co-curating the design section of the Vienna Biennale in 2015 and 2017. His research interests are design strategies for positive change and social design.

Barbara Hoidn founded the architecture firm Hoidn Wang Partner in Berlin, Germany, together with Wilfried Wang. After receiving her degree in architecture (Dipl.Ing.) from the University of Karlsruhe, Germany, she was a Loeb Fellow at the Harvard GSD, Cambridge, USA, and taught at the ETH Zurich, the RISD, Providence, RI, and the Harvard GSD. Since 2002, she has been Visiting Associate Professor at the O Neil Ford Chair at The University of Texas at Austin. From 1994 until 2000, she was head of the office of the Senate Building Director in Berlin. She has curated many exhibitions, symposia and conferences on architectural and urban design topics nationally and internationally, and is the editor of several books and exhibition catalogues.

Guy Julier is Professor of Design Leadership at Aalto University, Finland. Before this he was Professor of Design Culture at the University of Brighton and Principal Research Fellow in Contemporary Design at the Victoria & Albert Museum, UK.

He has over 30 years experience in design education and practice ranging from pre-University teaching to post-doctoral supervision. Formerly a Visiting Professor at the Glasgow School of Art, Otago University and the University of Southern Denmark, he has also advised on design policy to various governmental organisations and led strategy projects on developing design research for the Arts and Humanities Research Council. As Professor of Design at Leeds Metropolitan University until 2010, he established DesignLeeds, a research and consultancy unit specialising in developing new approaches to urban regeneration. His research sits at the meeting point of design and the social sciences, both in terms of its contemporary practice and historical enquiry. Most recently he has developed work on the role of design in neoliberalisation processes, resulting in his new book *Economies of Design*. He is also the author of *The Culture of Design* (3rd edition 2014) and co-editor of *Design and Creativity: Policy, Management and Practice* (2009).

Steve Lambert is a conceptual artist and professor of New Media at Purchase College of the State University of New York. His art has been shown everywhere from marches to museums both nationally and internationally, has appeared in over fourteen books, and four documentary films. Steve is the Co-Founder and Co-Director of the Center for Artistic Activism in New York City.

Fernando Luiz Lara is a Brazilian architect with degrees from the Federal University of Minas Gerais (BArch, 1993) and the University of Michigan (PhD, 2001). The author of several books and hundreds of articles, in academic and professional journals as well as the general media, Prof. Lara writes extensively on a variety of issues regarding the Latin American built environment. In 2015 Prof. Lara published, together with Luis Carranza, the first comprehensive survey of Modern Architecture in Latin America. A member of the Brazilian Institute of Architects, and the Brazilian DOCOMOMO, Lara has also been active in his native country as a critic, researcher and educator. A licensed architect in Brazil, Lara has designed many structures, alone or in partnership with others. His current interest in the favelas has turned into opportunities to engage with public policy at the municipal level as well as collaborations with local firms designing public spaces in informal settlements. In 2005 he founded Studio Toró, a non-profit devoted to the challenges of water conservation and urban flooding in Latin America. Since 2009 Fernando Lara has collaborated extensively with Horizontes Arquitetura, a Brazilian firm dedicated to public space, favela upgrades and social housing. Together they created the Laboratório de Urbanismo Avançado, a non-profit devoted to the creation of better public spaces. Fernando Lara is Professor at Universidade Federal de Minas Gerais and Associate Professor of Architecture at the University of Texas at Austin where he also served as Chair of the Brazil Center at the Lozano Long Institute of Latin American Studies from 2012 to 2015. At both universities Fernando Lara teaches seminars on 20th century Latin American architecture and urbanism, a doctoral course on the critique of architectural eurocentrism, as well as studios related to the continent's current urban challenges.

Prof. Dr. **Marcel René Marburger** M.A. studied Art History, German Literature, and Philosophy at the University of Cologne and did his PhD about the art theoretical relevance in Vilém Flusser's writings. He was scientific assistant at the Academy of Media Arts in Cologne, co-curator at the *Simultanhalle* in Cologne, lecturer at the Academy of Fine Arts in Dresden, lecturer and research fellow at the University of Arts Berlin as well as scientific assistant at the University of Potsdam. From 2007 to 2010 he was the scientific supervisor of the Vilém Flusser Archive. Since 2005 he has also been co-editor of the *International Flusser Lectures.* At present, he is lecturer at the University of Arts Berlin and professor for Design Theory and Cultural Sciences at the Design Faculty of the University of Applied Sciences and Arts Dortmund.

Thomas Markussen is associate professor of social design at the University of Southern Denmark. In his research and work, Markussen is interested in how design and art practices may be used to re-distribute power and orders of control so that marginalized and vulnerable groups in society can be empowered to have a say in processes of societal change. Currently, he is engaged in the 3-year EU-funded PROMETHEUS project (http://www.prometheus.care/), in which a cross-disciplinary research team consisting of health professionals and design researchers aim at increasing shared decision making for cancer patients at Danish and German hospitals. Moreover, he is managing the *Social Games against Crime* project (http://sacproject.org/). The aim of this project is to develop and implement a social game in the visiting facilities in top secure Danish prisons that can help children to maintain and develop proximal relationship with their incarcerated fathers.

Chantal Mouffe is Professor of Political Theory at the Centre for the Study of Democracy at the University of Westminster in London. She has taught and researched in many universities in Europe, North America and South America and she is a corresponding member of the Collège International de Philosophie in Paris. She is the editor of *Gramsci and Marxist Theory* (Routledge and Kegan Paul, London, 1979), *Dimensions of Radical Democracy. Pluralism, Citizenship, Community* (Verso, London, 1992) *Deconstruction and Pragmatism* (Routledge, 1996) and *The Challenge of Carl Schmitt,* (Verso, London, 1999); the co-author with Ernesto Laclau of *Hegemony and Socialist Strategy. Towards a Radical Democratic Politics* (Verso, London, 1985) and the author of *The Return of the Political* (Verso, London, 1993), *The Democratic Paradox* (Verso, London, 2000), *On the Political* (Routledge. London, 2005), *Agonistics. Thinking the World Politically* (Verso, 2013) and with Inigo Errejon, *Podemos. In the Name of the People* (Lawrence & Wishart, 2016).

Maziar Rezai is a Design-Activist, Design Researcher and Film Critic. He is a doctoral candidate in Design Studies at The Braunschweig University of Art (HBK) and currently a guest lecturer in Art University of Tehran in Iran. In addition, he works as Art Director and design counsellor and has led several consulting projects.

Dr. **Pierre Smolarski** is a scientific assistant at the University of Applied Sciences Bielefeld and the University of Wuppertal. In his research he mainly focuses on visual rhetoric and rhetoric of design, philosophical aesthetics and aesthetics of everyday life (such as pictures of labour). Publications: *Rhetorik des Designs. Gestaltung zwischen Subversion und Affirmation* (Bielefeld 2017), *Rhetorik der Stadt. Praktiken des Zeigens, Place-Making und Orientierung im urbanen Raum* (2017), and *Adbusting. Ein designrhetotisches Strategiehandbuch* (Bielefeld 2016) co-edited with Andreas Beaugrand.

Ann Thorpe is Deputy Director of the Transport Institute at University College London (UCL). She was previously with UCL's Department of Science, Technology, Engineering and Public Policy and UCL's Bartlett School of Architecture. She is the author of Architecture & Design versus Consumerism (Routledge 2012) and The Designers Atlas of Sustainability (Island Press, 2007).

* The *International Research Network on Design (and) Activism* was founded in 2017 by Tom Bieling (Berlin University of the Arts) and Andréa Poshar (Politecnico di Milano), at the Design Research Lab / Berlin University of the Arts. The main goal of the network is to encourage a continuous debate, investigation and publication of research related to design and its role within social, activist movements.
www.design-activism.org